TOWARD A SOCIALIST AMERICA

TOWARD
A SOCIALIST
AMERICA

A Symposium of Essays

EDITED BY HELEN ALFRED

". . . and they shall beat their swords into plowshares,
and their spears into pruninghooks; nation shall
not lift up sword against nation, neither shall they
learn war any more."   *Isaiah*, II, 4

PEACE PUBLICATIONS
New York 1958

LIBRARY OF CONGRESS CATALOG NUMBER 58-8936

412

CONTENTS

Notes are at the close of an essay

Introduction

FROM ALL PARTS OF THE WORLD come tidings of the progress being made toward socialism. In one country after another modern economies, that operate from a social base and are governed by social aims, are emerging. The old capitalist systems, pushed to the immediate goals of maximum profit—with incidental, if any consideration of the social costs involvel—are found to be socially inadequate and unworkable.

There is evidence of growing doubt among American working men and women, in all areas of occupation, regarding the efficacy of a capitalist economic system in maintaining high standards of life and labor and the constancy of production for peaceful uses. Faced with uncertain tenure of employment, with debt and, in tragically large numbers, with poverty, workers in industry and agriculture find it increasingly difficult to provide suitable conditions for themselves and their children. And now even greater sacrifices are being asked of them, as the conflict and temperature of the cold war are stepped up.

Small wonder that in industrial plants and on the farms, as well as in college, church, and on the street, questions substantially like these are being asked: Is it not manifestly impossible for the national productive plant to be kept running full tilt, and at inordinately high profits for the few, while the purchasing power of the many steadily declines? Can the American system of monopoly capitalism remain in motion only as long as it is geared to *organized obsolescence* in its most wasteful form—to a warfare economy and to production and distribution of the tools of human destruction? If not, what is the alternative? May it not be necessary to replace this wasteful and unstable system with one founded on the social ownership, planning and management of production that operates to improve the conditions of living and labor among all the people of the United States and to exchange, with all other nations, of the food, goods and services produced, all for purposes of building an enduring peace?

7

This symposium of essays on aspects of American socialism has been arranged in the hope that it may serve three general purposes: to widen public interest in the need, and to strengthen confidence in the practical possibilities of a socialist America; to define the main objectives and mechanics of a socialist economy and urge their adoption; to suggest political action to expedite the transition to such a system.

The reader will soon discover that the contributors are not all of one "hue" of socialist thought. Nor do they approach consideration of a socialist economy from the same, or even similar backgrounds of activity and experience. It may be said, however, that the authors are as one in the belief that the social ownership, planning and management of key sectors of production in the United States are essential, and inevitable.

No attempt has been made to prepare a road map to the new order. But it is hoped the book may at least serve as a weather vane, to show which way the wind of popular demand is blowing. Nearly every American believes himself to be as nearly right as the weatherman. We therefore venture, by way of introduction, to make a few predictions regarding the direction in which the people of this country may be expected to move, in their continuing pilgrimage to socialism.

It can never be forgotten that the socialist movement is international in spirit and in the scope of its goals. And it is imperative that world unity be promoted through the negotiation of arrangements with all nations—socialist and non-socialist alike—for social, cultural and economic cooperation. But, in characteristic American fashion, we shall in this country doubtless pursue a rather independent course toward a full-blown socialist economy. Thomas Jefferson, who never underrated the independent quality of the American people, in a letter to Samuel Kercheval, in 1816, wrote, "Each generation is as independent of the one preceding as that one was of all that went before."

But as one inspired, skillful and dynamic revolutionary to another, Mr. Jefferson might probably have been in agreement with Mr. Lenin who, a century later, adjured his people (in *Revolution and the State*) not to overlook "the mechanism of social management here already to hand". Lenin cited the post office "as an example of the socialist system", and suggested organization of "the *whole* economy like the postal system". He of course added that such organization must function under the power of the people, the workers.

In the more than one and one-half centuries since our national postal system was inaugurated the United States has ventured into many and diverse areas, and in varying degrees, of collective ownership and planning. An inventory of the programs and projects, approved and administered by federal, state and local governments would fill pages of this book. Their initiation and development have been manifestations of a continuous process, with ever more frequent rounds of periodic change. Despite the organized opposition of monopolists, their "institutes", and lobbies, and in the face of such indifference as that displayed by conservative administrations, these programs have been sponsored by progressive leaders; their acceptance by a cross-section of the American people is taken for granted.

These demonstrations of collective ownership and limited planning testify to the resourcefulness of the American people. While living under the reign of intense concentrations of wealth and power in the hands of the few, it has still been possible to achieve this degree of economic change without upheaval or chaos. It means that even the weak and scattered forces of the socialists and other progressive minded groups in the community have been sufficiently persuasive to sway wide areas of the voting public and their political representatives. Their influence by remote control requires assessment also. For it must be admitted that some of the proposals for "creeping" socialism nave been temporarily expropriated, without benefit of credit, by Democratic and Republican candidates who, while appealing for the support of the people, were not too sure of themselves or their party programs. Hard put to devise issues on which to invite popular support, more than one old-party politician has "stolen the thunder" and the votes of a socialist candidate by lifting a plank or two from his solid socialist platform. This is an old English custom—for the Tories to dish up the Whigs at election time.

The progress toward a socialist economy, while steady, has been distressingly slow. But our experience in the United States has made it manifest that such a system can be projected peacefully, within the present structure of our government, and be sustained by the Constitution. Sharp acceleration of the process through a greatly enlarged program of planned public production and distribution for promotion of the general welfare, *not* for warfare, could serve as a veritable life saver in this critical period. There is mounting concern over the possibility of a catastrophic war, with no apparently genuine diplomatic negotiations under way to prevent armed conflict. Capitalist economies are slipping. The majority of our people are in need not only of material security, but are also hungering for such hope and inspiration as are offered by socialist objectives.

To aid in averting disaster and to serve the long-term, as well as immediate needs of the American majority, a national people's party, geared to the labor movement and sparked by socialist aims, seems imperative. Such a party, skillfully organized to promote a nationwide, and industries-wide program of planned public production, would by the very nature of the case be required to undertake the following activities:

1. *Research*—social, economic and political—and the preparation of drafts of a sample national plan and of sample bills outlining the procedure for government acquisition and operation of a selected group of industries;

2. *Educational work*—related to the proposed plan and public ownership legislation, carried on through all available channels of commercial communication and through schools and colleges, churches and other community groups and organizations, and

3. *Party campaigns*—also organized on the basis of the program of the party, but carried on *continuously*—throughout the years, not merely in terms of the current campaign.

The campaigns conducted by such a people's party, open to candidates of high calibre, unquestioned integrity, and of proven fidelity to American working men and women and their families, could be expected to open fresh paths to political and economic democracy in the United States. Political and economic processes of government touch at many points, and frequently. Their close coordination, through the demands of socialist-minded voters and elected officials, would give promise of the reduction, and ultimate removal of human exploitation from all areas of American life.

The weather-vane indicates that the winds of public opinion and support are blowing in the direction of an independent people's party. Registration and voting records suggest that many Americans have lost interest and faith in the two old parties in their failure to face up to vitally important issues.

American labor is under attack, from corruption within and monopoly chiseling from without. Rank and file members, as well as officials of the unions, in many cases have indicated the need for a new political alignment of the workers. Public ownership is widely accepted and generally supported by the labor unions. Many public ownership and public welfare programs owe their inauguration and expansion to the incomparable organizational skill, and the political strength and sagacity of American labor. Labor's approval and active upholding of a great nationwide plan of public ownership of production and distribution would seem a natural and logical next step toward political control by the workers of the whole American economy. Their participation in founding a people's party would serve two specific and useful purposes, it is believed: it would strengthen the unity and influence of the majority of their members—*who are incorruptible,* and would provide a sure guarantee of the success, even some important victories at the polls, of a planned public ownership party and its program.

The discontent of the American working farmer and farm worker could be counted on to lead many of their fellow agriculturists to enter an alliance with labor in support of such a party.

Negroes and their organized groups could not do better, possibly, for their people at this time—as large numbers of them have long since recognized—than to associate themselves with a people's political party that sanctioned no barriers of race, creed or color, and stood foursquare for the rights and freedoms of all peoples, everywhere.

American socialists would endeavor to hold such a party to the course of long-range socialist aims. Socialists have learned that political organization is no sleight of hand performance. In large numbers, and throughout the country they have devoted years of their lives—during campaigns and between—to promoting popular acceptance of the principles and the policies they believe to be sound, essential and certain of ultimate incorporation into the law of the nation. Socialists are often asked why they never grow discouraged. The answer, of course, is that they never lose hope, a rare possession in these days of widespread cynicism and social irresponsibility.

Representatives of community organizations would surely be interested, even to the point of open support, in a party that existed for the protection of no special interests save those of the community as a whole.

It is even conceivable that many a born Democrat and Republican might be seen climbing onto the bandwagon, and with the greatest of ease.

Now—if only the AFL-CIO and its affiliates; and the independent unions; the progressive farmers and their organizations; the Negroes; the cooperative societies; the women; peace advocates; priests, parsons and rabbis; the teachers and students, and all others who may, were to meet in conference ere long, for the purpose of considering and organizing plans for founding a national party of the majority—we should be on our way. The winds might be wintry, the weather rough. But what more challenging crusade could we all join than such an expedition to a socialist America!

HELEN ALFRED

New York, March, 1958

HELEN ALFRED was born at Lake Geneva, Wisconsin in 1889. A "daughter" of 18th century American revolutionaries and granddaughter of an active New York City 19th century abolitionist, she has been a 20th century American socialist for many years (was a Socialist Party candidate for the New Jersey State Legislature from Essex County, in 1930). Miss Alfred studied at the University of Southern California, Columbia University, and London School of Economics; graduated from the New York School of Social Work. She was Headworker at Madison House Settlement on New York's lower East Side, a founder and organizer of the National Public Housing Conference and of the Citizens Conference on International Economic Union.

PART I. AMERICAN WORKERS NEED SOCIALISM

"LABOR IS PRIOR TO, and independent of, capital. Capital is only the fruit of labor, and could never have existed if labor had not first existed. Labor is the supporter of capital, and deserves the higher consideration."

From ABRAHAM LINCOLN'S *Presidential Message to Congress,* 1861.

WHY SOCIALISM? *by Albert Einstein*

THE INDIVIDUAL HAS BECOME more conscious than ever of his dependence upon society. But he does not experience this dependence as a positive asset, as an organic tie, as a protective force, but rather as a threat to his natural rights, or even to his economic existence. Moreover, his position in society is such that the egotistical drives of his make-up are constantly being accentuated, while his social drives, which are by nature weaker, progressively deteriorate. All human beings, whatever their position in society, are suffering from this process of deterioration. Unknowingly prisoners of their own egotism, they feel insecure, lonely, and deprived of the naive, simple, and unsophisticated enjoyment of life. Man can find meaning in life, short and perilous as it is, only through devoting himself to society.

The profit motive, in conjunction with competition among capitalists, is responsible for an instability in the accumulation and utilization of capital which leads to increasingly severe depressions. Unlimited competition leads to a huge waste of labor, and to that crippling of the social consciousness of individuals which I mentioned before.

This crippling of individuals I consider the worst evil of capitalism. Our whole educational system suffers from this evil. An exaggerated competitive attitude is inculcated into the student, who is trained to worship acquisitive success as a preparation for his future career.

I am convinced there is only *one* way to eliminate these grave evils, namely through the establishment of a socialist economy, accompanied by an educational system which would be oriented toward social goals. In such an economy, the means of production are owned by society itself and are utilized in a planned fashion. A planned economy, which adjusts production to the needs of the community, would distribute the work to be done among all those able to work and would guarantee a livelihood to every man, woman, and child. The education of the individual, in addition to promoting his own innate abilities, would attempt to develop in him a sense of responsibility for his fellow men in place of the glorification of power and success in our present society.

Excerpts from a statement published in *Monthly Review*, May, 1949 and in the collection of Dr. Einstein's writings, "From My Later Years," published by *Philosophical Library* in 1950. Quoted here with the permission of the Estate of Albert Einstein.

Is It Utopian to Advocate Socialism?

By Stephen Hole Fritchman

LET ME BEGIN WITH A WARNING. I write as a minister, as a parish parson working with men and women in their vicissitudes of daily living. My perspective is homely and pragmatic; I say this in no way apologetically, but for clarification. While priests and parsons admit that they can counsel and aid people under any system of government and industrial production, they naturally would prefer a social order which had fewer casualties and less insecurity for the average person living in it. I have been increasingly persuaded of the necessity of socialism by my day to day ministry, more than by Utopian constructions or idealistic creeds. Whatever I say comes out of a cauldron of experience, not out of an ivory tower. It is my thesis that it is no longer utopian to advocate a socialist America, it is imperative as good economics, good law, good government, good culture and good religion. It has long been good religion, but this alone has been irrelevant to the ruling powers, who have

STEPHEN HOLE FRITCHMAN was born 55 years ago in Cleveland, Ohio, of Quaker parents. He holds a B.D. degree from Union Theological Seminary and an M.A. degree from New York University. He has been pastor of the First Unitarian Church of Los Angeles for the past ten years, and previously served as minister of Methodist churches in New York, and Unitarian churches in Maine and Massachusetts. He has also been religious news editor of the *New York Herald Tribune;* has taught English at Ohio Wesleyan, New York, and Boston Universities; has served as Director of Youth Work for the American Unitarian Association, and as editor of the *Christian Register* (now the *Unitarian Register*). His published books include "Young People in the Liberal Church", "Men of Liberty", "Together We Advance", and "Axioms of Freedom". Articles by him have appeared in *The Nation, The Churchman, Mainstream, The American Socialist, Monthly Review* and various foreign publications.

thought of religion as a convenient anodyne, a happy substitute for those frustrated in other realms of life, or as an extension of the propaganda arm of the state.

I have noticed a shift during my lifetime on the matter of socialism and its prospects. In my childhood in the early part of this century many adults genuinely expected to live to see a socialist America. They were idealists or practical persons, as the case may be, but they were revolutionaries who saw the new order as something imminent. They were secular apocalyptics, if you will, who saw the end of capitalism around the corner. Today in this country there has been a sea change. Few of my seniors and fewer of my contemporaries hold to such an expectation. Hence the use of the term "Utopian" for those who talk of socialism. I am not a prophet nor the son of a prophet, and I haven't the remotest idea whether even with all the miracles of biochemistry and social security I shall live to see a socialist America. I do not dismiss the possibility as airily as many; but whether I see it in my day or not, I am thoroughly convinced that it is marching toward me at a rapid pace. And I wish to speak of the reasons for my confidence. It is interesting that in spite of the prevailing assumption of our public relations experts that socialism is an absurd mirage, our politicians seem genuinely frightened at the challenge of socialism, not on the other side of the globe, but here at home.

On April 15, 1956, former President Herbert Hoover spoke in Dallas, Texas, to the Inter-American Bar Association and delivered his sharpest barbs at the "hermit crabs" of socialism in the western hemisphere conspiring to overthrow the government. He castigated its advocates as a cult of disloyalty. Mr. Hoover charges that these hermit crabs propose a planned or managed economy. They are for nationalization of some of our industries. They favor a centralized government.

On March 11th of that same year, at a breakfast meeting of 5,000 Masons, Senator Karl Mundt of South Dakota cautioned his listeners about the socialist dangers in our federal government. He spoke of impatient men who are cutting the sound moorings of private enterprise, and the rewards of our merit system. These straws indicate a sensitivity to the issue which I think confirms my thesis that the socialist discussion is not a mere academic issue. For all of the silence about socialism in our mass circulation magazines or on TV screens, it is an issue which sober citizens should come to terms with if they care for the future, distant and immediate alike.

Anna Louise Strong in her May, 1956 issue of *Today* began her editorial: "History moves with a swift current since Christmas. Its direction is still the same. The Soviet world leads from strength and the West is dazed by it. The West has had the world by the tail for 400 years, but the tail has jerked loose. Basically, this power shift includes three aspects, inter-twined: A shift of power from imperial states to colonial peoples, a shift of power from the white to the colored races, the earth's majority, and a shift of power from the capitalist system to the socialist." She then says, "Such power shifts march inevitably; as long as men continue to live and move and strive on our planet, they are the essence of man's collective life. No man can halt them. They may be delayed slightly, but only slightly."

I was interested that the eminent and conservative Christian historian, Arnold Toynbee, in a broadcast on Town Meeting of the Air on November 27, 1955, noted this power shift from the West. He said: "In the last 41 years the West has lost power and the Western way of life has lost credit. It is plain to the rest of the world. We have allowed Western rulers to overthrow and abuse freedom." Those of you who have made a study of Toynbee's ten volumes, or even the summaries of them, know that he anticipates a new system of compromise and combination of capitalism and socialism.

Miss Strong and Dr. Toynbee are both saying, it seems to me, what Joseph Needham of Cambridge University in England said in 1937, "The disillusioned masses will never return to liberal individualism but may very well pass to true collectivism, hence the frenetic enmity with which fascist leaders pursue the spectre of Bolshevism." Now, 20 years later, it seems highly probable that the colonial peoples and colored masses of the earth will encircle America with a socialist society of some form or other, leaving us an island of "free enterprise" ever less free and faced with the challenge of transformation or death.

We need as Americans to face the facts of life overseas if we are to understand our own future. In the have-not three-quarters of the world the populations are multiplying rapidly, the standard of living is falling, capital accumulation falls far behind the most elementary needs, the peasant economies are dead. The colonial peoples are aware of their poverty and also aware of the possibilities of economic change open to them. They know that the state alone can adequately undertake the job of gathering capital investment and gathering the human resources. This is socialism; and the economists and states-men of the have-not nations know it well and have no illusions that there is any workable alternative. There are American busi-ness men and investors who have immense goodwill regarding the problems of mankind and its poverty, but few of them have the knowledge of what goes on in Burma or Indonesia or Costa Rica. They are victims of what the theologians used to call "invincible ignorance".

Certainly I have no illusion that American socialism will be ushered in by a new edition of Bellamy's *Looking Backward*, or a revival of the magnificent addresses of Washington Glad-den, or Henry Demarest Lloyd or George D. Herron. These men made thousands, nay millions of Americans, into rational humanists and sometimes Christian socialists, and their words watered the soil of a changing America. Thomas Wentworth Higginson, Walter Rauschenbusch and Dr. Harry F. Ward all helped thousands of preachers, writers and teachers to see the madness of our capitalist jungle. With Jack London, Upton Sinclair and Lincoln Steffens they educated millions to a con-ception of a new America where none were to ride on the backs of others, and where the storage of tons of surplus crops would never contaminate the land with its satanic contradiction of hunger in the midst of plenty. What I am saying is that the coming of socialism in the next few years will not be by the eloquent persuasion of idealists like those I have mentioned with honor, but by the necessities of history, the demand of masses of men who look at a world offering rationality and planning in-stead of irrationality and planlessness, masses of men sick with centuries of being on the outside, who repudiate utterly Edmund Burke's statement that the people "must respect the property of which they cannot partake". These awaking masses prefer the Bible to Burke. They remember the Scriptures when they say: "The profit of the earth is for all."

It is true that the socialist movement in the United States has declined to the lowest ebb in half a century. One looks back to Eugene V. Debs' million votes, while in jail, as something not of this century but some golden age in ancient times. But as we look at the sad estate of organized socialism here let us keep some perspectives. One third of the human family at least, more nearly two-fifths, are living under socialism now. Socialism is stronger than it was fifty years ago in almost every country on the globe except the United States, Spain, the Union of South Africa, Guatemala and Monaco. It is apparent to hundreds of millions of living people that socialism corresponds to the basic needs and aspirations of human beings under the demographic and technological conditions of the 20th century.

I know perfectly well that thousands of labor leaders who were once socialists (even voting socialists) have recanted, and now find America a paradise of Cadillacs and swimming pools, Ed Sullivanized culture and time-payment world tours by TWA. I know that we have come to believe that the bubble will never burst, that credit can be forever inflated and the two-car family become a reality in all forty-eight states. But a working minister who meets people when they have finished reading *Life* and *Look,* when they have no more credit and no job, has less reason to be dazzled by the mirage of "everlasting" prosperity. People come to my church as refugees from Mississippi and Alabama. I talk with folks who find it is true that real wages are lower, not higher, than a decade ago and who face financial disaster in spite of unemployment insurance and $85-a-month old-age pensions. (Have you tried living on $85 a month lately?)

Do not think my allusion to the socialist saints of the past 85 years are derogatory because they were philosophers instead of economists. As a minister I have a very high regard for the ideological argument for socialism. It is basic that we have it clearly in our minds as we look at the material necessities of the case. A nation, or a world, that flies in the face of human aspirations for equality will find no economics adequate to hold power over its people. Socialism will prevail, early or late, because it satisfies the equalitarian hungers of mankind. It is more consistent with the real needs of human nature than predatory capitalism, however disguised. I know that Thurman Arnold in "The Folklore of Capitalism" denies this, but I think Einstein was closer to reality than the former assistant Attorney-General. Einstein pointed out that "a predatory so-

ciety accentuates the egoistic drives of man's make-up while
his social drives progressively deteriorate. They become prisoners of their own egotism"; and that is what has happened
to millions of splendid Americans. By reading their news and
pre-digested opinions off the backs of advertisements called
newspapers, or getting their cultural entertainment between ever
longer TV commercials, they find the prison doors locked.
They actually come to believe that every other man is a com-
petitor, a rival for their job, a fellow out to get the customer's
order before they do. But throughout the world today there
is a decisive majority (counting millions living in capitalist
nations) who are ready to try something other than economic
anarchy, or a prosperity of time payments. Such a climate
breeds earthquake weather. Men are increasingly ready to
say that it is no longer safe to leave either the ownership of
the earth's resources or the tools of industrial production in the
private hands of irresponsible individuals or the legal fictions
of bloodless corporations, where whim or the desires of a
moneyed elite rather than the needs of the majority dictate
their employment.

It has long been recognized that men can be kept prisoners
for incredibly long periods, and that they will suffer intolerable
evils for years before breaking the bonds placed upon them by
their fellows. Historians have long pointed to the use of priests
in this process of inculcating patience among the exploited
and enslaved. I am not minimizing the importance of education of the masses (when the means for such enlightenment
can be secured). I remember the ancient answer of Confucius
when asked what one should do for the people: "Feed and enrich them . . . then educate them." To be sure the process of
education today is frustrated with great diligence. With unprecedented means of communication around the globe, millions
in our own land are bereft of even the clementary facts of their
own democratic, economic and cultural possibilities. The loyalty oaths fastened on churches and schools in California are
very immediate and familiar to me. The ostracism of the public speaker who says "socialism" even under his breath is not a
fiction but a very present reality.

But we see an America coming to self-knowledge the hard way
these days. Thousands upon thousands of colored citizens are
being educated in the South today to the possibilities of a

better way of life. The Montgomery bus boycott was a school
more effective than any seen in years. It may be that by the
hundredth anniversary of the Emancipation Proclamation (five
years away), Negro citizens will in actuality have the ballot in
all the Southern states.

We Americans cannot afford more "Little Rock" publicity
in the press of the world. After 388 years the Negro people
are not only losing patience with promises, they are finding
the peaceful weapons of resistance to second class economic and
social citizenship. If capitalism is what keeps them in menial
positions, then, say more and more Negroes, let us try socialism. They may not verbalize it so bluntly, but this is the gist
of their logic as they see a paradoxical culture of Continental
convertibles and Mississippi slums.

The Mexican-Americans of California saw one of their own
nominated for lieutenant governor on the Democratic ticket
two years ago. A large minority of white citizens in Virginia
voted for integration of schools a year ago. This is tremendous
progress and is a hint of majorities to come. The tidal wave
of resistance to the Confederacy mentality is something we have
not seen in this country before. The rule of Southern white
supremacists in our Congress is far from over, but it is threatened. The Democratic Party is riven by a moral principle.
The Jim Crow southern section of the party cannot "accept"
racial integration, the northern majority cannot win an election
without it. Integration cannot be avoided by lynchings, murders or legal tricks for many years more. But we may well ask
how much martyrdom must it take to bring the Constitution
into effective operation? We are not discussing socialism in an
abstract fashion. It is more than a matter of pamphlets. It is a
matter of lives.

The Negro people of Montgomery have shown America that
it is possible to have social change without force and violence
on their part. The Supreme Court is showing us that it is
possible to have social change without force and violence. But
White Citizens Councils, demagogues like Governor Faubus of
Arkansas, and nameless groups of diehard racists are insisting
that they want force and violence rather than any revision of
economic and social arrangements clearly repudiated by a majority of our people and our courts. The great Methodist
Church, with millions in its membership, has asserted the possi-

bility of an integrated church and set going the machinery for its fulfillment, without force and violence. None but the most blind and obdurate today in our own land are insisting upon the ancient weapons of rifle and rope, or the newest weapons of hydrogen fission to delay the equality now demanded by the American people.

The seven hundred capitalists who gathered in October, 1957, in San Francisco, under the aegis of Publisher Henry Luce, did not have any illusions about the ability of America to provide for the economic needs of our entire 170 million people. A nation that can hurl deadly missiles into outer space, a nation that can build vast military bases on scores of foreign shores and islands and equip them with thousands of nuclear bombs for instantaneous lethal delivery, can feed, clothe, shelter and educate its citizens from its rich natural resources and its technological skill. The ability is there, as every issue of Mr. Luce's magazine *Fortune* makes manifest to all readers. Whether the struggle for power by authentic delegates of the masses of the people succeeds without civil strife remains to be seen. The American capitalists at the San Francisco conference seemed on the whole to reveal no malice, just ignorance of the temper of many millions, in other lands and in America as well, millions without a chain of magazines at their command, or a network of TV and radio stations.

As these words are being written Aneurin Bevan, of the Labor Party in Great Britain, is visiting in California and pointing out some of the commonplaces summarized above. He is saying that private property, if irresponsible to social need, must yield to other power—to democratic forces represented by organized labor and an aroused electorate. The achievement of a socialist America can be a thing of peace, of law, of persuasion. This is not just a preacher saying so. It is a Justice Warren, a Senator Lehman, a Governor Williams, a Secretary-General Hammarskjold, and more important, the masses of enlightened men and women who support them, plain folk who may or may not have a schematic doctrine of socialism, but who know that present technology and industry and transportation and agriculture are capable of fulfilling their material necessities.

We are not today in a primitive society in which the pleas for sanity and brotherhood from an Asoka or an Iknahton or an Amos seemed hopeless idealism. Today their words jibe with actual possibility. Their aspirations become necessity if we are not to occupy an atomic grave of our own digging. There is no Negro diamond miner in the Transvaal who need be ignorant nor hungry, no Mexican farm laborer who need suffer the ravages of disease as have his ancestors for centuries. This we know is true: the demonstrations are not theoretical but history in our own time. Ministers of any conscience refuse to dismiss as Utopian the concept of a reconstructed social order which offers every possibility of a far healthier life for the people living in it, the workers who constitute its overwhelming majority, as well as the professionals and administrators who conduct its operation.

We have abundant evidence, that needs no detailed rehearsal here, of the tragic costliness of monopoly capitalism in human terms. A social order where vast wealth is concentrated in a few hands and daily insecurity is the fate of great majorities produces a warring, neurotic and vulgar civilization which is its own condemnation. I write these words while visiting a desert community where men in ten thousand dollar imported automobiles drive past fabulous ranch houses of movie and television stars in one block and then, in a matter of seconds, find the scene one of indescribably shabby slums, slums where Indians, Mexicans and Negroes fight the heat and insects without benefit of air conditioning or filtered swimming pools.

These contradictions may be so commonplace that they make no impression on a deadened conscience, but they reap a harvest nevertheless. Such a warring society of class against class leads by cruel logic to headlines about drug addiction, airline murders for a mother's insurance, sky-rocketing divorce figures, juvenile insecurity and crime, mass alcoholism and crowded mental hospitals.

We place strait-jackets on the minds of our teachers and public employees; we drive honest officials out of our foreign service with loyalty checks; we restrict the travel of scientists and scholars; we tie the hands of labor organization with repressive legislation; we cater to the pornographic in magazines and films, and generally advertise our sickness to a shocked world. The number of persons in every stratum of society seeking professional help from psychiatrists, psychologists and other counselors is all too familiar. Men and women might endure all of this stoically (as they did in the Dark Ages) if they saw no practical alternatives, but in spite of a conspiracy of slander and a curtain of silence, they receive tidings of quite workable alternatives. Even so obscure a person as myself was forbidden a passport to Australia a few years ago, but such capricious tricks, for all their inconvenience to us, are self-defeating. Ideas, as well as radioactive dust, sweep across all boundaries. Louis XVI and George III and later the Romanoffs found this to be true, and so will the passport division of the State Department and postal inspectors impounding books and pamphlets at our seaports.

Hardly a week passes without someone asking me: Why is socialism so unpopular in America in 1958? Why is America one of the few nations in the world in the mid-twentieth century with an almost non-existent socialist movement? The answers are many and taken individually may seem unconvincing. To take them together may explain the reason in part for the thundering silence in our country today about solutions which were once commonplace conversation in millions of American homes.

I have already spoken of the overt and familiar instruments of repression which make a man of modest means think twice about joining a party proposing radical reform. They are best symbolized by the Smith and McCarran Acts, aimed at silencing and demobilizing not only the Communist Party, but all parties with serious socialist intentions. A man thinks twice, whatever his philosophical principles, before writing a pamphlet, paying party dues, holding a political meeting in his home, or even preaching a socialist sermon, if he reads the news in the daily papers about the men and women now languishing in the common jail for these traditional activities of free-born Americans. He may be a convinced socialist and still be short of acting like a Christian martyr. He may not feel sufficiently affluent to bid farewell to a wife and three children, and enter a federal penitentiary for two years under a contempt of Congress citation for using his legal Constitutional privileges. I know and profoundly respect a number of writers and artists who have, without affluence, paid this price, but it is hard to mobilize sufficient votes to elect a socialist President when such a penalty hangs over the head of every proven voter in such an enterprise.

And it would be a little less than realistic to deny the rewards, bribes if you prefer, paid to those who will forget their dreams of a socialist society for the more immediate dividends that come from supporting the prevailing economic folkways, (whatever one may think of them *sub specie aeternatatis*). A very intelligent and charming woman came into my study a week ago and said that after 32 years of marriage to a labor official, during which time they had both been active socialists, she found herself deserted, and asked for divorce because her husband found her continued activities with public meetings "leftish", reading and radical table conversation an "embarrassment". Her husband was receiving an annual salary of $8,000, buying a new car every other year, and was satisfied to go along with the top echelons of his union's hierarchy, even though he knew it was a sellout of the socialism he once advocated with full heart and consenting mind. "It will not come in our lifetime, so why buck the way things are?" Beck and Hoffa are not alone. Their examples have been contagious to many a "pie card" in the lower echelons of labor.

This case study in the success of what Kenneth Burke calls the "cult of acquiescence" has, of course, its more flamboyant parallels from coast to coast. The purge of labor by the Truman and Eisenhower administrations is a familiar story, but it is related to the question "Why is socialism so rarely mentioned in public today?" It may not be Utopian to advocate American socialism, but it is certainly hard on the budget of those who believe life must include a motor boat and a deep freeze if existence is to be bearable. "What if there are layoffs and speedups? This is part of the grief." . . . "Why ask too many questions of the men on the picket line at Kohler and Westinghouse? They never had it so good." The cynicism of the man who has sold his vision of a socialist world is part of the social wreckage you and I must count as we ask, "What price a people's democracy?"

It is hard for the people of China or Burma to understand the paradox of a George Meany in a million-dollar office building in Washington, whose great union is made up of the men who must be foot soldiers in any World War III, who is more militant than the President in the White House in demanding a larger arms program and a more expansive military aid program overseas. Does all this mean that we should just sit it out and wait for our fellow citizens in other lands to win the battle for a classless society? Does this mean that we should seal the

lip and look the other way so as not to offend the oligarchs of
finance and industry who find this the best of all possible worlds
and are at ease in Zion, albeit a Zion which includes ulcers,
alcoholism and utter boredom when the last gadget has been
bought and the last tour of the Caribbean completed?

I think a great many people have been drained of their
courage and their faith in recent years, by devoutly hoping that
the organizational men in the gray flannel suits could keep
them happy with their gospel of an endless cornucopia called
prosperity and full employment, even if it be the employment
of tool makers for the jet fighter plane, the guided missile and
the cobalt bomb. The postponment of a welfare society, with
planned production of the things all men and women need,
includes an acceptance we too often forget: acceptance of need-
less misery, continued housing shortagages, curable diseases,
postponed higher education, shelved scientific research, and the
blunt control of impudent socialists in various Guatemalas.

I am not only protesting the shoddy substitutes for culture
and health and human character that the postponement of
socialism gives us. I am angry that we never say what is so
obvious to any thinking man: that American socialism could
and would outlaw racial and religious discrimination overnight;
that it would open hospitals to people irrespective of income;
that it would really open the doors to criticism and dissent; that
it would welcome creative experiment and exploration, not so
much of the stratosphere as of the earth itself for a more
abundant life, not for an occasional Grace Kelly and her Prince,
but for millions of children who yearn for a warm school lunch,
a public pool in the summer, a well stocked library and a father
not too exhausted to play games when he gets home from work.
It is perfectly true that a Socialist America could be stupid,
dull and mechanical, with a thin veneer of culture, and as
standardized as life has become for millions in our Sears, Roebuck
civilization of 1958, but this would be a risk we could take without too much peril, considering the vulgarization that goes on
in our public and private life today. Millions can be conditioned,
you may argue, to really like "rock and roll", sadistic comic
books and movies about space-borne monsters raiding earth for
its current crop of Sabine women. But it can be equally well
argued that millions could find their communication media and
schools, theatres and halls, used for the creative work of artists

and composers, playrights and actors at a level never yet attained. Economic slavery has for centuries been at the root of all other slaveries of the mind and body. The achievements of socialist nations in this century give us some reason to think that when a people have a chance to write a budget for their own cultural and social life, they will show a great amount of common sense. After ten years of cold war vilification of our friends behind the so-called "iron curtain" we are now finding that they have been quite successful in their pursuit of the fine arts: What a paradox that the Soviet "barbarians" have but to send over an Oistrakh, a Gilels, a Rostopovich, to pack every concert hall they enter.

Let me be as plain as I know how. It is not utopian to advocate any improvement over the present arrangements that seems practical, within the borders of possibility for ourselves with our present knowledge and power. While we still are living in what W. H. Auden in his poem on Spain called "the military empires of tiger and shark", we are also living in a time of unparalleled self-knowledge about the human heart and its glorious possibilities for decency and joy. We most certainly are not the crown of the evolutionary process, the highest production of which nature is capable. As Joseph Needham says in *History is on Our Side*: "If we look back upon the past as a chaos compared with our own high level of organization, it is extremely probable that men of the future will look back on our age as an age of chaos."

Personally, I think the hour is far closer than the public press or Congress or the union local admits, that it will be sooner than we think that the conscience of the world, and of our own people too, will be totally outraged at the spectable of natural resources being the property of private men, who from their chance ownership derive personal benefit, and who permit access to these resources only on their own terms. Let me say frankly that I do not minimize the value of the advances made toward socialism within our capitalist framework. I rejoice at Nebraska's first publicly-owned atomic power plant, at Tennessee's TVA, at the hundreds of city-owned power and light plants, and all the steps being taken to save our national forests, our waterways, our public schools and state hospitals (to mention at random a few pre-socialist ventures the American people can see with their own eyes.) I am for the pre-socialist demonstration—the city health clinic, the government life insurance policy, the state pension to the blind.

As a minister, a social worker if you prefer, I see a maturing of the world's conscience in my own time on this matter. It is now becoming a planetary scandal that men perish in the midst of wealth abounding. Socialism of a modern, workable, scientific form is sweeping the earth because there is no comradeship possible, no self respect or fraternity possible, in the chaos of capitalist organization. This is obvious now, not only to scholars in their academic lofts; it is a moral possession of tremendous masses who are walking out of deliberately maintained darkness into sunlight and knowledge.

I do not know the date of our American release from economic thraldom, but I do not place it in some distant time beyond the skies as did our primitive Christian brothers of the first century. The mystic, Julian of Norwich, once wrote: "In the end all shall be well, but not in our time." I feel his moderate optimism has been outstripped. The millions of people in India, in Africa, in China, in South America, are saying "Not tomorrow, but today." Whether by cataclysm or gradual enlightenment our own millions will soon say the same thing; this I truly believe. I know that many old socialists, once hopeful that they would see the dawn of socialism across the American plains, are now disillusioned. I know the statistics of minority party memberships and the withering fire that has made them the figures they are, but on sober second thought it would be well to remember the old revolutionary saying: "All the battles of the working class are defeats, except the last."

I do not subscribe to the fatalism of some of my socialist friends that we just wait for disaster to be the great teacher. There is something ghoulish and misanthropic about such a posture. I do believe we can all play a part at some point in working for the acceptance of a socialist America, even in modest ways. In the Congressional election year of 1958 and the Presidential election of 1960 millions of dollars will be spent on telecasts and broadcasts, on billposters and pamphlets, on polls and films. You may feel that the American public can be purchased in this fashion in spite of anything we can do about it. I do not. If several million Americans would speak out, ask questions, write letters, talk to their neighbors, ring doorbells, attend party caucuses, interview candidates, join delegations, the two major parties could be forced to positions they haven't otherwise the least intention of taking. The farmers of the midwest have already begun to demonstrate such energy. Many trade unionists of the rank and file are showing similar zeal, in spite of corruption and irresponsibility and collusion with management at the top levels.

If we are ever to have a militant party with a socialist platform it will be formed by men and women seasoned in political struggle, not by men and women sitting cynically at home on their hands and their ballots. The Negro people of Montgomery have shown us this truth. The NAACP has shown us this truth. The Quakers have been showing it for years. If socialism is possible in the 20th century in America, and I believe it is, it will be shaped and organized and won by a vigorous and seasoned body of shock troops who come from existing parties, who come from existing unions, who come from existing churches. It is sheer defeatism to say such a party cannot be built in a country of 160 million people.

We had better be getting to work and learning the skills of political agitation, persuasion and action at some level now, or we will trigger the very catastrophe any man of compassion would pray to avoid. We have an arsenal of political rights in our Constitution, and a magnificent Populist, labor-farmer, socialist tradition, small but enormously successful in getting reforms adopted in the century past. There is no reason for pessimism, even in these fat years of war-fed prosperity. We can have the commonwealth of justice for all the sons of men if we choose it. The decision lies with us today.

The American Family
and Socialism

By Bertha Capen Reynolds

IN THE UNITED STATES the comforts of living have multiplied within one lifetime. In rural or urban U.S.A. we have moved from water pails to hot and cold faucets, from privies to plumbing, from stove fires to automatic heating, from washboards to mechanized home laundries, from kerosene lamps to electric lighting, from cooling food in a tin pail hung in the well to refrigeration and packaged frozen foods. The telephone, radio and television have brought the happenings of the world into the family living room. Motor cars have vastly increased family mobility, and a few hours' flight by air takes us to any part of the globe. What more do we want?

This is called the American standard of living. Yet one can travel for days through rural states and see shacks unfit for human habitation, with none of these comforts. One can turn off the glittering avenues of our great cities into slums where the tenements are wretched, rat-ridden fire-traps, obsolete more than fifty years ago and still inhabited. It takes an income to provide for "the American way of life".

The Heller Committee for Research in Social Economics at

BERTHA CAPEN REYNOLDS, author of "Learning and Teaching in the Practice of Social Work", and "Social Work and Social Living", has been a psychiatric social worker, teacher and consultant in this field since 1913, contributing frequently to professional journals. She is a member of the *National Association of Social Workers,* and the *American Orthopsychiatric Association.* A New Englander by birth, she has been close to early-American traditions. She states that her "long experience with families and communities has convinced her that for prevention of human misery and for healthy national life only socialism makes sense".

the University of California priced its budget for a family of four, in September 1956, at $5593 annually, or nearly $108 per week. In the same period, 1956, weekly earnings in manufacturing averaged $80.13, and in non-manufacturing occupations tended to be still lower. According to the Federal Reserve Board sampling of consumer finances in 1955, half of all family spending units received a money income of less than $3960 a year, and 64 per cent had incomes of less than $5000.[1] Only about a third of the families in the United States, therefore, earned enough to equal the standard of the Heller Committee budget.

Statistics on consumer credit show by what means the American people live as well as they do. Mortgage debt in 1956 was 34.5 percent of the total personal income, after taxes, of the people of the United States. Installment debt, mainly for cars and household durable goods, amounted to 11 percent of the annual after-tax income of individuals at the end of 1956.[2]

The cost of credit, of course, adds materially to the cost of living. The rise in credit financing must mean that the American people insist upon a high standard of living at any price. If they are to feel that they *belong* in a country where corporation profits are the highest in history and a spate of advertising flows over radio, press and screen, they can not afford to "think poor".

As one answer to insufficient income, many fathers carry one or two extra jobs outside the working day—for the shortening of which labor fought bitter struggles a generation ago. Mothers also work outside the home. Of all mothers in the United States with children under 18 years, five and a quarter millon, or one in four, was in the labor force in 1951, and more than two million of these had children under 6 years of age. There are no statistics covering all facilities for day care of children, but limited surveys show that over 40 percent of those listed are operated on a commericial basis, and over half the facilities are in only six states.[3] What, then, is the cost to family life of the effort of mothers and fathers to keep up with the "American standard of living"?

If a comfortable life is the American standard, freedom from anxiety does not seem to be a part of it. Loss of income, whether by unemployment or business failure, is the wolf at the door of almost everyone. The United States Census Bureau, in 1955, estimated that out of a civilian labor force of 65.8 million an

average of about 4 percent were fully unemployed. Estimates
vary from 2.5 percent in a prosperous year to as high as 12 percent in depressed areas. These figures do not reflect irregular
and part-time employment. Business failures numbered over
12,000 in 1956, hitting most heavily the smaller firms.[4]

The history of labor struggles in recent years shows that
negotiations have been for such benefits as a guaranteed annual
wage, shortened hours to compensate for increased production
per man, pensions, sick benefits. These demands reflect the
anxieties of the nation's workers over cuts in take-home pay,
displacement of workers by new machines that almost tend
themselves, speed-up of machines to a pace that human flesh
can not bear, a pace that makes a man old at forty.

Farm owners were once thought more secure than other
workers. The trend, however, is toward elimination of the
family-sized farm, and increase in the number of farms of a
thousand acres or more, which can afford expensive mechanization. Average prices received by farmers for all commodities
in 1956 had decreased by 18 percent since 1948, while prices
farmers had to pay for what they bought increased 11 percent.
The per capita net income of the farm population in 1955 was
less than half that of the non-farm population, and nearly a
third of this income was from work for wages outside the farm.
For the Negro farm population incomes were less than half
those of the white farm families.[5]

Where to find a place to live is as critical a problem for
American families as how to meet the cost. An acute housing
shortage of many years' duration is not relieved by "slum clear-
ance" which replaces substandard dwellings by expensive apart-
ments, and drives low-income families into worse and more
crowded slums. Negro, Puerto Rican, Mexican and Oriental
families can not buy the housing of their choice at any price,
in most areas, because of discrimination fostered by real estate
interests. For families of any but the highest levels of income
there are not enough homes being built to keep up with the
increase in population, to say nothing of replacing the 15 million dwelling units below the minimum standard of decency.
Since government control of profiteering in rents has broken
down since the war, the governmentally subsidized low-cost
housing has become a necessity for working class families. Yet,

since the Housing Act of 1954, government plans have sharply cut public funds for low-rent rehousing projects.[6]

The American dream has been that every generation could look forward to a better life for its children. Is the dream becoming a nightmare? The relatively full employment of recent years has been geared to war and preparation for war. The United States appropriated 67 percent of its total budget for the fiscal year beginning July1, 1956 for war preparations (85 percent if one includes the obligations from past wars). while it allotted only 3 percent of its budget for social security, welfare and health.[7]

Even if war preparations create prosperity of a sort, must American families raise their children to be bomb-targets, crawling under the desks of their deteriorating schools for futile protection? Must they go without essential health care, education and homes to keep the war stocks booming? Must war scares, stimulated when military appropriations are sought, silence voices for peace by the cry of "subversive", and make destruction of civil liberties the price to be paid for "security"?

It is not surprising that children growing up in a world preparing for annihilation, their minds fed by comic books and television programs full of violence and crime, should want to live with excitement, even if briefly. The facts about juvenile delinquency are frightening. Not only did teen-age crime increase by 45 percent between 1949 and 1954, but more than a million youngsters who came in conflict with the law in the latter year were charged with more than usually serious crimes.[8] Parents (even if they are able to spend time with their children) can not control commercial seduction of young people to violence, vice and drug addiction. To what future can our children look forward under capitalism, even if they escape total destruction in war?

What vocational future? As mechanization increasingly displaces manpower in industrial production, unemployment must rise to menacing proportions unless vocations are developed to fill leisure hours and increase the world's store of knowledge and enrich its culture. In our present society, cultural and sports programs are now offered either as profit-making ventures which are quite inadequate to the need for them, or, if government undertakes them on a mass scale, they are attacked as that evil thing called "creeping socialism".

A war economy such as we have blocks education of large numbers of young people for creative vocations in two ways. First, education is deteriorating for lack of money for school equipment and teachers. Then, in hysterical search for "subversive" tendencies among educators, actors, writers and artists, those in power force workers in these fields to stifle independent and creative thinking, and to conform (or even to *inform* against others) or face loss of livelihood and possible imprisonment. At best, cultural activities must have sponsors, whose approval must be constantly sought—either advertisers who can spend millions, or government itself, which is already exhausting its resources for weapons of destruction. So, under capitalism, security in creative work seems a utopian dream.

Perhaps the best vocational future for young people is in servicing the new complicated machines, and in planning extended use of the new sources of power. Scientific and technical education will be required. In this, however, the United States lags behind the socialist USSR,[9] and is facing an acute shortage of science teachers and of students who elect scientific courses.

Suppose young people find the best opportunities in salesmanship, working on the minds of consumers to induce more buying and better "public relations", or selling insurance against every conceivable danger in a time when everyone is hungry for security. There are good money rewards in this field, but what haunting fear that one misstep, one big advertiser offended, will mean vocational suicide!

America is many things. Even if all we have said is true, it is also probable that nowhere in the world are so many people so well off materially as in the United States today. Why do we need socialism?

We spend vast and increasing sums for welfare services and grants, and yet those who administer those services know that they can do nothing about the necessities people lack. Capitalism can not keep its promises to more than a small top fraction of its population. Capitalism can not avoid a housing crisis that makes the word home a mockery to millions of families. Capitalism can not avoid laying off men in favor of more profitable machines. It can not avoid depressions, when consumers can not buy, nor threats of war to stimulate business. Capitalism can not avoid edging to the brink of war, constantly, to secure raw materials and markets, and to exploit the labor power of other countries. Capitalism makes a travesty of political democracy when a poor man's vote gives him choice only among candidates and polices which may be good for the largest corporations, but not for him.

We have a noble traditon of democracy in this land. The changes, as it has moved from an economy of scarcity in an undeveloped country to high production in a mechanized economy, demand that democracy be brought up to date. The rule of a few families controlling the nation's resources is not the same thing as the rule of the people of the United States over themselves. Either we must have economic democracy, or we shall lose the political democracy our fathers fought and died to win.

Socialism is economic democracy. Some say that socialism is only a utopian pipe-dream. It is not untried. One country has lived under socialism for forty years, and close to one half of the people in the world are trying out some form of it. Our press and radio exhaust themselves to convince us that socialism is the greatest of evils. Do we take the trouble to find out what it really is, and how it works?

Socialism means, first of all, that the people of a country own its natural wealth and resources for production, and have determined to use them, themselves, rather than to hand them over to a privileged class to divert to their private gain. The source of wealth in the labor power of men and women is not to be exploited for an employer's private profit. What workers produce is used by them for better living, or pooled for better common services for all. Under socialism, no man can deny another an opportunity to work, and an obligation to work according to one's ability is ingrained in national consciousness. Planned production is substituted for the anarchy of competition for profit. Making war loses its incentives when everybody loses and no one can profit from the destruction of war.

If the majority of the people of the United States want to develop a socialist system, in what ways will the lives of American families be different? Using the experience of countries now living under socialism, one can predict that certain characteristics of socialism will bring certain inevitable changes, along with differences due to national history and traditions. What are these changes?

1. There will be no unemployment. With profit no longer a motive, work that is needed will occupy people of all ages, according to their ability. If mothers choose to work outside the home there will be organized housekeeping and child-care services so that families do not suffer. Women will have the range of vocational choice now open to men, and a place in many new occupations. Work will be related to demand for goods and services, not limited by opportunities for profitable investment.

2. There will be leisure for everyone, not the bitter leisure of unemployment nor the aimless leisure of the parasite but the shortened hours of labor made possible by automatic machinery. A socialist society neither oversupplies its wants nor holds back technical improvements to protect former investments. With leisure, families need not be strangers to their children, nor be starved for culture, sports or challenging avocations.

3. The consumer's dollar, freed from heavy taxation to support a competitive struggle for national dominance, will be worth more to the consumer. Prices will be reduced when supplies are abundant, since there are no monopolies to control prices. Fixed charges on income, like rent, will be controlled under socialism, so that more of the family's funds will be subject to personal choice. Families will not have to pay the staggering costs of advertising to sell competing products.

4. Young men and women can look forward to exciting careers in science, technology and the arts. A socialist society explores the land which belongs to all its people, without having to ask any private corporation whether it expects to profit, or fears such explorations will endanger its present investments. Vast projects in flood and drought control, discovery of minerals, studies in plant and animal life, even changes in climate and topography, are characteristic of socialist countries. Education for careers in these fields is not limited to a privileged few, but open to all who show ability and are willing to work. Through public aid to the arts cultural workers will have an exciting audience of a vast population, previously denied access to the best in culture, keenly sympathetic and critical.

5. Under socialism, workers provide for themselves, collectively and completely, against the hazards of life. Unemployment is not a hazard, but for sickness there is comprehensive medical care which becomes preventive health care for the

whole population. There is complete social insurance coverage for old age and disability. All the benefits which workers begin to demand under capitalism, and secure only partially, become a reality when a nation's people possess the natural resources and the fruits of labor which actually belong to them.

Strangely enough, it is the very security of a socialist system that is most objected to in America today. Suppose people do have guaranteed employment, leisure, health care and old-age protection. Will they not deteriorate, lose initiative, become mass-minded robots? Are young people in socialist countries well off perhaps only because they have more done for them more consistently than is true under capitalism? And what does that do to them as persons?

Something more than freedom from fear of want *is* needed to produce happiness and personal growth. Psychiatrists and social workers have learned, through years of study of anxious and disturbed people, that economic security is not enough. For the emotional security which makes growth possible there must be a sense of belonging, of being worthwhile, a chance to love and be loved as an individual, a chance to achieve something of value to the social group which makes one's world.

We know that many children in America grow up without this basic emotional security and, if they escape a bed in one of our crowded mental hospitals, lead frustrated and unhappy lives. Perhaps their harassed parents can not love them; perhaps they have to live in slums where they are not treated with human dignity; perhaps they are children of minority groups, taunted for color or creed and denied the chance that others have, to be honored for fine achievement. What we have said about opportunities under socialism indicates that some of the emotional needs mentioned here would be met in that different mental climate. The critical question is whether young people under socialism stand a better chance of having the priceless ingredient for growth—achievement accomplished by struggle with challenging difficulties.

The outstanding fact is that far more is expected of people who are building a socialist society than in an economy where they are replaceable cogs in a profit-making machine. In jobs of responsibility and challenge they are accountable to their peers, for the work and its results belong to them all. Such jobs must be prepared for by years of work and study. Incen-

tives under socialism, for which men and women endure great
toil and hardship, are the rewards of recogniton for good work
in the public service.

How could a nation with the history and traditions of our
United States attain a socialist system provided it seemed to the
majority of the people to be desirable? Our brief survey outlining the very different conditions that prevail in countries
under socialism suggests strongly one thing: To administer an
economic, as well as a political system would require that a
whole nation participate more responsibly in government than
our experience under capitalism has prepared us to do. We
may well feel that the USSR, which has transformed a backward
nation into the second greatest world power in forty years, has
not solved all the problems of democracy. Neither have we.
Have we come to think of our government (from which the
benefits presently enjoyed by American families have been won
by organized struggle of working people over many years) as
indeed a "welfare state"? Is it best approved when it gives
"handouts", and when it lets alone the enrichment of large
corporations at the expense of the people as a whole? Do we
talk about "government interference", and "government inefficiency", and refer to politics as if it were a dirty job? Can we
ever take on added responsibilities as a democracy unless we
change the detachment of the average citizen to a realization
that the government is ours, and that it is *we* the people?

When we hear that socialism is impossible because "you
can't change human nature", a thoughtful appraisal reminds
us that we *have* changed as a people, as our conditions of
living have changed. Perhaps we have become "soft" since
the pioneer poverty of our ancestors. The struggle of several
generations of parents to give their children more "advantages"
than their parents had has done something to the mental climate
in which children grow up; even as increasing use of machines
has taken from them the necessity of hard physical labor. Perhaps the juvenile delinquency of comfortable neighborhoods
is youth's answer to being robbed of incentives for meeting
difficulty and danger.

The critical question for American families is: For what
are we training our children? Is it to live in ever greater personal comfort? Or is it to bear a fitting part with all other
human beings in the struggle to conquer nature for man's use

and happiness? Do we know how to teach our children self-discipline, courage, sharing, and consideration for others? Do we train them for social responsibility, even in little things such as picking up toys and using public property if, indeed, it belonged to all? Do we, in little daily decisions in the home, give first place not to self-advancement but to carrying out a trust with honor? A generation trained in such principles could know whether socialism would serve its purposes better than capitalism, would have learned how to work unitedly with others to achieve it, and could enjoy living responsibly in a socialist democracy.

A socialist democracy will never be handed to us nor forced upon us. The changes necessary to substitute for private exploitation of the nation's resources the planned use of them, for the welfare of all, will not come easily nor quickly. It is the American families of today who will prepare the responsible citizens of tomorrow. One of the worst effects of living under a competitive system, geared to profit even at the expense of the terrible threat of a war of annihilation, is that it has temporarily robbed us of our heritage as social human beings. We are driven apart from our neighbors by every conceivable prejudice and fear—fear of joining anything that requires energy and courage, fear of speaking out in the market place of ideas, fear even of thinking responsibly about our world. Nothing is more evident, in an age of mechanical power, than that one person or one family is helpless alone. Periods of crisis like a depression or a war have taught us that people united in common action can accomplish amazing things.

Organized effort is our only hope. The social benefits we enjoy today under capitalism have been won by the struggles of working men and women over the past hundred years. Not only economic betterment but public education, health protection, decent housing, protection from the threat of wars for profit are gained by determined struggle of organized bodies of people, getting together as workers, as consumers, as tenants, as parents, or as youth groups, demanding a future of opportunity instead of a wage slave's weariness or a death by violence. In this land of great traditions and great opportunities, we can have whatever we are willing to unite with others to work for with determination and courage.

Suppose we come to see that the times demand a political party that will represent the interests of the majority of the workers of this country, industrial workers, farmers, professionals. Such a party will be born out of the bitter experience that workers are living through now, out of struggles for food and shelter, for decency and the good life beyond stark necessity, struggles for democracy that include everyone without distinction of race, creed, or national origin. These battles will have to be fought in the present historical situation which is unprecedented in its assault upon the very means by which men must free themselves. A whole people has been conditioned to distrust organization, to fear each man his neighbor, to refrain from independent thought or forthright speech. A whole people has become accustomed to associate "welfare measures" with communism (presented as a bogy threatening from outside everything we hold dear), to hate monopoly (but to hate it as "bigness", or as "planned economy", not for its control by private interests), to equate government with inefficiency and corruption, not with a people's power to determine its own best interests.

Such conditionings will be burned out in the crucible of struggle for commonly-felt ends—the welfare of every man, woman, and child. The workers of America will come to find their high duty and privilege in responsible political action and public service. If what they build is socialism, need anyone fear such a future?

NOTES

1 *Labor Fact Book No. 13*, Labor Research Association, New York, pp. 22, 14.
2 *Ibid.*, p. 8.
3 *Bulletin*, Women's Bureau, U.S. Department of Labor, No. 246, pp. 6; 21-23.
4 *Labor Fact Book No. 13*, pp. 9, 11.
5 *Ibid.*, pp. 46, 48, 51, 52.
6 Helen Alfred, "Dynamic Housing", *The Nation*, Oct. 30, 1954.
7 *Labor Fact Book No. 12*, p. 17.
8 *Ibid.*, pp. 48-50.
9 Beatrice King, "Technical Education Under Socialism", *New World Review*, New York, June, 1956.

The Role of the Artist
in Social Change

By John Howard Lawson

HOW DOES ART RELATE to social change? Do American writers, painters, musicians, actors, dancers, direct their work toward improving the social situation? Do they dream of a more abundant future? Do they feel their creative efforts are part of creative processes that affect the course of social development?

It may be noted at once that the questions have "subversive" undertones. A large number of American artists would hasten to deny that they are interested in anything so suspect as wanting to change society. A good many of them, probably a majority in all fields of artistic endeavor, know little of socialism and are honestly convinced that it is alien to the American scene. Many believe socialism means regimentation and the death of art.

Are there other faiths and purposes animating the practice of the arts? Certainly there are aesthetic creeds. But these are canons of taste or technique, and are in large measure dedicated to the principle that art and social action are unrelated. The New Critics, ensconced in positions of authority in colleges

---

JOHN HOWARD LAWSON was born in New York City in 1894. He graduated from Williams College in 1914, served during the First World War in the American Ambulance Service with the French and Italian armies. In 1925, the Theatre Guild production of his *Processional* made theatrical history. His plays include *Success Story, The Pure in Heart, Marching Song*. Among his best known motion picture scripts are *Blockade, Action in the North Atlantic, Algiers, Sahara*. His book, *Theory and Technique of Playwriting and Screenwriting*, is a standard textbook, widely used in schools and colleges. In *The Hidden Heritage*, Mr. Lawson has explored the cultural origins of American history. These books, as well as his study of Hollywood pictures, *Films in the Battle of Ideas*, have been translated into many languages.

and the more influential literary magazines, seek the pure essence of art in "image, metaphor and myth." Among the schools of modern painting, the abstract-expressionists hold an honored place, subscribing (as a critic recently observed) "to the three D's, dehumanization, dematerialization, diffusion . . ." Musical fashions tend to accept Schönberg's view that "Music has no more relation to the external world than a game of chess".

It is not our purpose to discuss aesthetic theories, but rather to stress the present detachment of the arts from any concern with social issues. The divorcement is itself a barometer of the political climate. The idea of change suggests doubt of the *status quo,* and such doubt is discouraged by the dominant culture. The dim view of socialism is not counterbalanced by any other invigorating political faith or social passion.

The situation is new, and marks a break with earlier traditions. Dissent, protest, faith in progress, have shaped American thought over two centuries. We can look back only two decades to the hope and anger that stirred the conscience, and the art, of the thirties. The hope sprang from visions of change —the sight of it taking place, the sense that what was accomplished was small and what was impending was limitless. Anger was the engine of change; challenge and skepticism vitalized the arts.

Today, the dominant culture directs our anger to a danger which is said to originate abroad and to threaten all that is free and creative in our national life. We are told, by almost every means of instruction and communication, that socialism means war and tyranny, that it is a false and rigid dogma imposed on "captive" peoples by force or fraud, and that it will be imposed on us if we do not guard the ramparts of our freedom.

One would suppose that artists would be among the first to man the ramparts, calling all the resources of the arts to the great task of defending our national culture and human values.

Nothing of the sort has happened. We have noted that the arts tend to declare their independence, not so much from a foreign creed, as from their own society.

It is difficult to generalize about the arts in the United States, in view of the bulk and diversity of our cultural product. The plays of Shakespeare, Shaw and O'Neill attract crowds on Broadway. The mediocrity of radio and television is not infrequently broken by flashes of authentic drama and exciting knowledge.

It is hard to draw sober conclusions from the massive statistics of our mass culture. Tens of millions, tabulated by Thendex in the anonymity of their living rooms, are exposed to everything from Bach to Spillane. They seem, according to the statistics, to be receptive, or at least submissive, to the whole range of experience. But we have no way of telling what the experience means to them. We can judge their reaction only by the flick of their fingers on the dial.

However, there are tendencies in contemporary culture which are fairly generally recognized: (1) The anti-Communist witchhunt which has shadowed American life since 1947 has established a blacklist affecting hundreds of professional people in film, radio and television, and the climate of fear limits freedom in every field of art, science and education; (2) Opportunities for Negro artists are limited in many areas of artistic expression, and there are other areas from which Negro artists are wholly excluded; (3) Employment is spotty and economic opportunities are shrinking for American cultural workers; (4) Artists tend to avoid themes that are "controversial" or politically suspect, and emphasize erotic or psychological problems; (5) Critics are inclined to take a gloomy view of the status of the arts.

Defenders of the *status quo* find themselves preoccupied with the ethics and values of business. A stream of novels and studies examine "the Organization Man", the executives in gray flannel suits, the "patterns" of corporate humanity.

The *Saturday Review* recently published a special issue dedicated to "Education and U.S. Business: New Partners", announcing that "the time has come to end the graceless war which has raged for more than 100 years between the businessman and the scholar". Scholars who are unconvinced may be reassured by the leading article, "The Culture of the Business Man," by Crawford H. Greenewalt, President of E. I. du Pont de Nemours. Mr. Greenewalt says that Ralph Waldo Emerson would feel at home in a gathering of business people, and informs us that some business executives are "learned men of vast and unremitting scholarship".

The fact that the *Saturday Review* can so vulgarly applaud "the new partnership of Campus and Executive Suite" is a sufficiently devastating comment on the decline of American culture. The *Saturday Review* itself comments frequently on the sad state of the arts. Only two weeks after the tribute to Big Business, an editorial noted: it is "remarkable that so many of our post-war American writers have fallen by the wayside, or have failed to reveal in their work any continuity of ideas".

James W. Aldridge posed the problem more sharply a few years ago: Modern novelists, he wrote, "have inherited a world without values and since they have no choice but to find their material in that world, they have had to deal with valuelessness, and that can never form the basis for a successful literature".

Underlying the negativism of contemporary culture is the economic uncertainty that inhibits the pursuit of the arts. The difficulties can be documented in any field of artistic endeavor.

Although the Metropolitan Opera broadcasts to large audiences, its operation is beset by financial pressures. The United States has only two or three permanent opera companies, while Germany has fifty.

An American musician employed in a symphony orchestra earns about $1500 per year, and there are only slight hopes of advancement beyond that depressing sum. Young Americans are eager to study the dance, so eager that hundreds of skilled and unemployed dancers throng to every audition.

There are many university and non-professional theatre groups throughout the nation, but the National Council of Arts and Government warns that there are "great stretches of the country which today do not have any professional theatre".

Exhibitions of painting and sculpture attract public attention, but it is not easy to attract buyers. There are almost no painters or sculptors who make a living by their art. They must teach or work in other fields to obtain a livelihood.

To find opportunities for employment, the American artist must turn to mass communication, advertising, industrial design, commercial music, or similar business undertakings. This is the nub of the problem. Corporate power controls the main areas of employment and dictates the nation's cultural policies.

The corporate arts give and withhold jobs according to the conditons of the market. *Collier's* and other big magazines ceased publication in 1956, and others are prepared to die in 1957. When a magazine dies, professional careers die with it.

Thousands of talented people have been thrown out of work by the closing or reduced activity of the Hollywood motion picture industry. Most of them cannot be absorbed into television, which relies to an increasing extent on the back-log of films made under happier circumstances by the people who are now unemployed.

The artist who works under the fear of losing his job is not likely to go too far in asserting his creative independence. He must adjust his aspirations to the requirements of mass communication, which requires a varied program, extravagant in display, assuring the mass audience that all the resources of the world's art are at their disposal.

But the rich fare is ordered by the power that pays the bills. The artist is not a free agent. In certain instances, he is extravagantly paid. But, like the scientist in the commercial laboratory or in government service, he is not the master of his fate.

Our corporate culture includes everything from Shakespeare to *Queens for a Day*. All that it fails to include is the wholeness and intensity of life.

The artist is not forbidden to deal with any aspect of contemporary experience. He may see and depict what he will—provided he does not look too long or probe too deeply, provided he is not carried away by impolitic fervor, provided he avoids uncomfortable extremes of pity or anger.

The American heritage is largely rational and affirmative. It is also individualistic and combative, drawing its strength from controversy and dissent. This is *all* that is lost, the values we have lived by. Without values, the artist loses his purpose and power.

As long as political or corporate influences limit the creative life to the political-corporate view of man's destiny, the passion of the creator is functionless.

William Faulkner has written nobly of the function of the writer. But in a recent interview he scoffs at moral responsibility: "The best job ever offered to me was to become the landlord of a brothel. In my opinion it's the perfect milieu for an artist to work in".[2]

Faulkner has a dour irony. He may be suggesting that the art of our time is suited to the moral climate of a brothel. Underlying the irony is the social comment, the tragic dilemma. Faulkner's dream of the writer's function as prophet and guardian of truth is an empty joke if the only truth is negation and the only assurance death.

The American artist's despair or frustration is not an accurate mirror of the environment. American life is not lived in bawdy houses, nor in executive suites, nor in the crumbling Southern mansion where "Baby Doll" discovers Sex.

The arts do not reflect the whole truth of life in the United States. This is the basic reason for the confusion and bitterness in the realm of art. The creative spirit is shut off from the life-giving truth. But artists do reflect, one-sidedly and subjectively, the tensions, weaknesses, fears that afflict our society.

The family in Tennessee Williams' *Cat on a Hot Tin Roof* are not Russian peasants. We may question whether they are Americans, in any profoundly perceptive sense. But this is the heart of the matter. Williams may be insensitive to American reality. But he projects what he sees: a society without values, driven by rudderless impulses.

Walt Whitman wrote in 1855: "The United States themselves are essentially the greatest poem." Has the poem become a song of unreason, of juvenile crime and suburban maladjustment, gadgets and time-payments and automation, good wages and uncertain employment, fear of depression and the warning splendor of the mushroom cloud that rose over Hiroshima?

The poetry of American life lies in the spiritual and moral strength of the American people, pitted against the pressures and dangers of the time. The source of these pressures and dangers is monopoly capital, the vast power that exploits the people and prevents the flowering of art and life.

Let the artist walk our city streets and country roads. Let him observe the slums where ten million American children live in unsanitary shacks or tenements. Let him walk through the state where the Negro boy, Emmett Till, was killed, where the average per capita income in 1954 was $812, and more than thirty percent of the rural population earned less than $500 in the same year.[3]

Let the artist note the contrast between conspicuous wealth and grinding poverty, between the towers of industry and the dwellings of the poor. The contrasts in the human geography of our country are as strident as the pattern of the rivers and mountains and deserts.

The time will come when American artists will paint and

write and sing the greatest poem, the song of the proud land.

For the artist, freedom is the breath of life, the first pre-requisite for performing his function. Unless the artist is free to create out of the turmoil of humanity, as it is seen and felt and known to the individual creator, he is dying in the midst of life.

This would seem to be a simple truth. But it is far from simple—not because it requires crippling modifications, but be-cause it is bound to another simple truth: in the words of John Donne, "No man is an island, entire of itself; every man is a piece of the continent, a part of the main."

Lenin said it is impossible to live in society and be free from it". Since we cannot be free *from* society, and since past history offers little assurance that we can be free *in* it, we tend to hedge our concept of liberty with amendments that negate its pure meaning. The contradiction between personal liberty and the social structure is schematized in various ways. In gen-eral, the folklore of capitalism associated freedom with the hard competition of the marketplace. The individual may hope for a measure of freedom if he can outrun his competitors in the race for profits and prizes.

The idea of freedom must itself be freed, purified from encrusted lies. It must be seen in its simple glory, as the to-getherness of people, resolving their differences in the urgency of their common need to work and create and build.

No one can do this alone. For man alone is impotent. Even Robinson Crusoe on his desert island, had to organize in order to survive. This is as true for the artist as for all others. Indeed, it is more profoundly true for the artist: his function is not merely to imagine and devise, but to communicate and teach. An individual can create a poem if he has writing materials. He may even invent and memorize a poem without these tools. But the development of the arts, like every other aspect of civilization, tends more and more to involve complex processes of cooperation. Scores of artists are required to perform a sym-phony, or to complete a motion picture.

The concept of human liberty is meaningful when it is placed in the context of a free society, in which all forms of organization, including production and distribution, government and the state, serve to nourish and advance the creative po-tentialities of every individual.

There is nothing startlingly new in this concept. It is the
right to personal fulfillment which the Declaration of Indepen-
dnce describes as the "pursuit of happiness". The phrase is
vague, because the achievement of happiness for every citizen
in terms of comfort, opportunity, spiritual enlargement and
cultural experience, was beyond the material resources or social
perspectives of our nation when it declared its independence
in 1776.

But Jefferson and other signers of the Declaration believed
in the ability of people to work together, and the document
affirmed their faith in reason and cooperation, as the means of
improving society and thus advancing toward the goal of personal freedom.

The historical development of the past hundred and fifty
years has taken the personal right to the "pursuit of happiness" out of the realm of theory, and placed it on the agenda
of history as a practical Twentieth Century proposal. The advancement of science toward an economy of abundance offers
the possibility of guaranteeing the reality of freedom, not to a
class or group, but to every member of the human family.

A free society implies democratic control of the whole
social process, economic as well as political. The power of the
people assumes a new dimension when it extends to industrial
power, public power, atomic power. People are the masters
of their fate when they are the masters of the energies they
have called into being.

Freedom is not solely a matter of material resources—as we
have learned in our own country. But a society organized to
serve all its members must have the economic means of satisfying
their needs. Otherwise, men and women cannot be free to
choose their work, adequate leisure canont be provided, technical
and professional careers must be limited, and there is neither
time, money, nor public taste for the full flowering of the arts.

This is the essence of socialism. It is a design for human
liberty, "securing for every member of society", as Engels said,
"through social production . . . the completely unrestricted
development and exercise of their physical and mental facul-
ties—this possibility now exists for the first time, but it *does*
exist".[4]

Those who discuss socialism and human rights without reference to the economic base are ignoring its historical signifi-

cance. In fact, they are turning their backs on history, on humanity's long struggle to improve the conditions of life.

The function of the artist demands sensitivity, courage, moral passion, untrammelled imagination. A clod, a brute, may have full freedom to write a sonnet, but the work will be wasted. We all recognize that art involves values. But how are the values determined? What is the measure of sensitivity? Who is the arbiter of visions, the assessor of dreams?

Artistic freedom in the abstract means that everyone can print a book, regardless of its length; everyone can conduct an orchestra, make a film. The idea is absurd. But it defines freedom-in-the-raw.

The question of values is primary. It determines the public response to a work of art, but it also goes back to the origin of the creative process. Artistic effort demands a degree of concentration and technical mastery which is achieved by long apprenticeship. In one way or another, there must be selection of persons for artistic training. Art education, techniques learned and approved, the goals to which the artist aspires—all these are matters of values, governed by the level of artistic feeling and understanding in the whole society.

Art is a discipline. There is no harder discipline than the self-imposed order and direction of the creative spirit. The extent to which the artist is encouraged to give his best (and the measure of what the "best" means) is the gauge of the social response to art, which in turn is the key to creative freedom.

Artists have often worked in solitude and neglect, in opposition to a society which gave them neither respect nor liberty. But the value of their effort is judged in the long run by the social response, the recognition that society was wrong.

A free society, then, is one in which every talent is nurtured and encouraged. This means that the social order is dedicated to the highest aesthetic standards, and constantly strives to enlarge the area of aesthetic experience—which, by the same token, enlarges the freedom of the creator.

The function of art resembles the function of science, in its responsible relationship to the community. No one would argue that the scientist is "free" from the methodology of science. Nor would any sane person defend the scientist's "right" to privately invent a death-ray capable of wiping out cities. Whether the invention of more lethal instruments of war, under governmental or industrial supervision, comes within the proper function of science, is a more difficult question. But it indicates the social urgency of the usage of culture.

Socialism dedicates culture to the people. Only the enemies of democracy can argue that this is a debasement of art, or that it limits the artist to the lowest level of mass taste. The struggle for freedom begins with the elementary struggle for subsistence. But it looks to the stars. If people can never rise above the standard of comic books, we may despair of democracy.

The crisis in the arts in the United States arises from the increasingly commercial character of the dominant culture and the consequent erosion of cultural freedom. "Independent" artists are as impotent as small businessmen in attempting to oppose the concentrated power of vested interests. The partial democratization of the arts can be won only by the conscious will of the people.

Public sponsorship of the arts, on a national and local basis, offers salvation to talented and unemployed artists. And it can encourage public interest in forms of creative activity that may counteract the deadly glitter of mass communication.

The belief that art serves a public function in a democratic society goes back to the early days of the republic. In 1792, when colonial laws forbidding dramatic shows were still in force in Massachusetts, a pamphlet was published in Boston demanding that a great building be erected to house both the state legislature and a splendid theatre:

> The building should be surrounded by a piazza, whose pillars, at twelve feet distance, should help support a grand dome or roof. . . . The first floor on one side will accommodate the whole legislative assembly. . . . That part of the building devoted to the theatre, being very capacious, lightsome, and excellently fitted for such use; the galleries will be so constructed that the feeblest voice below, will be very audible. . . .
>
> It is designed to have a lower floor that will contain two thousand spectators, and three galleries to contain fifteen hundred, fifteen hundred and twelve hundred spectators. . . . If the legislature of Massachusetts established such a theatre . . . its effect on the manners of the people must be truly astonishing. . . . History will undoubtedly

mark an era so favorable to the intellectual powers of man,
in this western world. . . . The history of the stage will
ever after have a conspicuous place in the history of
America.

Alas! The pamphleteer's dream remained unrealized, in Boston or any other American city. There was an interval of
a hundred years before even the most modest recognition was
accorded to the place of the arts in our national life. In 1891,
after fifty years of agitation, a bill for a national conservatory
of music was signed by President Benjamin Harrison. But Congress refused to make any appropriation for it. Out of this first
hesitant step toward public art, came Anton Dvorak's *New
World Symphony*, composed during the time he served as director of the conservatory. Dvorak's paean to democracy did
not compensate for the lack of funds, which doomed the plan
for a musical center serving the people. After three years,
Dvorak admitted failure and returned to Europe.

Congressional distaste for culture was again demonstrated
in 1919, when Congress refused funds for a Council of the Fine
Arts. In 1910, President Taft replaced the Council with a
Commission serving without pay. Since no money was involved,
Congress authorized the commission, which has done effective
work in developing a public buildings program. The beauty
of the nation's capital today is in part due to the work of the
Commission.[5]

The first serious step toward national development of a cultural program came as part of the clamorous movement of the
people that transformed the nation under the leadership of
Franklin D. Roosevelt. In 1933, a prominent painter, George
Biddle, wrote a letter to the President urging the United States
to emulate Mexico and permit artists "to express the ideals of
their time and country" in the decoration of public buildings.
In response to Biddle's proposal, the Section of Painting and
Sculpture of the Treasury Department was established, and
empowered to employ a limited number of artists.

A year later, the more comprehensive Federal Arts Project
was inaugurated under the Works Progress Administration. It
was a depression measure, designed to give employment to professional artists. But it was an integral part of the new and almost revolutionary thinking of those fruitful years. Its origin

in Biddle's letter suggests the impact on American culture of the great movement of Mexican painting that arose from the struggle for a publicly sponsored people's art.

The Federal Arts Project, reflecting and strengthening the desire of artists "to express the ideals of their time and country", had a creative effect on American life that has never been adequately recognized. The twenty-five million Americans who attended concerts and studied music were participating in a New World Symphony that surpassed Dvorak's dream of a people's music. The Federal Theatre reached thirty million people, more than half of whom had never before seen a dramatic presentation.

The production was tremendous in quantity. It was often of striking quality, and initiated vital experiments in form and content. In every field, there are eminent artists who began their work under the auspices of the WPA.

The destruction of the projects in 1939 was not accompanied by proper measures for the protection of these treasures of American art. Where are the 48,000 easel paintings, the 84,000 prints, the 3,562 works of sculpture, the 28,000 posters produced by the 5,000 artists during years of earnest effort? Some of the sculpture is in public parks. Some of the paintings are in schools, hospitals and libraries. But much of the work is gathering dust in warehouses, or is damaged or wantonly destroyed.

The Congressional storm that crushed this flowering of democratic culture revealed the intense animosity toward the arts motivating a majority of the nation's law-makers. Congressman Martin Dies inaugurated the work of the Un-American Activities Committee by demanding that Christopher Marlowe be called to explain the Un-American propaganda in his plays. The gross ignorance of Dies, matched or surpassed by his successors in Congressional investigations, cannot be dismissed as a casual example of the incompetence of so many politicians.

The Un-American Activities Committee was established to destroy the Federal Theatre. In a larger sense, it was an attack on the whole cultural upsurge of the thirties on "the treason of ideas" which, according to Whittaker Chambers, persuaded a majority of Americans to vote for Franklin D. Roosevelt.

The history of Congressional investigations shows the interrelationship of art and politics: know-nothing Congressmen, misusing the power of their office to destroy the professional lives of writers and educators, make no secret of the fact that their contempt for writing extends to the words of the Constitution itself.

The interrelationship of art and politics is as important for the average citizen as it is for the politician. Unhappily, Americans are not aware of the role that art can play in the enrichment of their lives and in every phase of social development. Although millions were stirred by performances and exhibitions and training programs of the Federal project, they did not see that culture is the beating of the nation's heart, which is therefor a matter of public interest and national survival.

The political onslaught on the projects in 1938 and 1939 was evidence of their democratic service. Of course, there were people who held that art cannot be "free" unless it is controlled by private enterprise. An article entitled "Pork Barrel Renaissance", by F. H. Taylor, in *Magazine of Art* for March, 1938, referred to "this lotus of the American Renaissance, flowering in a cesspool of art politics".

But the work of the projects proved that they could not be controlled by politicians. Indeed, this was the complaint of reactionary Congressmen. The debate on a bill for a permanent Arts Project, introduced in 1938 by Senator Pepper and Congressman Coffee, centered on two provisions: one related to the right of organizations having the greatest number of persons employed in the art enterprises to nominate the administrative personnel; the other provided for union wages.

Democratic control is a key question in any Federal, state or municipal program of the arts. It arose in one form or another in most of the fifteen bills seeking to transform the temporary Federal undertaking into a permanent plan, which were debated in Congress from 1935 to 1943.

Public sponsorship of the arts is not a socialist proposal. Accuracy is required in political definitions, especially at a time when reactionaries cry out against every move for the welfare of the people on the ground that it is "creeping socialism." Socialism is achieved only when people assume effective control of the resources and productive capacities of their society.

The definition shows the long road to be travelled. At the same time, it rejects the reactionary view that "rugged indi-

vidualism" is the law of democratic development. On the contrary, the increasing concentration of economic power demands
increasing public control in order to protect the people.

There has never been, and never could be, a democratic
government (in the classic bourgeois-democratic meaning of the
term) which does not perform certain services and control certain economic activities. George Bernard Shaw has observed
that, "Though each family buys its own beer separately, they all
get their water communistically."[6]

Our culture would be more impoverished than it is if government abandoned any concern with the arts. Most of our
cities maintain museums. There are about a dozen civic theatres
in the United States, which are partially supported by municipal
funds. Many organizations, such as the American National
Theatre and Academy, work closely with the government, and
in some cases the relationship is formalized in legislation. 1956
saw the establishment, by act of Congress, of a Federal Advisory
Committee of the Arts, to aid and support cultural interchange
with other countries.

In every nation of Western as well as Eastern Europe, state-
subsidized theatres and other art enterprises are accepted as a
matter of course. In England radio and television are public
institutions, and it is only recently that private competition,
with its accompaniment of vulgar advertising, has been permitted to enter the field. The Arts Council in England has
a very limited budget, but it has done a great deal to foster
creative effort in drama, music and the dance, as well as promoting art exhibitions and aiding painters and sculptors.

France has an older and more serious tradition of national
responsibility for cultural activity. The French government's
aid to theatres and production of new plays in Paris alone is
about twice the whole cultural budget provided in England.

Canada's parliament has recently allocated $100,000,000 to a
newly formed Arts Council "to foster and promote the study and
encouragement of, and the production of work in the arts, humanities, and social sciences".

The backwardness of the United States in respect to the arts
may be attributed to the structure of corporate power, which
seeks to make even the soul of man a robot on the beltline of
profit. But it should be evident to thoughtful Americans that
the development of the arts is a matter of public concern af-

fecting the welfare and future of the nation.

There were signs in the skies, in the fall of 1957, that shook our confidence in the pre-eminence of American science. Intensive discussion of weaknesses in science and the need for a new approach to education has pointed to the relationship between scientific progress and the whole climate of culture. Science cannot flourish in an atmosphere of anti-intellectualism, derision of "egg-heads", and neglect of the arts. A democratic culture provides the faith, the dynamic purpose, which give meaning and direction to creative effort, linking science and art in a community of culture dedicated to humanity.

Recent efforts to establish some sort of Federal Arts Foundation are encouraging, although these proposals are of a limited character and do not give adequate recognition to the importance of artistic experience as an "inalienable right" of all the people.

The Javits-Clark Bill, introduced in the Senate during the first session of the 85th Congress, is one of a number of measures which seek to establish a "United States Arts Foundation". The bill provides for assistance to the "performing arts", theatre, music, opera, dance and ballet, ignoring other areas of aesthetic effort. Nonetheless, the bill deserves support as a first step toward solution of an urgent problem.

What is needed is a United States Arts Authority, a government department with representation in the President's cabinet, empowered to carry forward a comprehensive program of cultural study, professional training, assistance to individual artists, and sponsorship of production or exhibition of works of art, with public funds for the acquisition of land and construction of buildings, with power to make federal loans and grant subsidies to localities for regional, state or municipal development of artistic projects.

A broad campaign for the establishment of an arts authority would help to educate the public in the value of the arts, their place in our history and traditions, and the extent to which the people of the United States are culturally underprivileged.

Where are the present opportunities for young artists in this "land of opportunity"? Where is the contact between the artist and the people which serves to stimulate the individual creator and to raise the level of public taste?

When we deprive the artist of the right to create, we deprive the whole society. The unwritten dream, the unpublished poem, the painting put away to collect dust, the talent deprived of training, are denials of liberty.

In 1891, William Dean Howells spoke of his hopes that a "communistic era in taste" might be approaching. He was not speaking of Communism as the term is used today. But he was stirred by Edward Bellamy's *Looking Backward,* with its picture of a socialist America, a land of shining cities and equality for all.

The vision inspired Howell's conviction that art draws its strength from the people. He urged "the portrayal in every art of those finer and higher aspects which unite rather than sever humanity. . . . The arts must become democratic, and then we shall have the expression of America in art".

The full flowering of the arts will come only at the moment foreseen by Engels, when "men, with full consciousness, will fashion their own history. . . . It is humanity's leap from the realm of necessity to the realm of freedom".[8]

NOTES

1 *After the Lost Generation,* John Watson Aldridge, McGraw Hill, New York, 1951.

2 Cited, *Saturday Review,* July 7, 1956.

3 *Characteristics of the Low-Income Population and Related Federal Programs,* U.S. Government Printing Office, 1955.

4 *Anti-Duhring, Frederick Engels.*

5 Reports of the Commission of Fine Arts may be obtained from the Government Printing Office, Washington, D. C.

6 *The Intelligent Woman's Guide to Socialism and Capitalism,* George Bernard Shaw, Brentano's, New York, 1928.

7 *Criticism and Fiction,* William Dean Howell's, 1891.

8 *Anti-Duhring.*

Alternative Approaches

By John Thomas McManus

ON SOME LEVEL OR OTHER, all people in the United States must be aware, acutely or dimly, of serious shortcomings in their society. All are under an unprecedented tax burden. All live in an uneasy militarist prosperity which, by its own terms, must verge into war or collapse; and which, for many, is more than offset by taxes, by heavy installment debt and depreciation of savings, insurance, etc., through inflation. For perhaps the lower third of the population, even such prosperity as this does not exist: these are the families whose earning power is limited by discrimination for reasons of race, color, national origin or politics, or by peonage systems prevailing in many areas of the nation.

Under a two-party politcal system over which the voters have no power of sanction save to choose periodically among the candidates of one or the other party, the people have a representative government in name only. At only one period in recent years, in the early New Deal when the people's power began to assert itself through the Democratic Party after the economic

JOHN THOMAS McMANUS was born in New York City in 1904, was educated in the New York schools, graduated from Marietta College in Ohio. He went to work at the *New York Times* at the age of sixteen as an errand boy, then copy boy; while at college was a reporter for the *Marietta Register;* returned to the *New York Times* after graduation, as reporter; was Cinim Editor of the magazine *Time,* 1937-40; and was with *P.M.* from the time it was founded until the paper was discontinued. Mr. McManus is General Manager of the *National Guardian,* which he, with Cedric Belfrage and James Aronson founded in 1948. He was a charter member of the New York Newspaper Guild and its president for several years; was also an international vice president of the American Newspaper Guild, and an officer of the New York CIO. He served as congressional secretary to Representative Leo Isacson, A.L.P., at Washington while the latter was a Member of the House.

collapse of the '30's, has there been a glimmer of truly representative people's government, under the leadership of Franklin Delano Roosevelt. Since Roosevelt's death, both Democratic
and Republican parties have collaborated in the decimation of
New Deal gains; and repression of opposition opinion and activity has reached a crest not attempted since the earliest years
of American government, when the Federalists sought to suppress the following of Jefferson and Madison.

A form of universal military service and an education program officially geared to the needs of a war economy impede
the natural, healthy development of American youth. Public
works and development of natural resources are at a standstill.
Military programs serve to rationalize the largest and most
blatant profit-feeding by government of big business in the
nation's history.

What is called full employment—some 60-odd million jobs
with a "normal float" of unemployment variously calculated
at from 2-5 million—is threatened momentarily by the advance
of automation. If the system under which Americans live has
prepared solutions for sustaining its wage-earners under automation, the wage-earner has yet to learn of them.

To guarantee this way of life against any competition, the
people are forced to prepare for, and pay for, the possibility
of hydrogen war, with the best prospect for victory being
50 million casualties to inflict 200 million on the "enemy,"
meaning the Soviet Union as the chief bastion of the socialist
third of the world.

The alternative to the risk of remaining one of the two out
of three Americans who can hope to survive a hydrogen war
is to turn the minds of the American nation against the degradation, depredation and destruction implicit in this situation,
and together to seek the means to an alternative way of life—
not only for all Americans but for the 200,000,000 we might
have to kill so that two-thirds of us might survive.

Such an undertaking requires in advance a realistic estimate of the forces available to carry it on; and the kind of
initiative which can evoke the participation of an optimum
portion of those forces in the difficult, beginning stages.

The reservoir of forces who could be drawn on to undertake
this task is impressively large: it includes the millions still living and active who tipped the politcal balance in the New

Deal years, who helped build the CIO, who have come into (and for the most part since gone out of) the orbit of the American left in the last 25 years. There is no reason to believe these people have altered basic convictions. Rather, one must respectfully believe that most of them are awaiting developments sufficiently promising to warrant resumption of participation in mass activity in behalf of their convictions.

Probably the single most reassuring development to win these people to participation in the struggle for social change would be agreement on a common program by all, or at least the most significant, of the various socialist groupings in the country. Correctly or not, many Americans of the independent left of center in the country regard this as the principal reason for the existence of such groups. If their function is not to generate—or indeed to have already generated—a mass movement for social change, most Americans will regard them as non-essential. Yet agreement among socialist sects on a common program for the United States is a Utopian hope; hence the least the independent left must demand is non-interference with such a long overdue movement, if participation is withheld.

I believe millions of Americans today would welcome, and at whatever level possible participate in, any move in our country toward a wholesome and not fratricidal approach to the application of socialist solutions to our society's ills. As the manager of a publication—the *National Guardian*—which reaches an active 50,000 people nationally each week who would be at the core of such a movement if it should develop, I can speak with some certainty about their views, which are expressed to us freely and regularly from all parts of the country.

These are people who "wi' Wallace bled" in '48 in an effort to start a people's party; and who stood their ground when Wallace left them in 1950 on the grounds that "in any contest between the East and the West, I am a man of the West." They are one-worlders, to use the most common form of castigation short of red-baiting. They are friends—critics perhaps but not enemies—of the socialist world. They believe with Dr. W. E. B. Du Bois, many of them, and with Anna Louise Strong that the Soviet Union for nearly 40 years—and the People's Republic of China in the last decade—have wielded the instrument of socialism significantly and well for the future health of all humanity.

They are not ready, as are some whose argument I have heard, to write off four decades of Soviet power. They are not ready to deny or disavow their friends and associations of years of one-world conflict. They are not quick to adopt and further the propaganda of the anti-socialist machinery of government or of the well-kept press because it is a handy stick with which to beat the Stalinist dog. Their courage in their convictions is unquenchable, yet having been frustrated once in a mighty try at mass, independent people's organization, they will not settle for less than the best the next time.

If there is to be a new movement on the left in our country, these will be the ones to move it initially—as they brought the Progressive Party of '48 into being in 48 states, as they moved a world to humane action in behalf of the Rosenbergs in 1952-53.

But they are not buying anything any of us have offered to date in the direction of new political organization. They are waiting—waiting for assurances against disruption, against manipulation and liquidation, and for a positive program for America which can be sold inevitably to the majority of Americans who are determined for a world of peace, freedom and abundance.

This positive program—which would be most significant if concurred in by the significant left organizations—is now the property of no one. At least none has convinced the other that we have such a program nor has any of us convinced a sufficient number of Amercans of this to prompt others to concur in the interest of progress. It is, in point of fact, a program for which not even the initial analysis now exists in any available form. It requires study, an analysis in American terms of an American situation, and the ability to sell it as preferable to what our people have today, and as what they would want for their children and the children of others. If we have scholars and social scientsts among us, this is the challenge to them; if we are politicians, then this is the real and unique political problem, not to be avoided by submerging our aims for the purpose of electing perennially the less worse of the machine party candidates.

Vincent Hallinan, California lawyer who was Progressive Party candidate for president in 1952, sums up the present situation this way:

"Fundamentally, and on a broad basis, the conflict now dividing the world is one between the public and private ownership of the means and instruments of production and distribution. An analysis of the other issues will convince one that they will resolve themselves upon a solution of this primary conflict. In this country the public ownership forces are small and without adequate resources. The champions of private ownership embrace every vested interest in the country, all the media of mass communication, and the tremendous repressive machinery of Government. Here are the elements against which the struggle must be waged."[1]

None of us, not even Mr. Hallinan from his considerable eminence—can summon a new national political party or movement into being without wide concurrence. Yet Mr. Hallinan's forthright summing up of the issue of the day could be the nub around which it may be possible to get immediate and significant concurrence on the local level in virtually any large community in the country.

The public ownership argument, carrying with it the obvious parallels to socialism and the similarly obvious imperative that public ownership may be entrusted only to a government responsible to the people, brings the community close to the heart of the argument which divides the world today. Mr. Hallinan and other noted independents are working on a program which will seek concurrence in all the communities of the country. The ultimate emergence of a nationwide movement to intervene as widely as possible in national elections may well turn on the acceptance of such a program.

Meanwhile, the only program before progressives throughout the nation is the Communist Party's proposal for the building of an "anti-monopoly coalition" among labor, farmer, Negro and other groups, directing their efforts within the framework of the Democratic Party. The proposal seeks to "curb the power of Big Business", "limit the economic concentration and power of the trusts" and to "reduce their incredibly swollen share of the national wealth". Presidents Lincoln, Theodore Roosevelt, Wilson and Franklin Roosevelt all professed similar aims, and as long ago as 1943 I heard Morris Ernst expound them, so they can hardly be considered "vanguard" objectives.

More to the point today, perhaps, may be the kind of program offered by the sociologist C. Wright Mills of Columbia

University in the *Nation* of December 9, 1957. Professor Mills, author of *The Power Elite* and several other challenging analyses of the socio-economic makeup of the United States, called for:

East-West coexistence based on negotiation.

"Some 20 per cent of the current U.S. military budget should be allocated to the economic aid and industrial development of underdeveloped countries."

Increased exchange of citizens and U.S. passports and visas to all who wish to travel.

Removal of "security and loyalty restrictions" and exchange of scientic information.

Removal from private hands to public control of scientific research and development related to the military.

Cessation of "all further production of 'extermination' weapons".

Abandonment of all U.S. military bases abroad.

Promotion of disarmament.

Acceptance of Moscow's proposal for arms embargo to the Middle East; joint guarantee of all frontiers in the area; drafting of regional and international wealth—if necessary the expropriation of local oil concerns—for a Middle East development program.

U.S. recognition of China "and of all other Communist-type states. Without what the peoples of China and India have to offer, the world is too poor to get along properly".

The U.S. should announce some such program now, then "earnestly seek meetings with the Russians, with or without other nations present".

Professor Mills said he did not suppose his "proposals will be acted upon this week by the power elite of the U.S." on the ground that they are utopian. But, he said, "precisely what they call utopian is now the only condition of human survival."

Professor Mills' program is not an alternative to, but a different, more inclusive program that the "anti-monopoly coalition" envisions. It stresses peace, which is uppermost in the minds of most people, despite the labor leader who recently said peace would be a catastrophe to American labor. Further it proposes a measure of public control of scientific research and military development and calls for an increasingly representative United

Nations. With backing, it has more than a good chance of finding expression in the voting process if it can be put forth by independents inside or outside the machine parties.

The same C. Wright Mills, in works previous to *The Power Elite*, has correctly identified labor leadership in the U.S. as, in general, aides de camp of the power elite, whose function is to keep labor from carrying out effective action against monopoly or monopoly-run government. Further, Mills has called attention to the changing character of the "working class" in America, pointing out the huge shift to white collar work. A full, new study of the nature of the 70,000,000 wage-earners who create America's wealth is indicated as the basis for future consideration of the "basic law of socialist development", so recently as Nov., 1957, restated from Moscow as an "alliance of workers, farmers and other working people led by the working class of which the Marxist-Leninist Party is the core".

To wait, as the traditional left admonition goes, for "labor" to lead such a people's movement into being, may be to accept indefinite postponement of this high objective if not perpetual stalemate.

For the purposes of development of a people's movement or political party for social change, the stratification of American society must be correctly assayed. The concerns of women, youth, foreign-born, Negro, Puerto Rican, Mexican and other minorities, rural and urban peoples, etc., can be discovered and channeled into political action without waiting for the nod of the "labor statesmen" so accurately depicted by C. Wright Mills.

Rather this leadership and the broad spectrum of American labor—ranging as it does from charwomen to airline pilots—may be much more apt to recognize and turn toward a movement genuinely established by the basic elements in American society; and these basic elements may on the other hand find no expression in and may therefore reject the kind of movement which might emerge on the say-so of present-day labor leadership in the Unted States.

---

1 To hair-splitters on the left, Hallinan, himself a professing socialist with a small "s," in 1956 offered these two parables and a drop of advice, all from the pages of history:

" . . . the manner in which the left in this country has allowed itself to

be torn and divided and to waste its energies in such conflicts [is reminiscent of] the perils which the Earl of Dundee faced when . . . in the midst
of battle, his left flank fired on his center in revenge for a wrong committed 200 years before.

"Gibbon relates the conflict between the Christians of the 5th Century,
which erupted into riots in which thousands were killed. The conflicts arose
from the argument as to whether the Holy Ghost proceeded from the Father
and the Son through a process designated as 'Homousion' or through that
known as "Homoiusion'. We are unable to learn from the most eminent
of those who care to devote themselves to such concerns just what the distinction was. I feel that the liberal people of the United States are now
concerned with very grim and practical problems, and not whether a particular political party derived from the Father or the Son."

PART II. TRANSITION TO A SOCIALLY BASED ECONOMY

"In throwing open our ports to the commerce of the world we shall far better secure their safety than by fortifying them with all the "protected" plates that our steel ring could make. . . .

"The dangers to the Republic come not from without but from within."

From Protection and Free Trade *by* Henry George. *First published in* 1886. *Reprinted by The Robert Schalkenbach Foundation,* 1941.

"Our industrial and economic order in all its phases—industrial, agricultural, and financial—is not democratic. It is neither owned nor administered nor directed democratically. It functions in an autocratic manner. It is at variance with our social and political ideals. Its prime objective seems to be the concentration of wealth and power in the hands of a decreasing number of individuals. It breeds poverty and want, scarcity and insecurity, but by necessity. It can no more eliminate unemployment, short of the emergency created by war (and then only temporarily), than an engine can run without fuel. We need to refashion this economic order to a more democratic pattern by democratic means and for democratic objectives. If we fail to do so, the shadows are likely to lengthen across the land."

From Ill Fares the Land, by Carey Mc Williams *Little, Brown and Company, Boston,* 1942.

"The realization of the truth that socialism is not necessarily involved with the form of governmental organization ought to go a long way to remove some of the current objections to it, which assume that a socialist philosophy is inimical to 'the American way' of government, and really threatens to undermine our Constitution. In point of fact, a completely socialistic economic system could be introduced in the United States tomorrow, without a single important change in the form of government."

From *Economics For the Millions,* by Henry Pratt Fairchild

KARL MARX

in *Capital*

That which is now to be expropriated is no longer the labourer working for himself, but the capitalist exploiting many labourers. This expropriation is accomplished by the action of the immanent laws of capitalistic production itself, by the centralization of capital. One capitalist always kills many. Hand in hand with this centralization, or this expropriation of many capitalists by few, develop, on an ever extending scale, the cooperative form of the labour-process, the conscious technical application of science, the methodical cultivation of the soil, the transformation of the instruments of labour into instruments of labour only usable in common, the economizing of all means of production by their use as a means of production of combined, socialized labour, the entanglement of all peoples in the net of the world market, and with this, the international character of the capitalist regime. Along with the constantly diminishing number of magnates of capital, who usurp and monopolize all advantages of this process of transformation, grows the mass of misery, oppression, slavery, degredation, exploitation; but with this too grows the revolt of the working-class, a class always increasing in numbers, and disciplined, united, organized by the very mechanism of the process of capitalist production itself. The monopoly of capital becomes a fetter upon the mode of production, which has sprung up and flourished along with, and under it.

Centralization of the means of production and socialization of labour at last reach a point where they become incompatible with their capitalist integument. This integument is burst asunder. The knell of capitalist private property sounds. The expropriators become the expropriated . . . capitalist production begets, with the inexorability of a law of Nature, its own negation. It is the negation of negation.

From *Capital* by KARL MARX
English edition, Vol. I
International Publishers, 1947

Socialism, American Style

By Broadus Mitchell

BEFORE WE CAN ENTER on the American scene we have to go back some hundreds of years to the Mercantilists, statesmen and writers of Europe. They stood for regulation of economic life by national and local authorities. Government promoted and corrected for the furtherance of deliberate ends, such as the import of the precious metals, and the breeding up of a vigorous, industrious population that would produce cheaply and furnish ample recruits to armies. But their regulations, reaching to the minutest matters of trade and even to personal expenditures, became pestiferous. A school of philosophers in France in the middle of the eighteenth century—called the Physiocrats—rebelled against hampering controls and a multiplicity of taxes.

By this time capital had accumulated in private hands. Merchants and bankers were restless to hazard their wealth in unrestrained ventures. The economists supplied them with a logic, the law of nature, *laissez faire,* or the rule of no rule. Men should make their own economic choices, government should not interfere. This became the maxim of the so-called classical writers in both France and Britain. Chief among these believers in the doctrine of public benefit to flow from private

---

BROADUS MITCHELL is Professor of Economics, Rutgers University, New Brunswick, New Jersey. He was born in Kentucky, received his B.A. degree from the University of South Carolina (1913) and Ph.D. from The Johns Hopkins University (1918). At intervals he has been newspaper reporter, member of the staff of the Division of Industrial Analysis, U.S. Department of Commerce, and ran on the Socialist ticket for Governor of Maryland. His publications have been chiefly in the field of economic history. His latest books, both appearing in 1957, are "Alexander Hamilton, Youth to Maturity, 1755-1788" and "Heritage from Hamilton".

selfishness were the Scots professor, Adam Smith, author of the *Wealth of Nations;* Thomas R. Malthus, the clergyman and teacher best known for his *Principle of Population;* and David Ricardo, the London stock broker, celebrated for his rigorous analyses of the shares of wages and rent.

With these and their lesser confreres individual free will was sacred, but social free will was sinful. Combined action, in any of its forms, announced disbelief in this theology. Public relief of the poor, protective legislation for women and children in factories, labor unionism, even corporate business enterprise were suspect. The historically minded, who declared that these and similar institutions were useful, were profane. William Godwin, who held that human society could be perfected, and Robert Owen, the industrialist who made practical reforms pointing to a new moral world, were discounted as dreamers. Other utopians, like St. Simon and Fourier, were put down as fanatics. Those in America, followers of Alexander Hamilton, who urged a degree of planning for national prosperity, especially a protective tariff, were throwbacks to practices which were condemned by the enlightened.

However, by the time of Karl Marx these heresies had reached a certain respectability. He took foundation stones of his revolutionary system from Ricardo. His sweeping defiance of capitalism was supported, in a distant, academic fashion by the social ameliorations espoused by his contemporary, John Stuart Mill. Radical workingmen kept up a clamor for the People's Charter, demanding correction of economic evils by means of a revamping of Parliament. The nobleman Shaftsbury and the fervid propagandist Oastler plugged in season and out for the ten-hours law to prevent the worst exploitation in cotton mills. In France national workshops, such as they were, did not spell ruin.

In the next two generations collective practices, voluntary and governmental, proliferated. In Britain labor unions were fully legalized, while the corporate form of business enterprise grew from occasional into universal use. Bernstein modified Marx to suit the parliamentary penchant of the English. On the Continent tariffs and cartels were matched by statutes providing compensation to the unemployed. This last device leaped the Channel, and the Fabians projected a socialist United Kingdom to be achieved piecemeal. Examples were not wanting in Amer-

ica, where Grangers and Populists provoked regulation of railroads and industrial combinations. Soon the Federal Reserve
reformed the National Banking system.

This pattern of progress—slow and selective, but solid—
seemed pedestrian by contrast with the swift Soviet Revolution.
Russia had lagged, and made up lost time on the double quick.
Of course the Bolsheviks did more than reorganize their own
economy. Their heavy doctrinal emphasis reached to the whole
world. Marx's red beard had previously been shaved, as it were,
but now it grew bushy again and in the West inspired horrid
fears.

In the United States our violent repulse of Soviet ideology
has been accompanied by conspicuous advance in economic
planning nevertheless. In the very moment of theoretical re-
jection we honored the Russian impulse in manifold practical
interventions of government in our economy. The main cause
was the Great Depression of the thirties which left us no choice.
Even President Hoover, reluctantly bowing to necessity, entered on relief and financial subsidy to big business in distress.
The bank closings ushered President Franklin Roosevelt into a
wider program of economic and social rescue than he had thought
for. The New Deal was all the more comprehensive and influential because unpremeditated. The British were more conscious of their further resort to collective correction of capitalist
misbehavior. Capitalism, they discovered, tended to stabilize
at less than full employment. This was the technical, academic
way of admitting that capitalism, whatever its merits in other respects, left to itself would consign millions to starvation.

So events proved to be our teachers. American ingenuity
and adaptability were never better shown than in the New Deal
when a Democratic administration forgot old preferences for
passive government and enlarged federal responsibility into the
engine of recovery and reform. The prediction that public
relief would pauperize the population was disappointed. Not
only did the destitute accept assistance as a matter of course,
but members of the middle class rejoiced to have mortgages
adjusted and refinanced, and the topmost business enterprises
found rescue in the Reconstruction Finance Corporation. The
zest with which farmers (traditional symbols of individual self-
reliance) promoted benefit payments has become a byword. It
is true that important business interests were the first to become

restive and declare that government could withdraw its helping hand. The President so far agreed that public spending was sharply reduced, with the result that in 1937 we suffered an abrupt recession and national largesse was reinvoked.

However, in a further effort "to get government out of business", removal of abuses in private enterprise loomed as a promising prospect. The federal authority, in suspending enforcement of the anti-trust acts, and in the operation of the National Industrial Recovery Act, had done everything to encourage collusion and combination. But now, heedless of consistency, the Attorney-General mustered resources for an all-out assault on monopoly and semi-monopoly. The Temporary National Economic Committee, patronized in the highest official quarters, professed the fatuous belief that our troubles sprang from violations of competition. Hardly had means of undoing this mischief been explored than the war in Europe called us to a defense program in which the bulk of production orders were issued to a hundred biggest firms so lately called miscreants. The last monographs depicting the ill deeds of monopolists had not been printed before the crusade which they were to document was gratefully forgotten.

World War II, coming on the heels of depression, confirmed America in the practice of national economic planning, on a scale hitherto unknown. "No need for alarm", cried corporations that fattened on military contracts. "American free enterprise is not selling its birthright. This is an emergency war economy. After victory we shall return to self-sufficient private initiative." But little business was not lulled. Efforts of the Smaller War Plants Corporation to keep minor producers in a healthy way of business were often uneconomical. They amounted to a sort of industrial social work, and could be only half-heartedly pursued while the overweening purpose was speed and volume of output. Sub-contracting to make sure the little fellows got something was hard to promote and harder to police. The fact was that a fractionalized economy is not adapted to war demands. It must not be forgotten that the federal government built outright and owned $16,000,000,000 of war plants. That was the fast way to do it. Some of these were located with exigencies of war chiefly in mind, and would never have been constructed by private enterprise. However, the fury of war and then the satisfaction of victory covered up the departures from economic and political tradition. After V-J Day we could relax, sell publicly-owned plants to corporations at a small part of their cost, demobilize material orders, undo price control and ostensibly begin where we left off before the war concentration.

But post-war was never like pre-war. After World War I, Harding had sighed for return to normalcy. Coolidge gave business its head, and the engineer Hoover preached system which partook of trade-association selfishness. The debacle of 1929 taught a severe lesson. So following 1945 we guarded against relapse. The Employment Act of 1946, even as reduced in the legislative rolling-mill, proclaimed more governmental responsibility than we had relished before. True, Uncle Sam did not guarantee every worker a job, but engaged to make a climate favorable to full use of our human resources. The President's Council of Economic Advisers was set on the ramparts to give warning of approaching economic danger. The congressional committee on the President's economic report accepted detection, diagnosis, and therapy of economic ills. Social security, no longer a debatable expedient, was taken for granted as an institution calling for expansion. The project of augmenting it was no longer ideological, but merely technical, with billions of money ready to be recruited under compulsion for the protection of millions of men, and incidentally for the welfare of the economy.

The prescription by John Maynard Keynes, the British adviser, was as puzzling to the patient as the Latin squiggles of the physician, but the import was plain. The notion of the self-regulating social body was abandoned. Henceforth government was to be the doctor in frequent attendance, administering now stimulants, now sedatives. The digitalis and barbiturates were to be monetary and fiscal, with massage to supply less indirect manipulation. "Propensities" in the economy were to be prodded or forbidden, induced or interdicted. The Bretton Woods conference of finance ministers of many countries, conducted under the eye of Keynes himself, took all into the international realm. The gold standard was a memory, management had supervened. Free will was exploded, policy was the palladium. The International Monetary Fund relied on contrivance to defeat the hazards of cupidity.

Not completely, because nations—unequally developed and suffering from various holdovers, political and economic—could

not swing from accustomed orbits in a twinkling. Purely national imperatives must be allowed for. National currencies
would be deliberately depreciated for supposed internal health
and to clutch at vanishing supplies of exchange. To an extent,
the International Monetary Fund was compelled to overlook
such emergency action, even to make itself partner to dangerous
measures. What long-time solution could be offered for the
problem of national immaturity coupled with national pride?
President Truman responded with "Point Four" and related
plans for grants for overseas economic development. The United
Nations chimed in with technical assistance. Hopefully the
dollars would reduce dearth and disease, induce industry and
more productive agriculture, and greater well-being would encourage democracy and attachment to the western powers.

Increasingly our aid was earmarked for military objects, so
that the experiment in economic promotion never had a full
trial. But we must pause to note the point to which the program
brought American capitalism. Our motive was to give rather
than to get. We could generously divest ourselves of super-
abundance. More than philanthropy moved us. We were canny,
too, for the policy of give-away postponed saturation of American markets. We cast our bread upon the waters, hoping that
the day of its return was distant. This was a transformation of
old axioms. Here was a rival to the doctrine of economic
change through revolution. Instead of the resentments of hunger, we used the persuasion of plenty. Ironically, to rescue foreign peoples from the blandishments of communism, we would
finance economic planning in a considerable part of the world.
I have known only one Turk in my life. He was a worthy fellow,
but I never felt a commitment to his country. Yet I could pay
my income tax, stroll two blocks to the New York piers and see
my darling dollars, in the form of trucks and tractors, loaded
for Istanbul.

At home, the welfare state, damned by Republicans, was not
discontinued when they were returned to national authority.
True, they separated tidal oil lands from federal oversight, but
they soon realized that even an oblique attack on the Tennessee
Valley Authority was unpopular, and they embraced ten million
more Americans under Social Security. Maybe the profoundest
remark of the 1956 presidential campaign was that of Eisenhower
that he did not care which political party introduced Social

Security; it is right and he proposed to espouse and extend it. The old order changes, we give allegiance to new patterns ot behavior.

Britain displayed the same willingness, or necessity, ten years before, with the adoption of modified socialism on a national scale. The victorious Churchill was ushered out to make way for the unglamorous Attlee and piecemeal conversion to a planned economy. Reinstatement of the Conservatives could not undo the program thus commenced.

The new departure in Britain has had deep effect in America. Because of ancient cultural ties, events there sent vibrations through our public life. Socializing crucial sectors of the economy, with more to follow, surprised but did not shock us. We had been prepared to witness something of the kind. Left as the last great capitalist country, we felt lonely, but not resentful. Then and there, perhaps, we reconciled ourselves to a mixed economy, the only question being how the scales might be tipped toward the public or the private weight. The progress of events in the short run is in doubt. Under our constitutional system state sovereignty favors the private pan of the balance, federal authority favors public auspices. Over a period, the indications are that we shall place increasing reliance on federal control, subvention, promotion, protection. Only the federal government has the resources, or the responsibility, to produce atomic fission, and where that power lies our destiny is determined.

We have become so acustomed to subsidies to farmers, credit assistance for housing, policing promotion of new corporate enterprise, aids to scientific research, expenditures for conservation, supervision of trade practices, and a hundred other services of the central government that we do not recognize the degree of the break with old passivity. We are more alert to $45,000,-000,000 of defense appropriations, but forget how far this prodigious spending props prosperity. We debate new proposals, such as federal grants to public schools, or socialized medicine, but with a suspicion on the part of opponents that these measures are likely, soon or late, to be entered upon. The desegregation decision of the Supreme Court will have profound economic results in raising the competence of millions of Negroes, improving their standards of living, increasing output, and stimulating market demand.

Parallel to enlargement of the functions of government—national, state, and local—is the collectivism of big business. The American people fought its conspicuous beginnings seventy-five years ago, as manifested in the combination in railroads, industry, and commerce. The common law held monopoly odious, statutes defined and condemned restraints of trade, the hustings rang with denunciations of wealth contemptuous of commonwealth. But gradually assault sank to toleration and finally to acceptance. The economies of large-scale production, redounding to the benefit of consumers, proved supreme. Courts, with a deal of rationalization, acquiesced. Foremost financial and industrial tycoons, long called ruthless, died as noble philanthropists. Others applied their skill and prestige in public assignments in war and peace. Within their business empires competition is annihilated, and long-range planning is installed. Actual operation is in the hands of salaried personnel, from the worker at the bench to the scientist in the laboratory. Only topmost decisions are referred to representatives of widely dispersed owners. The profit motive presides, with advertising its ally but these efficient mechanisms are far removed from the dog eat dog perversity of earlier American capitalism. "What is good for General Motors is good for the American people" was a resented remark, but it indicates the degree to which private and public interest are blended. The National Planning Association and the Committee for Economic Development are expressions of this fact.

What is set down above does not add up to socialism viewed as a complete ideological system. Elements of socialism are embodied in the relative displacement of competition by planning, in the high degree of governmental responsibility and solicitude, and in the extent to which production for use has modified production for profit. It is the way in which America increases reliance on cooperation in one form and another. Socialism in this country is not a proposition, but a process. At one end of the scale is dependence on private means to reach public ends; at the other end employment of public means to achieve private ends. In moving from the first to the second, if that is what we are doing, much reform, correction, and opportunist adjustment will appear, with small benefit of theory. The development will be slow, but promises to be a transformation.

None of the foregoing means to say that social advocacy in

America and elsewhere has been unimportant in determining practice. Philosophers, and those who have translated their principles into the language of the street, have been influential in conditioning the public mind and removing inhibitions to reform. The New Deal borrowed, of course without acknowledgment and probably unconsciously, from previous socialist analysis and recommendations. Likewise long but ill-defined familiarity with such reasoning and proposals speeded acceptance of the emergency program. The New Deal, with its intervention of the federal government to rescue the economy, was compounded of many elements. Its chief significance, for history, was in application of organized effort for social well-being. Trust in curative processes through uncoordinated private motives was for the nonce thrust behind us.

That much agreed, many subsidies and concessions went to bolster the very private initiative that had brought us to grief. Some policies sought to induce scarcity in the reliance that this would indirectly minister to need. Others, notably unemployment compensation, social security, and the Tennessee Valley Authority, bespoke immediate and positive planning for plenty. But all, whether makeshift or designed for enduring benefit, testified to the conviction that we as a people could act collectively in our own behalf. How much of this was suddenly concocted in the face of imminent peril, when old reliances had demonstrably failed, and how much was prompted by prior thought and propaganda, it is impossible to know. Both ingredients were present.

The opposite of the material is the moral. Marx has been identified with materialism. The future of society seemed fated. All must get worse before it would be better. Predicted disaster—demonstrated by observation of history—enveloped the philosophy in a sort of gleeful dread. Millions were fascinated by the prospect of the mass of mankind brought by relentless increase of misery to the desperate remedy of revolt. This was the inexorable process of capitalism. Of course the foreboding was mixed with hope. The seizure of the machinery of the state by the hitherto exploited would install the classless society, with freedom, plenty, and ceaseless happiness for the future. But this joyous eventuality was not to be looked for until the workers had been ground in predestined suffering.

Much of the appeal of rigorous Marxism in western Europe

was, ironically, to endurance rather than to the expectation of release. It almost seems that mankind prefers to bow the neck instead of lifting the head. Is not Christianity in large part a religion of sorrow? We clasp to our bosom the cross, symbol of burden and pain. We console ourselves with the promise of life, but that is to ensue only after death. In the Europe of Marx the protracted experience of deprivation made people love their misery. Following Marx's forecasts, they invited more affliction before the bright day of escape could dawn. An impotent defiance sustained them in their wretchedness, but this was a meaner thing than the springing human spirit. Resurrection was foretold, but ill-defined.

This mental overcast resulted from a deficit economy. Aspirations of progress were reproved by the teachings of the classical economists that only so much could be wrung from the earth. Each addition to the stock of food would be won at the cost of increased toil. The law of diminishing returns presided over the scene of human struggle. This was in the genius of things, to be encountered but never conquered. At the same time, within this closed economy contrivance was at work. Men had brought mechanics to their rescue. Power machines redoubled mere animal exertion. But whose was the reward? That was seized by the merciless owners of the new means of production. The spectacle of the few profiting while the many were penalized rankled. There was not room for permanent, progressive gain of both capitalists and workers. In fact, in the striving to squeeze a little more from ever-resistant nature the masses were being consistently robbed to contribute to the affluence of their cruel masters. So the cheated were by turns sullen and fierce.

This weight of oppression, these fateful fears belonged to Europe of the nineteenth century. America offered a different outlook. A new continent of prodigious and varied resources, occupied by an ingenious population inheriting the blessings but not the banes of ancestors in old countries, promised increasing returns. Effort was repaid by ever ampler output. Each addition to production and transport was more than proportionately beneficial. The combination was more than the sum of the parts. Ebullience took the place of gloom, resilience dispelled resistance. Yet this was not at first apparent to all who essayed to draw the economic picture of America. Such was the transposition of European thought to the new land that academic writers, anyhow, parroted the old gloomy preconceptions. Their books were in effect carbon copies of classical texts. This continued into a late generation of students who went to Europe. for their university instruction. This lag is not yet overcome.

The American professional economists would have done better to take lessons from their own native environment, which was giving the lie to what they learned abroad. Or they could have listened to men of affairs who in their actions and in systematic economic writings proclaimed optimism. Alexander Hamilton, the first Secretary of the Treasury, in his reports to Congress at the outset of the nation's career planned for plenty. His assistant, Tench Coxe, alive to the uses of machines, exerted himself to introduce the industrial revolution here. Friedrich List, for some years a visitor from Germany, taught by observation and example, showed how the American society could mount in riches. Mathew Carey, the Philadelphia publisher and pamphleteer, combined industrial promotion and confident economic prophecy. His son, Henry C. Carey, after early amassment of a fortune, quit business for economic study and advocacy. He challenged the dismal analyses of Europe, declared that the order of the universe and of social organization was from less to more. Even in the South, Edmund Ruffin, dirt farmer and geologist, preached means of replenishing depleted soils, replaced stupidity with agricultural science. John Rae, a teacher who lived in several countries in the course of wide wanderings, summed up better than others the delightful destiny of America.

These men stressed not just the physical resources of our continent. They were more perceptive. For them our chief opportunity lay in social organization for productive competence. Here, sprung from the American soil, was a forecast similar to that of Marx, but omitting the economic breakdown which Marx considered must be the preliminary to regeneration. The Americans said that transformation from poverty into plenty should not come through desperation, but by rational design. Prosperity, not proletarian pauperism, opened the pleasant vista. Ever-increasing social efficiency invited our best endeavors.

So it comes that in America capitalism is technological more than ideological. It is a scientific release of energies, not a sociological repression of rights. As progress in standardized, large-scale production necessitates, we move, selectively, to socialize sectors of the economy. Occasions differ. In the beginning the vast western domain could not be other than public. Then it was disposed of to private owners to forward settlement and to induce construction of railroads to span the continent. When population pressed into dry areas we entered on large publicly constructed irrigation projects. As ranges were over-grazed we limited flocks and herds to preserve the vegetation and hold the soil itself from being lifted by the winds. We planted shelter belts of trees in the same behalf. Scenic areas were kept as national or state parks for public enjoyment.

We not only protect but positively improve our natural resources by public construction. The great all-purpose dams, serving not localities but regions, are of a different order of magnitude and object from the most ambitious private capitalist works. To begin with, they are beyond the financial competence of individual or corporate enterprise. More important, they provide social betterments which would not stimulate the profit motive. These huge public undertakings are comprehensive, embracing in their plans electric power, transportation, conservation, population resettlement, improved agriculture, development of industries of many sorts. They extend to building of new towns, renovation of education, develop respect for civil rights.

The Tennessee Valley Authority is the nearest completion of several plans for river systems. Here parts of six states were rescued from economic and political decay. The federal government brought sense and science to a region which, for the lack of these, had become the nation's No. 1 problem. In this undertaking not only did the public buy out private claimants, but contiguous states were induced to act as one for the common advantage. The St. Lawrence Seaway displays international public development. It is planned in every feature to make ocean ports of inland cities, to supply power to areas which will now augment agriculture with industry. Towns whose sites will be flooded are being moved bodily to higher ground.

The progress of public ownership and sponsorship is taken for granted. The physical facilities, varied and extensive as they are, form only the visible evidences of a growing social responsibility. Less tangible but even more important are recognitions of governmental obligation for expanding social services. A chief one is to secure stability in the economy itself. The president of a principal life insurance company, in a speech in the autumn of 1957 before the Economic Club of Detroit, called loudly for governmental prevention of inflation. Inflation destroys the expectations of his policy holders. He did not say so, but the fact is that there is no private insurance against this and other hazards which lie in what is truly the public domain.

Governmental purchases of goods and services on account of national security alone have risen since 1950 from less than 20 billion dollars to more than 45 billion dollars in 1957. State and local public purchases, which at the earlier date were larger than federal, have risen steadily to 35 billion but, significantly for the scale and focus of our operations, are now below expenditures of the national government for the objects of security alone. It is universally agreed that development of atomic energy, for good or ill, is in the public province. Minor experimentation and application will be farmed to private enterprise, but only the organized society has resources and responsibility for major exploration and production of this supreme force.

What does all of this come to? America exhibits in preparatory stages and promises further development of a socialism born, not of desperation, but of opportunity, nursed not in bitterness but in calm expectation. It is not sudden but gradual, on the whole, in spite of emergency spurts. Not without the benefit of theory, it is practical and progressive. It springs from the engineer's drawing board, from the scientist's laboratory, from the finance minister's budget. It is a socialism not of the closet, but of the street. It is a socialism not of brooding, but of burgeoning. In the common concerns of life it may be not the less potent for these surprising means of its accomplishment.

Monopoly, Oligarchy and Socialism

By Herbert Aptheker

THE CONTRADICTION BETWEEN socialized production and individualized appropriation is the cancer guaranteeing capitalism's demise and its replacement by socialism. Other considerations of a political or historical nature may hasten or postpone this process but the fundamental and ultimate source of the process lies in the material contradiction mentioned.

The two main economic manifestations of this immutable contradiction are the trends towards monopoly and oligarchy. The development of capitalist economy in the United States strikingly confirms this observation.

The fact is that the ownership and control of the American economy is highly monopolistic, and the trend for the past half century has been in the direction of intensifying the monopolistic character of that ownership and control. The distribution of wealth in the United States is decidedly oligarchic, and the trend in that direction has also been increasing steadily for the past fifty years.

Data proving the monopolistic character of American capitalism are abundant. Some of these will now be offered; the

HERBERT APTHEKER was born in New York City in 1915; received his B.S., M.A., and Ph.D. degrees at Columbia University; was awarded a prize in history by the Association for the Study of Negro Life, and was a Guggenheim Fellow. The following are among Dr. Aptheker's dozen published works: "American Negro Slave Revolts", "To Be Free", "A Documentary History of the Negro People in the United States", "History and Reality", and "Toward Negro Freedom". His articles and reviews have appeared in most of the leading historical journals, including the *American Historical Review, Political Science Quarterly, Journal of Negro Education, Journal of Negro History, Phylon,* and *Pennsylvania Magazine of History.* Dr. Aptheker is on the Editorial Boards of *Political Affairs* and *Mainstream.*

reader will observe that they demonstrate not only what exists, but also what the trend has been for the past decade, namely, intensified monopolization.

The Federal Trade Commission, in its report for 1949, declared there were 13 industries in which "extreme concentration" existed. The definition offered by the Commission for this category certainly justified its title, "extreme". This was reserved for those cases in which *no more than three* corporations owned at least 64 per cent of the net capital assets in the industries. In tabular form, this is the result:

Industries in which *three firms or less* owned stated
percentages of assets in 1949

Industry	Percentage	Industry	Percentage
Aluminum	100.	Plumbing Equipment	71.3
Tin Cans & Tinware	95.3	Rubber Tires	70.3
Linoleum	92.1	Office Machinery	69.5
Copper Smelting &		Motor Vehicles	68.7
Refining	88.5	Biscuits	67.7
Cigarettes	77.6	Agricultural Machinery	66.6
Distilled Liquors	72.4	Meat Products	64.0

In 1950, there were 587,000 corporations reporting to the Federal Bureau of Internal Revenue; the top 250 (less than 1/20 of 1 per cent) owned 42 per cent of all the assets of all the corporations in the United States.

In 1947, manufacturing corporations with assets of $100 million or more owned 40 per cent of the assets of all manufacturing concerns; at the end of 1953, companies in that category owned 54 per cent of all the assets of manufacturing concerns. Further, at the end of 1953, the top 2 per cent of manufacturing corporations owned over 76 per cent of the total assets of all manufacturing concerns in the country.

The most recent of a whole series of governmental committee reports on economic concentration, which have been appearing for some sixty years, is that issued in 1957 by the U.S. Senate Anti-Trust and Monopoly Sub-Committee (Senator Estes Kefauver, Chairman) and entitled *Concentration in American Industry*. Here are some of the findings announced in the Report:

In 1947, the four largest automobile manufacturers con-

trolled 56 per cent of the American market; latest available figures (end of 1954) showed they controlled 76 per cent of that
market. In 1957, the four largest steel corporations controlled
45 per cent of the domestic market; the latest figures showed them
controlling 54 per cent. The top 200 corporations accounted for
30 per cent of all value added by manufacturing in 1947; they
accounted for 37 per cent in 1954.

This study not only demonstrated the great increase in the
trustification of those industries long notorious as monopolized;
it showed the swift concentration of ownership in areas hitherto
relatively free of such domination. Thus, for example, in the
rapidly expanding paper and paperboard industry, the Report
noted that the four largest firms had lifted their share of total
business from 15 per cent in 1947 to 25 per cent seven years
later. Again, in electrical appliances, while the four major
companies controlled 36 per cent of the market in 1947, they
controlled 50 per cent in 1954.

Very striking was the fact that the fifty largest corporations in the United States made sales, in 1955, totaling $86
billion, or fully 28 per cent of the total gross national product
of the country.

Monopolization of ownership means monopolization of profits. Thus, companies with taxable yearly incomes of $50,000
and over, in 1949, equalled 13 per cent of all corporations, but
they received 50 per cent of all taxable income in the United
States; companies with incomes under $25,000 a year make up
78 per cent of all corporations, but they receive 6 per cent of corporate income. *At the close of 1953, the manufacturing concerns with assets of $100 million or more accounted for 70 per-
cent of the net profits made by all manufacturing concerns.* Actually the proportion of profits garnered by the biggest corporations is much higher than the already swollen proportion
they represent of the total assets and total sales of all corporations. This is due to the fact that the larger the firm, the greater
its rate of profit. Figures demonstrating this for 1949 are typical:

RATE OF PROFIT FOR CORPORATIONS

With assets under $250,000 . . . . 8.4 per cent
With assets up to $100 million . . . 10.0 per cent
With assets of $100 million up . . . 14.0 per cent

While, as has been stated, the whole trend of the American

capitalist economy has been in the direction of greater and greater concentration, the merger movement has been especially noteworthy in the 1950's. The Federal Trade Commission, in a release dated June 18, 1956, reported that there had been 846 corporation mergers in 1955—"the highest in the five years the Division has been tabulating them". In those five years, from 1951 through 1955, the total reported mergers came to 3,781. In its 1957 report the Commission announced another record year for mergers: in 1956 there had been 905.

Moreover, not only is there a steep rise in the number of mergers year after year; there is also a trend for the mergers to occur more often than before among the top-ranking corporations. The 1956 Trade Commission release, cited earlier, presents a table which demonstrates this fact:

ASSETS OF ACQUIRING CONCERNS	PERCENTAGE OF FIRMS		
(millions of dollars)	1940-47	1948-54	1955
50 and over	29.3	29.4	33.2
10 to 49.9	28.6	36.1	36.8
5 to 9.9	12.8	13.9	9.8
1 to 4.9	17.7	13.3	12.9
Under 1	11.6	3.2	1.5

(some assets are unknown)

From these figures it appears that 57.9 per cent of the mergers, 1940-47, had acquiring concerns with assets of $10 million or more; 65.5 per cent in 1948-54; 70.0 per cent in 1955.

Another very significant fact about these latter-day mergers is that many of them represent the combining of gigantic financial and banking institutions—the creation, as Victor Perlo demonstrates,[1] of a veritable *Empire of High Finance*. Former Senator Herbert H. Lehman of New York, an extremely wealthy man himself, with banking background, noted in an address delivered in April, 1957 that, in the six-year period from 1950 through 1955, inclusive, 830 banks, with assets of $18.6 billion, were merged, consolidated or acquired. And that, within this period itself, the merger rate kept rising, so that in the single year, 1955, there were the mergers or consolidations of 225 banks having assets amounting to $9.6 billion—over half of the merged banking assets in the entire period. On this aspect of the merger picture, Mr. Lehman commented in these words: "The end re-

sult is not only a decreased number of banks and less competition, but a more highly centralized control of the nation's
financial system, *with mounting danger to the entire national
economy if a relatively few individuals should decide, for whatever reason, to misuse their control over the lifeblood of our
economy.*"[2]

The obverse side of the coin of greater and greater concentration is the increasing troubles of small business. We have
noted above the sharp differentiation in the rates of profits
shown in 1949 by relatively small, medium, and large concerns.
This differentiation has been intensified with the ensuing
years.

Fortune Magazine, in its issue of May, 1957, points out that
the sales of small manufacturing concerns have been falling
steadily since 1951. The number and rate of small business
failures have been rising throughout the 1950's. It is significant
that, for example, the number of new businesses started in 1955
exceeded the number begun in 1952 by less than 3 per cent, but
the number of business failures rose by 44 per cent. And in the
first half of 1956 there were 6,496 business failures, which was
15 per cent more than there had been in the same period of
1955. Senator John Sparkman of Alabama reported in May,
1957, that, whereas big business realized a net profit of 9.3 per
cent in the last quarter of 1956, companies with assets of under
one million dollars, showed a net profit of 1.2 per cent (*N. Y.
Times,* May 23, 1957).

We have indicated above that notable concentration has gone
on in certain business areas that were traditional strongholds of
smaller capitalists. This is strikingly true in the information,
entertainment and propaganda industries—publishing (newspapers, magazines, books), movies, TV, and radio. Back in 1947,
when the Commission on Freedom of the Press, headed by Robert M. Hutchins, made its study, it concluded, "The agencies
of mass communication are big business and their owners are
big businessmen." Today in all these areas effective control
is in the hands of a few directly-participating corporations,
and is further concentrated within financial institutions whose
domination of credit give them life-and-death power.

Having pointed out the tremendous concentration of ownership and control of the industrial plant and the communications
media, with the apex of this in the tight banking empire, there

yet remain other facets of monopoly domination that must be noted. The vast majority of the hundreds of thousands of smaller businesses are dependent upon Big Business, not only because of a tight-money policy and because of the cost-price squeeze, but for more overt and direct reasons. The fact is that smaller business finds its retail prices set by the monopolists, and the prices of what it buys set administratively— not through non-existent competition—and set uniformly. It finds that through tie-in sales, withholding supplies, credit squeezes, etc., it is in fact an appendage to Big Business.

A striking example of this occurs in the oil industry, where the American Petroleum Institute, sensitive to the developing public awareness of the outrageous practices, powers and privileges of the oil barons, likes to prate about the 200,000 "independently owned or operated" service companies, and the alleged existence of 42,000 separate "oil companies". Actually, of course, the overwhelming majority of these "oil companies" are nothing but distributors of the products of the Big Ones, and the 200,000 station owners operate under license and restrictive contracts with the Big Ones that make of their "independence" a farce. The fact is that seven enormous corporations (with some interlocking) control the production, distribution, and price of the "Free World's" oil: Standard of New Jersey; Standard of California; Texas; Gulf; Socony-Mobil; Anglo-Iranian; Dutch-Shell.

The realities of monopoly capitalist domination of the American economy—what Herbert Lehman called "their control over the lifeblood of our economy"—and of the high degree of concentrated ownership are more and more penetrating the public consciousness. This alarms the proprietors and servitors of this Power. Hence they develop apologias which in the historic field transform Robber Barons into Creative Industrial Statesmen; in the economic field transform Free Enterprise into Responsible Enterprise, Monopoly Capitalism into People's Capitalism; and in the moral field make of a rapacious and selfishly-motivated system, one which really "has been shaped by the simple, humane principles of the Judaeo-Christian faiths and by the disciplines of the American democratic tradition".[3]

The Industrial Statesman who penned these immortal words was concerned, as he said, with the widespread "prejudice against bigness" in business and he wanted a large-scale educational campaign to be directed against this. The Chairman of Socony-Mobil continued, "I believe there is a certain urgency about this for the reason that, in many industries, the tendency toward 'bigness' is bound to become increasingly apparent in the next few years. Something must be done to allay the fear with which the public may be expected to regard this development." The Chairman's other contribution, also far from original with him, appears in this paragraph:

" 'Free enterprise' is the term which we use most frequently in describing ourselves and our economic system, but surely the term 'responsible enterprise' would be equally accurate. In using it we merely examine the thing from its other side. The other standard phrase, 'private enterprise', suffers, I think, from its suggestion of exclusiveness and the implication that its activity is no one's business but its own. We all know that that is a misleading implication."

This brings us directly to the claim reiterated by Big-Business propaganda to the effect that the giant corporations are really owned by the people at large—"people's capitalism"—and not by any ruling class. Certainly the reality of the effective domination of American politics, foreign policy, culture, and the economy generally by Big Business is indubitable; this does not mean, of course, that the power is not challenged, but it does mean that the effective power is where it is. The reality of class stratification in the United States is also indubitable, and has once again and most recently been documented by the anti-Marxist scholar, Professor Joseph Kahl, in his *The American Class Structure;* the sociological impact of this has been delineated in C. Wright Mills' illuminating *The Power Elite,* while features of the consequent moral behavior and ennobling private pursuits of the Elite were described with great sympathy by Cleveland Amory, in *The Last Resorts.*

But specifically on the point of widespread "public ownership" of the great monopolies: this, itself, is quite false. The Federal Reserve Board, in its *Bulletin* of October, 1949, stated: "Stock ownership is largely concentrated in a small proportion of the population, particularly in high income groups." The fact is that only about 4 per cent of the population has any stock-holdings at all; that is, 96 per cent of the American people own no corporation stocks whatever. Of the 4 per cent who do hold some stocks—making a total of six million people—the vast majority own a fractional quantity. Thus, 75,000 stock-owners (about 1.3 per cent of the total) own 50 per cent of all corporate stock; and of the 200 largest non-financial corporations, the top 1 per cent of the shareholders accounted for 60 per cent of the total common stock.

These figures alone effectively refute the "people's capitalism" propaganda. Nevertheless, it is important to observe that the same figures do show a wider dispersion of corporation-stock ownership than is true in any other capitalist country. While such dispersion actually helps monopolization of control (by reducing the percentage of stock ownership needed for effective control), it simultaneously offers an objective base for widespread petty-bourgeois feelings and aspirations.

A further fundamental feature of American monopoly capitalism is its domineering and parasitic role *vis a vis* the rest of the "Free World", and especially that portion of it that is still colonial. Confining ourselves, for the purposes of this paper, to the economic aspects of this question, one observes these highlights: The investment of American capital in foreign countries has reached colossal proportions in the past decade. This is done through Government grants and guarantees, through the direct absorption of firms overseas, and, more commonly, by the direct investment by American corporations in foreign properties, resources or concerns.

The most thorough and recent study of this subject appears in Victor Perlo's already cited volume. He demonstrates that total foreign investment has reached an all-time high, and that it is now at least four times greater than it was in 1939. The announced net profit from this investment in 1956 came to $3.2 billion, or nearly 15 per cent of total corporate profits. Hidden forms of profit are especially numerous in the foreign investment field; Perlo believes that adding this to the admitted net total would give a figure approximating an $11 billion profit each year for American corporations from foreign investment.

More and more this enormous foreign investment is being made by fewer and fewer American corporations—a further indication of the mounting monopolization of the American economy. Thus, in 1947 (according to the Department of Commerce publication, *Survey of Current Business*, November, 1949), there were 2,500 American companies with foreign subsidiaries and branches. But over 75 per cent of the net outflow of American direct-investment capital came from just ten of these corporations.

The rate of profit from foreign investments is very high. Thus, as one example, the Department of Commerce declared that in 1948 the average rate of return on all direct investments outside the country was 15.6 per cent—double the average rate of profit within the United States.

Foreign investments are especially important in oil, first of all, and in copper and iron ore, with considerable amounts also going into some manufacturing efforts, especially automobiles. Canada, Latin America, Africa, the Near East are especially lucrative areas of investment. Special economic privileges accrue, of course, to American firms doing business in colonial possessions, as Puerto Rico and Hawaii, or in quasi-colonial possessions, as the Philippines, South Korea, Taiwan, etc.

Cartels of an international nature—with "Free World" control over prices, patents, supplies—are growing. They are now very important in oil, electrical equipment, chemicals, rubber, tin, aluminum, etc.

Challenges to world domination of raw materials, technical know-how and equipment, and fluid capital are coming with gathering momentum from the Socialist world (especially, of course, the USSR) and these are having devastating effects on traditional imperialist practices and policies. Rising intra-imperialist disagreements also mark the present era; the sharp differentiations within each of the national capitalist classes similarly are mounting. These factors, plus the decisive challenge of the colonial liberation movements, are intensifying the crisis features of world capitalism and are basic considerations for all partisans of socialism. Detailed inquiry into these questions is outside the scope of this paper.

Capitalism is hostile to agriculture. No better illustration of this truth is possible than that of the United States, for here, in capitalism's paradise, agriculture has been for generations and is today in chronic crisis. Agriculture is becoming increasingly commercialized and its ownership more and more concentrated. More and more, great capital outlays are necessary; more and more, governmental policy favors the biggest farmers; more and more, Big Corporation domination is destroying the traditional American Farmer.

Lauren Soth, editor of the *Des Moines (Iowa) Register and Tribune*, in his recent study, *Farm Trouble*,[4] finds the "major farm problem" to be "low income—poverty—and what we may call non-commercial agriculture". In commercial farming he recognizes heavy "imbalances", with particular reference to the especially favored position, from the viewpoint of costs and government assistance, of the biggest rather than the smallest of the commercial farmers.

The fact is that the farm crisis is drawing millions of people from the land—120,000 farm families each year are giving up and moving out. While our farm population was 30 millions in 1940, it was less than 23 millions in 1956. Much of this results from enhanced technology and from normal processes of urbanization; but the greater part of it comes from the farm crisis, and represents tremendous human tragedy and waste.

All the figures demonstrate that the so-called Class I farms (defined by the Government as those which sell $25,000 or more of produce a year) are growing bigger and bigger, richer and richer, and are absorbing a greater and greater share of agricultural production and, especially, of agricultural income. More and more, too, the greatest of these giants are tied in with enormous industrial and financial combines. Meanwhile, governmental price and subsidy policies made by and for these great farm-corporations intensify the process of monopolization.

The government favoritism manifested towards the largest agricultural producing units is present also, of course, when it comes to industrial production. Tax, depletion, amortization, tariff, procurement policies of the Government all favor the greatest corporations. So intense is this favoritism that it amounts very nearly to an identity of policy and personnel between the richest corporations and the governmental apparatus.[5] This is so glaring that an article in the liberal Catholic weekly, *The Commonweal* (by Lawrence T. King, in the issue of November 8, 1957) concludes that "the suspicion must persist in the minds of many that an alliance is being forged between government and corporate power".

The obverse side of monopoly capitalism is mass deprivation. Monopoly capitalism means the existence of an oligarchy; the existence of an oligarchy carries with it the presence of immense numbers of impoverished persons.

It is true that the resources, physical plant and productivity of the United States are the greatest in the world. This, plus certain favoring historical conditions (as separation from the devastations of two World Wars, and the garnering of immense profits therefrom), together with the results of imperialist exploitation, make possible in the United States a higher standard of living, in terms of physical perquisites, than exists anywhere else. We do not here consider such matters as insecurity, speedup, corruption, delinquency, immorality, mental illness, alcoholism and drug-addiction, broken families—not to mention such an abomination as racism—all of which, of course, directly affect the standard of living in any rounded, human sense, and in all of which the United States is among the "leaders".[6] But in the sense of physical provision, and in that sense alone, the American standard of living is the highest in the world.

Nevertheless, there is the sharpest kind of inequality in the distribution of wealth in the U.S. and there are large layers of the population (not merely "pockets,"[7] as is sometimes said) who live in terrible poverty.

One of the reflections of extreme inequality in wealth distribution are the figures on family-held liquid assets. The Federal Reserve Board reported that as of the end of 1955, the top 10 per cent of American families owned 65 per cent of all family-held liquid assets (that is, government bonds, bank accounts, postal savings, shares in savings and loan associations and credit unions); the next 20 per cent owned 27 per cent; the next 30 per cent owned 8 per cent, and the bottom 40 per cent owned less than 1 per cent.

Savings themselves constitute another index of wealth distribution. The magazine *Business Week*, in its issue for June 16, 1956, published a report on this matter. Said the magazine: "At income levels below the $7,500 mark, savings are trivial." Self-employed Americans having incomes below $4,000 a year operate on a *deficit* of $706 annually—the annual average income in this group is $2,112. Others with incomes under $4,000—mostly wage and salary workers, end their year with a *deficit* of $149; the average annual income for this group is $2,311.

Self-employed persons having incomes from $4,000 to $7,500 have average savings of $293 annually (average income $5,508). Wage and salaried people in this level save $190 yearly (average income $5,240). In the upper brackets the savings become appreciable, both absolutely and relatively. Thus, self-employed persons with incomes in excess of $10,000 save on an average $6,380 yearly (average income $17,826).

People live on more than they earn (and this the vast majority of Americans do), through installment buying, revolving credit, personal loans at banks, etc. To cite the figures for but one method of borrowing: total outstanding personal loans, being paid back on the installment plan, came to $5.8 billion at the end of April, 1956—a total 105 per cent higher than in 1950.

The figures on actual income distribution for 1955 provide the following picture: First of all, a very low estimate, for that year, of the requirements of a multiple-person family for a minimum adequate living standard came to about $4,000; actually the Heller Budget, calculated at the University of California, placed the need at $5,400 a year. But taking the $4,000 figure one finds that, according to the Government figures, 32 per cent of all multiple-person families received an annual money income, in 1955—*before taxes*—of less than $4,000. Taking $3,000 as a minimum for single-person families, the government reports show that 68 per cent of such families had total money incomes, before taxes, of less than $3,000. As a matter of fact, taking the $2,000 level of yearly income, before taxes—which in 1955 certainly represented extreme impoverishment by American standards—9 per cent of multiple-person families (4 million such families) and 45 per cent of single-person families (that is 4.3 million persons) belonged in this category.

On September 9, 1957, the Census Bureau released income figures for 1956. According to this Government report, 8 per cent of the nation's families had incomes of $10,000 or over (before taxes). But 20 per cent of all families (seven million families) received incomes (before taxes) of less than $2,000; indeed, three million American families in 1956 had total money earnings, before taxes, of less than $1,000. The median family income was $4,783; at the same time, 42.7 per cent of all families had total incomes, before taxes, of less than $4,000. The particularly and chronically depressed nature of the farming population is indicated in the fact that the median farm income for 1956 came to $2,371, also before taxes.

In any discussion of the American Standard of Living, special note must be taken of the particularly exploited position

of the 18 million Negro people. Perhaps one table will be sufficient for present purposes to illustrate the nature of this situation:

MEDIAN MONEY INCOME, U.S. FAMILIES 1954 (Before Taxes)

	White	Negro	% Negro of White
Total U.S.	$4,339	$2,410	56%
Total Urban	4,827	2,876	60
in South	4,428	2,425	56
West	4,812	not available	
North Central	5,059	3,283	65
Northeast	4,837	3,243	67
Total, rural-farm	2,157	763	49
in South	1,516	742	49

(Source: Eli Ginzberg, et. al., "The Negro Potential" (N. Y., 1956),
p. 16.)

The preceding data, taken altogether, show a high per-
sistence of real poverty, a very widespread degree of bare minimum standard of living, a notable minority in the "middle-class"
bracket (about $7,500 to $20,000 a year, in 1955 dollars), and
a very small minority in the rich brackets. These figures point
to acute instability in the economy; they help explain the profound sense of insecurity afflicting most Americans who remain
above the poverty level.

As we have already indicated, the entire policy of the Government, in all areas, is geared towards the further advantage
of the very rich. One of the striking illustrations of this is the
nature of the Federal budget, which is notably deficient in terms
of human welfare (and the trend in the past several years is
to reduce further the percentage of funds allocated for this
area), and devoted largely to military outlay. Thus the budget,
starting with the fiscal year July 1, 1957, contemplates a total
expenditure of $83 billion. Of this over half—$43.6 billion—
is to go for military purposes. On the other hand, less than
one-sixth of the budget—$13.9 billion—is to go for human needs,
and this includes the total federal outlay for pensions of all
kinds, assistance to the poverty-stricken aged, blind, to the unemployed, to education, to disabled people, for medical research,
to libraries, museums and all cultural endeavors, school-lunch
programs, hospital building, and all "other welfare activities."

We conclude that the evidence shows that, in terms of what

we have and can do, but what capitalism actually does, it is woefully deficient as an economic order for the service of man. And this is true in that land where the system—for a great number of reasons—has been able to do the most. Given social ownership and rational planning, given the devotion of the enormous American resources and human capabilities for human welfare rather than capitalist profit, the actual well-being in economic, medical, educational and cultural terms of the American people would be incalculably advanced. This observation is all the more true now that we are entering into the age of atomic energy, automation and electronics (and the **uncovering and harnessing of** additional sources of energy and productivity). While these pose terrifying problems for monopoly capitalism, they assure unprecedented rates of production growth with Socialism and, indeed, the relatively rapid creation of that material abundance, justly distributed, that will be Communism.

N O T E S

1 *The Empire of High Finance,* by Victor Perlo. International Publishers, New York, 1957.

2 A very considerable portion of the speech takes up three pages in *The New Leader* (N. Y., April 29, 1957). Italicized words were omitted from this version, but appear in the *New York Times* (April 3, 1957).

3 B. Brewster Jennings, Chairman of the Board, Socony-Mobil Corp., in *U. S. News & World Report,* Feb. 22, 1957; reprinted from the *American Petroleum Institute Quarterly,* Winter, 1956-57.

4 In addition to the Soth volume, very important information will be found in the "Statement of Ernesto Galarza, Secretary, National Agricultural Workers Union, AFL-CIO" to House of Representatives, May 15, 1957. Available from the union in mimeographed form.

5 For a good recent study of "the government as promoter" of *Monopoly in America,* see that book by Professors Walter Adams and Horace M. Gray, Macmillan, N. Y., 1955; the writings of T. K. Quinn also are useful in this connection. See, for example, his article, "The Strangling Power of Corporate Giants," in *The Progressive,* March, 1957.

6 For some data on this, see the editorial, "Suicide, Homicide and Beer," in *The New Republic,* Sept. 9, 1957.

7 A kind of "pocket" which often goes unreported in government figures is the population of the numerous "Skid Rows" in the U.S. The men and women, completely broken and abject, in this kind of "pocket" must number many scores of thousands. One of the few good studies of this question is *Skid Row, U.S.A.* by Sara Harris (Doubleday, N. Y., 1956).

What Is Socialism?

By Paul M. Sweezy

This is a slightly revised text of a speech delivered at the University of New Hampshire on May 22, 1956, and published in *Monthly Review*, November, 1956.

Mr. Chairman and Ladies and Gentlemen: It is not my habit to read prepared lectures, and I would prefer not to do it tonight. In view of the extraordinary publicity which has surrounded this event, however, I could not refuse the request of the press and wire services for an advance text. And in view of the no less extraordinary interest which certain official quarters have in the past shown in whatever I happen to say at the University of New Hampshire, I think it may be wisest to stick to the text so that at any rate there need be no disagreement about what I am saying tonight.

First, let me say that I am very happy to be here at the University of New Hampshire again. For several years up to and including 1954, it was my privilege and pleasure to come here every spring to lecture in the humanities course and to participate in less formal student and faculty discussions. Due to circumstances over which neither I nor anyone here at the University had any control, these visits were interrupted—to my loss and regret. I hope tonight's meeting marks the renewal of an association which I have always found both enjoyable and fruitful.

PAUL M. SWEEZY taught courses on American corporations and socialism at Harvard University for more than ten years. He worked for the National Resources Planning Board, the Security Exchange Commission and the Temporary National Economic Committee, investigating monopolies from 1943 to 1945. He was with the Office of Strategic Services in England, France and Germany. Among his books are "The Theory of Corporate Development", Socialism", and "The Present Is History". At present Dr. Sweezy is co-editor with Leo Huberman of the magazine, *Monthly Review*.

But there is another reason why I am glad to be here tonight. Through no virtue (or fault) of mine, my appearance on the campus at this time has become a clear test of the quality of academic freedom that exists at the University of New Hampshire. Academic freedom, let me remind you, is not, at bottom, a matter of my freedom to speak my mind. That freedom, I am glad to say, I still have; and nothing has yet prevented me from making use of it. Academic freedom is fundamentally the freedom of the academic community to employ or otherwise bring before it anyone whose ideas and opinions it may think of interest or importance. It is a part, and a very important part, of the freedom of the sovereign people to educate itself for the responsibility of governing, and as such it is protected by the First Amendment to the Constitution of the United States. The essence of the matter was well stated by America's greatest civil libertarian, Alexander Meiklejohn, when he recently told a Congressional Committee that

> in the field of public discussion, when citizens and their fellow thinkers "peaceably assemble" to listen to a speaker, whether he be American or foreign, conservative or radical, safe or dangerous, the First Amendment is not in the first instance concerned with the "right" of the speaker to say this or that. It is concerned with the authority of the hearers to meet together, to discuss, and to hear discussed by speakers of their own choice, whatever they may deem worthy of their consideration.

If for any reason this meeting had been prevented from taking place, it would have been *your* authority and *your* freedom that would have been abridged and violated. The fact that it is taking place should prove to the people of New Hampshire that you still have and mean to use that authority and that freedom to hear "whatever you deem worthy of your consideration." I am not now concerned to thank anyone for arranging this meeting and inviting me to address it; but I am very definitely concerned to congratulate those who have been responsible —particularly the members of the short-lived Committee for Academic Freedom and of the Senior Skulls Society—for fighting the matter through and thus proving beyond any doubt that academic freedom is still alive at our state university.

I turn now to our topic for this evening, and I think perhaps the best way to proceed is to try to answer the question: What is Marxism?

Marxism is a body of ideas about the nature of the universe, of man, of society, and of history. It bears the name of Karl Marx, a German who was born in 1818 and died in 1883, and who lived the latter half of his life in London. Marx was a man of prodigious learning and enormously powerful intellect, one of the greatest thinkers not only of the nineteenth century but of all recorded history.

Marx combined in his system of ideas the realistic philosophy of the English and French Enlightenment, the comprehensive and dynamic point of view of the German idealists and particularly of Hegel, and the hardheaded analysis of the capitalist economy which we owe to the great British classical economists. The result was a brilliant new synthesis which is both highly original and at the same time stands squarely in the mainstream of modern intellectual development from the Renaissance onward. Here, in desperate brevity, are what I understand to be the central elements of the Marxian view of society and history:

The universe is real and existed for eons before there was human life, or for that matter life of any kind, on our planet. Life here on the earth is a natural by-product of the earth's cooling, and humanity is the result of a long process of evolution. In the earliest stages of society, human labor was still so unproductive that it yielded no surplus over and above the requirements of life and reproduction. As long as this was true, men lived in a state of primitive communism—cooperating, sharing, fighting, but not yet exploiting each other.

Later, techniques improved so much that a man could produce a surplus over and above what he needed for himself, and from this dates the beginning of economic exploitation and social classes. When one tribe fought and defeated another, it was now worthwhile to take captive the vanquished and force them to work for the victors. Some men became rulers living off the surplus produced by others; while the actual producers lost their independence and spent their lives toiling for their masters. It was in this way that exploitation of man by man and the division of society into classes originated.

But the form of exploitation has not remained unchanged—indeed, nothing remains unchanged, everything is in a constant state of flux. The exploiters seek to expand the surplus at their disposal, and with this end in view they invent and introduce new and better techniques of production; the exploited seek to improve their condition and therefore carry on a never-ending struggle to enlarge their share of the product. As a result the forms of exploitation change, and with them the whole structure of society. At first it was slavery, in which the laborer is the property of his master. Next came serfdom, in which the laborer has attained a certain degree of freedom but is still tied to the soil. And finally there is wage labor, in which the laborer is legally entirely free but must work for the profit of others because he lacks means of production of his own.

A society based on private ownership of the means of production and wage labor is called capitalism. It came into the world first in England and certain parts of Western Europe, not all at once but gradually and painfully between the sixteenth and nineteenth centuries. It brought with it social and political upheavals, new ways of thinking, and a deep awareness of the vast creative potentials of human labor and industry. Historically speaking, capitalism was a long leap forward. In the words of the *Communist Manifesto*: "It has been the first to show what man's activity can bring about. It has accomplished wonders far surpassing Egyptian pyramids, Roman aqueducts, and Gothic cathedrals; it has conducted expeditions that put in the shade all former migrations and crusades."

But capitalism contains within itself what Marx called contradictions which prevent it from fully realizing the potentials which it was the first to uncover. The capitalist class, comprising those who own the instruments of production and set them in motion, is and must be concerned with making profits, not with the general welfare. Capitalists subordinate other aims to the maximization of profit. In pursuit of this objective, they pay workers as little as they can get away with and steadily introduce labor-saving machinery. The consequence, of course, is to hold down the consuming power of the working class. At the same time, the capitalists restrict their own consumption in the interests of accumulating more and more capital. But accumulating more and more capital means adding to society's productive capacity. We, therefore, have the paradox that capitalism steps on the brake as far as consumption is concerned and on the accelerator as far as production is concerned. This is its basic contradictions, and it cannot be eliminated except through changing the system from one of production for profit to one of production for use.

On the basis of this analysis, Marx believed that it was to the interest of the workers to organize themselves politically in order eventually to gain power and replace capitalism by a system based upon common ownership of the means of production and economic planning, a system to which he and his followers came in time to give the name of socialism. Moreover, Marx had no doubt that the workers would in fact follow this course, and that their growing numbers, importance, and discipline under capitalism would sooner or later ensure their victory. As to *how* the transition would be effected, Marx at first thought that it would have to be everywhere by means of a violent revolution. But as political democracy spread, especially in the English-speaking countries, he modified this view and in the last decades of his life believed that a peaceful and legal transition was quite possible in some countries and under some conditions. "We know," he said in a speech at Amsterdam in 1872, "that special regard must be paid to the institutions, customs, and traditions of various lands; and we do not deny that there are certain countries, such as the United States and England, in which the workers may hope to achieve their ends by peaceful means."

So much then for Marxism. Naturally, my account is oversimplified and very incomplete, but I hope it may serve to give you some idea of the scope and quality of Marx's thought—so different from the impressions which demagogic opponents have always sought to convey. Let us now ask: What is socialism?

Socialism, according to Marx, is the form of society which will succeed capitalism, just as capitalism is the form of society which succeeded feudalism.

The fundamental change would consist in the abolition of private ownership of the means of production. Please note that neither Marx nor (so far as I know) any other modern socialist of importance ever advocated or expected that private ownership of consumer goods would or should be abolished. On the contrary, he favored the multiplication of consumer goods in the hands of the lower-income groups, hence a great extension of private ownership in this sphere.

As to the form of ownership of the means of production

which would characterize socialism, Marxists have never been dogmatic. Ownership must be by public bodies, but that does not necessarily mean only the central government: local governments, special public authorities of one sort or another, and cooperatives can also own means of production under socialism. And there can even be a certain amount of private ownership, provided it is confined to industries in which production takes place on a small scale.

A corollary of public ownership of the means of production is economic planning. The capitalist economy is governed by the market, that is to say, by private producers responding to price movements with a view to maximizing their own profits. It is through this mechanism that supply and demand are adjusted to each other and productive resources are allocated to various industries and branches of production. But public bodies have no compelling reason to maximize their profits (though, admittedly, under certain circumstances they may be *directed* to make as much profit as they can). In general, therefore, they must have some other principle to guide their economic conduct, and this can only be the following of a plan which coordinates the activities of all the public bodies.

Now socialists claim that it is precisely the freedom from the necessity to make profits and the coordination of all economic activities by a general plan which allows socialism to overcome the contradictions of capitalism and to develop its resources and technology for the greatest good of the people as a whole. Under such a system, crises and unemployment could only result from bad planning; and while bad planning is certainly not impossible, especially in the early stages of socialist society, there is no reason why planners should not learn to correct their mistakes and to reduce the resulting maladjustments and disproportions to smaller and smaller dimensions.

What about the non-economic aspects of socialism? Here Marx had a well-developed theory. He expected socialism to come first in the more advanced industrialized countries and to build on the political foundations which they had already achieved. Since in such countries the workers were in a majority, he believed that the taking of political power by the working class would mean full democracy and liberty for most of the people, though he also expected that there would be a period of greater or lesser duration when the rights and freedoms of the former exploiters would be subject to certain restrictions. As to the longer-run future, he reasoned that the full development of society's economic potential under socialism would gradually raise the well-being and education of everyone so that eventually all classes and class distinctions would be done away with. When that happened—but not before—the state as a repressive apparatus for dealing with class and other forms of social conflict would "wither away". The final goal of Marx and his followers can therefore be said to be the same as that of the philosophical anarchists. It would be a state of society in which, to quote Marx's words, "the free development of each is the condition for the free development of all" and in which distribution takes place according to the principle "from each according to his ability, to each according to his need".

Others before Marx had had a similar vision of a good society to come—a society of abundance and brotherhood in place of the society of scarcity and alienation which the human race had always been condemned to live in. What particularly distinguished Marx from his predecessors is that he purported to prove that this society of the future, which he called socialism, is not only a dream and a hope but is in fact the next stage of historical evolution. It would not come automatically, to be sure —not as the result of the blind decrees of fate. It would come rather as the result of the conscious, organized activity of working people, the vast majority of mankind. Given this perspective, the task of the humanitarian could only be to devote his energies to educating and organizing the working class to fulfill its historic mission. That, in a word, is what Marxists have been trying to do for nearly a hundred years now.

Marx's prophetic forecast of the end of capitalism and the opening of a new era in human history was given to the world in the *Communist Manifesto* in 1848. More than a century has passed since. Do the facts of this intervening period permit us to say whether Marx was right or wrong?

In the broadest sense, I do not see how it can be denied that Marx has been brilliantly vindicated. A mighty socialist movement based on the working class grew up during his lifetime. The crises of capitalism, far from abating, grew in intensity and violence, culminating in the holocausts of two world wars. Beginning with the Russian Revolution of 1917, more and more of the earth's population has withdrawn from the orbit of capitalism and has undertaken to reconstruct its economy and society on the basis of public ownership and planning. Today, something like a third of the human race has definitely abandoned private enterprise and, under Communist leadership, is building up a network of planned economies.

But it is not only in Communist-led countries that this is happening, though elsewhere the pace is slower. Since World War II, Great Britain has moved a considerable distance along the road to a socialized economy, and one of the two big political parties is a socialist party. Even more recently, India, next to Communist China the most populous country in the world, has adopted a Five Year Plan which the sober London *Times* calls "India's Socialist Plan".

The fact is that over most of the world's surface the trend is now visibly away from private enterprise and toward public ownership of the means of production, away from market-dominated economies and toward economic planning. Only in the United States and a few countries closely allied to the United States does the trend seem to be in the other direction. Here, it is true, the socialist movement is at a low ebb, and private enterprise is very much in the saddle.

Should we perhaps conclude that Marx was right for the rest of the world but wrong for the United States? Are we the great exception? Or are we merely lagging somewhat behind in a movement which eventually will be as universal as Marx predicted it would?

These are crucial questions, especially for us Americans. In what time remains to me, I shall attempt to indicate some possible answers.

There is one respect, and it is an important one, in which Marx was certainly wrong. As I noted earlier, he expected socialism to come first in the most advanced industrial countries. It did not. For reasons having to do with the late 19th- and early 20th-century development of relations between the advanced countries and the colonial and semi-colonial countries, the revolutionary movement grew more rapidly and had more opportunities in the backward than in the advanced regions. When the capitalist system was wracked by the destruction and disasters of the two world wars, it broke at its weakest points not at its strongest. Socialism came first to the Tsarist Empire, and spread from there to Eastern Europe and China.

This has, of course, meant that the early stages of the development of socialism have been very different from what Marx foresaw.

The new order could not build directly on the achievements of the old. It had no developed industrial base, no educated and trained labor force, no political democracy. It had to start from scratch and work under conditons of utmost difficulty.

Many people, including Marxists, expected socialism to proceed at once, or at any rate within a short time, to achieve its great goals: an economy of abundance, increasing democracy and freedom for the workers, a richer life for all. It could have happened that way if Britain, Germany, and the United States had been the first great socialist countries. But it could not possibly happen that way in backward Russia standing alone for a whole generation. The industrial base had to be built, and that meant belt-tightening. The Russians had no traditions of democracy and civil liberty, and under the difficult conditions of the '20's and '30's it was natural that a new police state should arise on the foundations of the old Tsarist police state. Moreover, like all police states this one committed excesses and horrors which had little if anything to do with the central tasks of construction the regime had set itself.

Under these circumstances, socialism in practice had little attraction for the people of the advanced countries. The standard of living of those living under it remained abysmally low, and political conduct, both among leaders and between leaders and people, often seemed closer to oriental despotism than to enlightened socialism. It was widely assumed in the West either that the Soviet Union was not socialist at all, or that socialism had been tried and failed.

In the underdeveloped countries, however, the USSR made a very different impression. They saw rapid economic advance, a vast process of popular education, some improvement in living standards—and never having experienced democracy themselves, they hardly noticed its absence in Russia. Communism was imposed on Eastern Europe by the Red Army chasing Hitler back to Berlin, but in China it was the product of a great popular revolution. And it is now expanding its influence throughout the underdeveloped regions of the world.

The two systems of capitalism and socialism exist side by side in the world today. They are competing for the support and emulation of the backward and uncommitted countries. They are also competing in terms of absolute performance. How will this contest turn out? Will those now in the capitalist camp remain there? Or will they tend to join the socialist camp as time goes by? And finally, what about the United States, the leader of the capitalist camp?

These are questions which every serious person in the world is asking today. I predict that they will be increasingly the center of attention in the years and decades ahead.

The answers, I think, will depend very largely on the relative success of the two systems in the following fields: production and income, education, and liberty. I believe that socialism will win out in this great world-shaking contest, and I am going to conclude my talk by trying to give you some of the reasons why I hold this view. I should add perhaps that I don't expect you to agree with me at this stage of the game. The decisive forces and trends are still operating for the most part below the surface, and it will be some time yet before they can be seen and evaluated by all. But I hope that I may succeed in making you *think* seriously about these matters. It is, I believe, important that Americans should be put on notice that things are happening in the world, and will increasingly happen, which contradict their established thought patterns and expectations. You may not believe me yet, but at any rate if you pay serious attention to what I say you should not be surprised when things turn out differently from the way you have been taught to expect.

Let us first look at the relative performance of the two systems in the economic field proper. It will be generally agreed, I suppose, that United States capitalism has been doing about as well as can be expected in the last decade. Let us assume for the sake of the argument that it continues to do as well (though I myself think a good case can be made out for the view that this is too favorable an assumption for capitalism). Let us also assume that the USSR continues to grow at about its present rate, though I believe this is likely to be an under- rather than an over-estimate. On these assumptions, what will be the outcome of the economic competition between the systems?

The answer is clear and unambiguous. Here is the way the Oxford economist, Peter Wiles, put the matter in a broadcast over the BBC last fall (I am quoting from the October 20th, 1955, issue of *The Listener,* weekly publication of the BBC):

> Perhaps the most important fact in all modern economics is that the rate of growth of productivity is higher in the Soviet Union than in any important free country at the period of its maximum development, let alone now. That is, whether we take roughly comparable circumstances or the present circumstances, the Soviet superiority remains. The best performance by a large non-Communist economy for a long period together appears to be that of Japan: between 1912 and 1937 she grew by about 3 percent per annum. The Soviet economy grew by about 5½ percent per annum before the war and by about 7½ per cent since 1948. For mining and manufacturing alone . . . the figures are: Japan 7 per cent, USSR 12 percent.
>
> We see that the overwhelming Communist superiority in industry alone leads to a great overall superiority (in the whole national income). The effect of compound interest is very great over a few decades. Thus, growing 3 percent per annum faster than the United States, the USSR could catch up from a starting point of half the United States national income per head in 23 years.

These facts are not widely known in the United States, I am sorry to say, but there is no doubt about their authenticity. Thus, for example, the *New York Times* of a few days ago (May 18) quotes Mr. Hugh Gaitskell, leader of the British Labor Party and himself a trained economist, as having told the Convention of the International Ladies Garment Workers Union, meeting in Atlantic City, that "Soviet national income was going up 10 percent a year, double the United States rate". If this continues, the USSR will overtake and surpass the United States *in per capita income* in about four more Five Year Plans.

Let us turn now to our second field of competition, education. Developments here are no less startling, and unfortunately no better known, than in the field of economics proper. So far as the Soviet Union is concerned, I can do no better than quote from what former Senator William Benton of Connecticut wrote in the *New York Times* Sunday magazine section on April

1, 1956, after a trip to the Soviet Union to study educational developments there:

> What is it that most impresses the foreign observer about the Soviet school system? In less than forty years, starting with a population about 50 percent illiterate, the Soviets have built a seven-year primary school system rivalling our own in universality, with nearly 100 percent enrollment.
>
> Since World War II, the Soviet secondary school system has mushroomed amazingly. By 1960 the basic ten-year school is to be compulsory everywhere. In spite of acute labor shortages, all children are to be kept in school from 7 to 17. Every Russian youngster is to be given an education—a Communist education, of course, but comparable in its high standards of study and learning to an English public school or a French lycee. . . .
>
> Further, the USSR is on the road to surpassing the U.S. both in the number and percentage of students enrolled in institutions above the secondary level. Indeed, when high level extension-correspondence students are included, the Soviet total of 4,300,000 enrolled in 1955 is already 70 percent over our 2,700,000. The Soviet Union offers as much training to every boy and girl as his or her talents and abilities will absorb. . . .
>
> Eighty to 90 percent of all students at Soviet higher institutions have been on state scholarships, which included stipends rising slightly from year to year. In February we learned from the Party Congress that beginning this autumn all education is to be free.

This speaks for itself, and all I would add is that the standards of the English public school and the French lycee are far above the average of our public schools.

The results of this enormous educational program are already beginning to show. According to Sir John Cockroft, head of Britain's Atomic Energy Establishment at Harwell, "Britain's output of graduate engineers was about 2,800 a year, while the figure for the United States was 23,000 and for the Soviet Union 53,000", (*New York Times*, April 14, 1956.) In other words, the USSR is already turning out more than twice as many engineers as the two most advanced capitalist countries combined. In science proper, Sir John estimated that the Soviet output was about ten times that of the British, and that the Russian scientists were fully as well trained as their British counterparts.

But maybe the capitalist countries are doing something to catch up in this all important field of education? If so, there are few enough signs of it. The secret of the Russian program, of course, is to train and vastly expand the number of teachers. To this end, teachers are treated with the greatest respect and are among the highest paid groups in Soviet society. The best graduates are enticed and urged into teaching: I have even heard from an American doctor who recently visited the Soviet Union that in medicine the top 3 to 5 percent of each graduating class is not permitted to practice but is, so to speak, drafted into the medical schools. How is it with us? How do we treat our teachers? What inducements do we offer to young men and women to enter the teaching profession?

Alas, I am afraid I hardly need speak of these matters to an audience like this. Whether faculty or students searching out what career to follow in life, you know all too well the answers to these questions. I will simply quote a few brief passages from a letter I happened to see in the *San Francisco Chronicle* (April 20) when I was recently in that beautiful city. It is signed by "A Math Professor, Ph.D.":

> A teacher of science in the Soviet Union is reported to have an income in the very highest brackets, as compared with other occupations, whereas in the United States, a teacher of science usually finds himself in the lowest income bracket; often he finds it impossible to maintain his family on a minimum living scale. . . . I have myself arrived at a certain eminence, with my Ph.D. in mathematics along with ten years of actual engineering experience besides 12 highly successful years as a professor. . . . Accordingly, I have been honored by the offer, which I have just accepted, to assume the position of chairman of the mathematics department of a leading private university on the West Coast. The job pays $5,500 a year. My son-in-law, who graduated from high school a few years ago and is now a bookkeeper, earns almost precisely the same amount. . . . Let us face the result: an economy which cares so little about its professors of science as to

place them on a bottom rung is not entitled to ask for a leading world position in science, and we shall not achieve it.

It is a sad story, but all too easy to understand. There is no profit to be made out of education—not directly anyway. And it is profit that guides a capitalist society. As long as we have capitalism, we shall undoubtedly treat our teachers as second-class citizens, and educationally we shall fall farther and farther behind a society which puts science and education above dollars.

We come finally to the question of liberty. Here the advanced capitalist countries started with an advantage over the Soviet Union no less enormous than in the field of economics. And on the whole, they have succeeded in preserving their lead more successfully here than in economics. The Soviet police state certainly has an unenviable record of arbitrary arrests, trials, purges, shootings, labor camps, and all the rest—you are much more familiar with this than with the Soviet Union's record in production and education. The question for the future really is whether these are necessary features of socialism as such or whether they result from Russia's dark past, from the almost unimaginable difficulties of building an industrial economy in a backward country against implacable outside hostility, and from the tensions and fears of a world in which war is an ever-present threat.

There is no certain way of answering this question yet. I can only say that as a convinced socialist, I see no reason for despair and every reason for hope. I do not myself attribute much of the Soviet Union's record in the field of liberty to the evil doings of any one man, including Stalin. One-man interpretations of history are too easy—and really explain nothing. And yet there is no doubt that the last few years, which happen to be the years since Stalin's death, have witnessed a considerable change in the Soviet world, and the pace of this change has been sharply stepped up in recent months. Many of the abuses of the past were sharply denounced at the February Congress of the Communist Party. Since then, we have been told that a new judicial code is soon to be promulgated which will bring the USSR closer to our idea of a government of laws rather than of men. The labor camps have mostly been closed, and it has just been announced that they will soon be abolished altogether. Workers can now leave their jobs by simply giving two weeks notice. A friend of mine who is a professor at Stanford University happened to be in Moscow on his way to India in December and again in March on his way back. He reports that the whole atmosphere, and especially the attitude toward foreigners, had undergone a startling change for the better.

Is all this merely a temporary aberration, or is it the beginning of a new trend toward liberalization in the socialist countries? I myself firmly believe the latter to be the correct interpretation. And I think the cause is clear: the forced march in the economic sphere is drawing to a close; Soviet citizens now constitute one of the best educated publics in the world; the achievement of atomic parity with the United States has given them an unprecedented feeling of security; and the Soviet Union, far from being isolated, is now surrounded by friends and allies, including the most populous country in the world. The preconditons for internal relaxation and liberalization are there. What is especially encouraging to all who love liberty, and that certainly includes the vast majority of the world's socialists, is that relaxation and liberalization *are actually happening*.

I believe that the trend is here to stay, barring another war which I think increasingly less likely. In the long run, it will present capitalism with the greatest challenge of all. Up to now, the defenders of capitalism have always been able to counter arguments for socialism with the reply: "Look at the slave labor camps in Russia!" And there's no doubt that it has been an effective argument. Now, however, the camps are disappearing. Suppose all that they symbolize also disappears? Suppose socialism shows what Marxists have always maintained, that it is possible to have economic collectivism *and* freedom? Suppose the socialist world overtakes and surpasses the capitalist world not only in production and per capita income, not only in education and science, but also in freedom and respect for the dignity of the individual? What then?

You may think these questions fantastic now. Perhaps. But let me make a suggestion. Let me propose that you file them away in the back of your mind and then bring them out, say once every year, and check the answers you are able to give on the basis of the latest facts available to you. I have no doubt what the answers will be, sooner or later. If I am right, it will be facts and not my arguments that will convince you. And I am very glad to leave it to the future to decide.

The People and Planning

By Victor Perlo

SOCIALIST ECONOMIC PLANNING is the dovetailing of all the production and distribution requirements of an expanding economy of publicly owned enterprises. The plan is drawn by a central planning body, but requires the active participation by workers in all areas and on an industry-wide basis in deciding what they can contribute and what they need for that purpose, and must accurately take into account the composite wants of the population. It provides for full employment, but each individual has the maximum freedom of choice in deciding where he will fit into it. (*Socialist economic planning is truly of, by, and for the people.*)

For many years anti-socialist propaganda in the United States attacked the very idea of economic planning. A picture was conjured up of some dictator making people cogs in the wheels of an arbitrary master scheme. This line of attack has not been abandoned. But the emphasis has shifted to the new argument that capitalism now has its own planning. Indeed business executives who decry the one extol the other.

What is the nature of this supposed planning under capitalism? Corporations establish five-year expansion plans, budgeting new factories and modern equipment in relation to anticipated increases in markets. An industrial giant schedules the flow of raw materials it owns in several countries to processing

VICTOR PERLO is a New Yorker, an economist (M.A., Columbia University), consultant, author and lecturer. He was one of the group of young government economists who assisted in the preparation of New Deal measures. Among his published books are "The Negro in Southern Agriculture", "The Income Revolution", "American Imperialism" and, the most recent (1956), "The Empire of High Finance".

and fabricating plants, while long-term contracts assure a steady supply of purchased materials and equipment. The flow of goods through all stages of production and distribution in world markets is set in advance. All of these elements of planning are centrally coordinated by a top managerial staff. For such corporations as the American Telephone and Telegraph Company, or Standard Oil Company of New Jersey, they involve as large a volume of goods, and as many people, as would a complete national plan for entire countries the size of Bulgaria or Denmark. In a capitalist country like the United States government regulations operate on a still higher level, controlling the supply of money, allocating scarce materials, establishing all sorts of quotas and subsidies for foreign trade, and in armament industries controlling the level of production.

We can best understand socialist planning by examining the differences between the capitalist and the socialist method. All of the partial plans of capitalists and their governments do not add up to a coordinated, viable, national program. Giant corporations' schedules leave much to the vagaries of the marketplace. And in the many small-business sectors of the economy everything remains hit or miss. Government regulations under capitalism are actually fragmentary, influencing economic activity, but scarcely involving overall controls. Moreover, there is no systematic coordination between the partial plans of individual corporations, nor between government regulations and corporate programming. *Planning in the fine, but a higher anarchy in the whole—that is the rule of modern capitalism.*

Under socialism, common public ownership of all major areas of industry and finance permits and calls for an all-embracing national economic plan. This would actually be a composite of plans covering production, labor, investments, and finance. The production plan would schedule output of each major commodity, and allocate the flow of goods between the various stages of production. Thus, the scheduled uses of steel would match the planned output, with a certain allowance for accumulation of reserve supplies. The investment plan would include the decisions as to how much expansion is desired for each commodity, and what new products should be brought into production, and schedule the machinery and construction needed for that purpose. The manpower plan would balance the supply of labor with the needs in different industries, taking into account the increased productivity of labor expected from introduction of improved equipment and methods. The financial plan would set prices, calculate the revenues to be collected from sale of products to consumers, the payment of wages, the turnover of money, and the amount of currency needed to balance these transactions.

Tentative drafts of each of these plans would be modified to ensure that all ingredients were harmonized. The supply of finished goods would be calculated to conform to the needs and purchasing power of the people, the level of earnings to fit in with the possible supply of consumers goods, and the number of jobs to equal the number of people seeking work. As in all activities involving human beings and the vagaries of nature, reality would vary from even the best of socialist plans. However, the use of reserves of goods and money would provide the flexibility needed to adjust to these variations, without unemployment or any interruption to the overall economic advance.

A technically expert central planning body would be responsible for the final plan. But as we shall see, its work could be meaningful only if based on the large-scale participation in the planning process of millions of people in different areas and in different lines of work.

There is another difference between capitalist semi-planning and socialist planning that is even more important. That is the difference of *aim*. Capitalist plans are prepared by representatives of corporate owners for the primary purpose of increasing the owners' profits. Socialist plans are prepared and developed by representatives of the working population for the purpose of improving the material well-being and opportunities for human development and enjoyment of the population.

Capitalist plans express the will of a small minority, and make pawns of everybody else, including the small firms surviving under the domination of monopoly. Socialist planning expresses the will of the immense majority, suppressing the initiative of only the former aristocrats of wealth.

Private ownership and production for private profit contradict the technical mode of production, a social process involving millions of people who are objects rather than beneficiaries. So the partial economic planning under capitalism does not bring economic stability. Each great corporation plans to maximize its *own* profits, necessarily involving conflicts with the plans of other corporations. For example, in 1956 the total sum of the "plans" of the automobile corporations involved a 10 per cent rise in the total sale of cars. But working people lacked the funds to buy the cars, and sales fell 20 per cent. The elaborate scheduling of General Motors fell flat on its face as orders for steel were cancelled and tens of thousands of workers were laid off. When one corporation "realizes its plan", others necessarily fail to do so. Plans of corporations using purchased raw material are often wholly uncoordinated with the production of these raw materials, resulting in sharp price gyrations affecting the livelihood of hundreds of millions of small producers the world over.

Still more significant, capitalist plans, if they are to succeed, must succeed in lowering labor costs to the utmost. They therefore involve a continuous basic conflict with the workers whose labor creates the values and profits in our society. They can only succeed, if at all, by preventing workers from sharing proportionately in the fruits of their labor and in growing efficiency.

Thus capitalist plans not only fail to provide for the purchasing power of the mass market, but continuously attempt to undermine it. And they must do so, or else they fail in their main purpose. So capitalist economy proceeds but haltingly, in a series of booms and depressions, with all the consequent hardship entailed for the population. And it proceeds in an inevitable environment of class struggle which, no matter how quiet on the surface, in one place or another and from time to time, comes to the fore again more violently than ever.

Socialist planning means continuously increasing production and productivity, fully in harmony with its aim of raising living standards. And its beneficiaries, the population, are in turn the market which is a necessary balancing factor for any production plan.

The possibility of significant conflict between plans of separate socialist enterprises, or different geographical areas would be minimized by the coordination of national planning, and by the fact that under socialism there would be no motive for one enterprise trying to drive another out of business or capture it.

Therefore *stable growth* is completely natural under socialism. Indeed the experience of the Soviet Union, which is the subject of controversy in many respects, leaves no doubt on this score. All observers agree that the Soviet economy has grown more rapidly, and more regularly, than that of any other country in history, and without the alternate booms and depressions of capitalism.

In recent decades much has been said and written about the increased role of our government in the economy. The part played by capitalist government has multiplied, but mainly in a particular way, through militarization of the economy. All other federal government measures of economic intervention, taken together, pale into insignificance in comparison with the military budget. The $40 billion plus of annual "national security" expenditures equals 7/8ths of the total federal outlays for goods and services. If we have had 15 years of sustained prosperity it is because we had the stimulus of huge arms spending, spending for reconstructing other peoples' war damages, and spending to arm other peoples for war, without yet suffering any war damages ourselves.

Our long boom has been the rest of the world's tragedy, and of course the personal tragedy of the few hundred thousand American victims of war and their families. Surely this is a fool's paradise. For now we all know that we cannot escape frightful damage in another global war. Spending for armaments is a "natural" for capitalism. It contributes greatly to profits, while the market is provided by the government, run by representatives of the giant corporate beneficiaries of arms orders, and paid for out of taxes collected from the entire population.

Spending for armaments is an economic misfortune under socialism. It diverts production from goods which would otherwise be available to raise living standards and to provide the means for still more efficient production. It benefits nobody. Under socialism disarmament is greatly desired by the rulers of the government, the working people. With socialism prevailing in the most powerful countries, including the United States and the U.S.S.R., complete disarmament would become quickly realizable and the danger of major wars sharply reduced thereby.

More than ever, our economy is today linked to the world's. Giant corporations supported by the government carry out international cartel arrangements for the control of raw materials. The international division of labor is dictated by these cartels to the greater profit of their members. It consigns most of the world's population to poverty, to being miners of metals and oil, or producers of tropical crops taken with little compensation by the cartel partners.

Each corporation of the cartel seeks a larger share, a major cause of wars. Other wars arise because of the conflicts between the corporations and the countries from which they get their raw materials. Our military bases dot the globe, creating the proper "climate" for corporate investments. Because we have the richest corporations and the most powerful armed forces the United States gets the lion's share of the raw materials, and is the center of most international conflicts. However, the benefits to the American people are small and fleeting, because so large a proportion of these raw materials is used for armaments, and because benefits only "trickle down" to the extent that American workers, through unions, strikes, and other methods, force them to.

Socialist planning would adjust to a different international division of labor. Each country would be aided to develop a more balanced economy and would be supplied on reasonable terms with the machinery and other commodities it needs, for use under its own control, in exchange for the goods we obtain from it. The international traffic in armaments would be eliminated, as would the waste of raw materials in arms production and the existence of foreign military bases.

At present there are two world markets—that of the socialist countries and that of the capitalist countries. Moreover, the capitalist world market is subdivided into various trading blocs, impeded by an increadible jungle of trade discriminations, tariffs and quotas, currency restrictions, and customs regulations —the whole dominated by a few giant internatoinal cartels which alone have the power to override national boundaries in their operations.

As socialism becomes the rule in more and more countries, the tendency will be to establishment of *a single world market,* with no restrictions imposed by greedy interests, but required to protect people from unemployment. National plans can take into account those of other countries, and the foreign trading programs of our country can increasingly be dovetailed into those of others. The volume of world trade would increase as the people of each country began to realize the benefits of those products which other countries could make more efficiently.

Socialist planning in America would devote much attention to the further development of our own untapped resources. Through water power, flood control and irrigation works, through investments in huge secondary reserves of shale oil and taconite and, most powerfully, through peaceful uses of atomic energy we would create a far richer life than we now enjoy, and without monopolizing the world's raw materials. The economic sources of war would be dissipated.

How rapid a rise in living standards could socialist planning provide? With the transition from capitalism there would be a sharp immediate gain for the majority, especially for those now living in poverty, and to the majority of the population making less than the Labor Department's budget for a workingmen's family. This would be provided out of the diversion of resources from military to peaceful use, from the curtailment of the extravagant living of a wealthy minority, and from the elimination of the waste of capitalist unemployment and "sub-marginal" employment.

For the longer pull the perspective of gains would be really spectacular. Industrial labor productivity in the United States increases by about 4-5 per cent per year. Certainly with the benefits of national economic planning and the elimination of the business cycle, this would be surpassed. *But even a 5 percent annual gain, properly distributed as it would be under socialism, is sufficient to guarantee the doubling of living standards every fifteen years.*

Does socialist planning mean the subordination of the American people to the dictate of a bureaucratic clique? Beacuse of the particular character of anti-socialist propaganda, this is perhaps the most crucial question on the minds of millions. The answer is an unequivocal no. The people, individually and collectively, would play a larger part in determining their economic destiny than could even be dreamed of in a capitalist society. It is probable that complete "freedom" for the individual cannot exist and that the attempt to realize it would merely substitute a different kind of anarchy for that which prevails under capitalism.

The difference between capitalism and socialism in the freedom and initiative of the individual is this: In the United States, under capitalism, a handful of individuals—perhaps a few thousand at the most—have an enormous degree of freedom of choice and scope for the exercise of their initiative, in economic and political affairs. They are the aristocrats of capitalism, the inherited overlords of American corporate economy. At the same time, the rest of the population has virtually no freedom, virtually no scope for the exercise of initiative in economic or other affairs.

Under socialism each person could have equal freedom and opportunity with others to exercise his initiative, the essential limits being his own ability and the requirement that his efforts fit within the framework of a broad plan.

The central planning body would have to decide issues of great importance, without asking for majority opinion. Economic planning is a science, based on the understanding and application of economic laws. One cannot decide many questions of economic planning by voting, any more than one can decide what medicine to take for an illness by referendum.

Essentially, everything concerned with the balance of the economy, the proportions and sequence of growth in various industries, must be decided centrally. For example, people might *want* a doubling of consumers goods production immediately. But that would be impossible. Beyond a certain initial gain, it would be necessary to increase the supply of machinery and to build factories so that consumers goods output could be increased. The planners would also have to provide for installation of new and more efficient machines, and "automation", so that each worker could produce more in a given time.

In this and other ways, the central planning agency would be a body of enormous scope. But it would not be a new dictatorship arising over the body politic. In the first place, it would be democratically controlled, either by direct election, or by appointment of officials—the people, of course, deciding which way they preferred. And since the government would be a people's government, the planning agency would be responsive to the people's needs, not to vested interests, as are many regulatory agencies of the government today.

Despite its wide range, the central planning body would not in any sense blueprint the details of everybody's life. Vital aspects would be determined democratically, some by majority vote, others by individual choice.

For example, suppose that economic planning indicates the possibility of increasing the per capita supply of consumer goods and services over a five year period by 50 per cent. This could be matched by a scheduled 50 per cent increase in weekly wage rates. But the majority might prefer—for example—to increase their supply of goods more slowly and take part of the gain in productivity in the form of increased leisure. So an alternative plan would be—increase consumers goods production and wages by 32 percent, cut the standard workweek from 40 to 36 hours, and raise the standard paid vacation from 2 to 4 weeks yearly. This kind of question, under socialism, could be settled democratically. It might be decided by direct referendum, or the policy to be followed might be enacted by Congress in response to public opinion.

Unions would have a scope of democratic action difficult to imagine under present conditions. Not that they would determine everything. For example, the general level of wages would have to be calculated scientifically by the central planning agency, so as to balance the supply of consumers goods, at stable prices, with the purchasing power of the population. And differentials in wages between industries would have to be determined, in large part, centrally, so as to insure an adequate supply of labor everywhere. For example, economic *pressures* today drive millions of workers into unpleasant or dangerous industries, such as fertilizer factories, stevedoring, and foundries. These are manned not at particularly high wages—in some cases at very low wages—and by people suffering under disadvantages such as economic and social discrimination, particularly by Negroes.

With all kinds of discrimination eliminated, unemployment ended, and the doors of opportunity opened to everybody, these industries would be left without workers, given the present wage structure. The planning agency would have to increase wage levels in these industries, and at the same time provide the means for rapidly overcoming the disabilities associated with them—means which are known to science, but not applied adequately because there is no profit in doing so.

Unions would negotiate with the government concerning the application of the general wage scale to their industry, and concerning the differentials according to skill. They might decide which occupations should be paid by the piece, and which by the hour, and the rate of progression in piece wages. And they would negotiate concerning the production plan for their industry and for particular factories. Is a particular factory being asked for too much? Do the workers wish to try a new method of production through which they believe their output and earnings can be raised without strain? These and many other questions would come within the scope of labor's economic democracy.

In the Soviet Union and countries of Eastern Europe, a whole range of activities is carried out by unions, the details varying greatly from country to country. A common practice is for a part of the receipts from each factory's produce, geared to its success in meeting or exceeding quotas and in keeping down costs, to be allocated to the trade unilon fo its own use. The funds provide vacation facilities, housing, clubrooms, and many other amenities. Different degrees of participation of labor in factory production management prevail.

Without very high productivity and a technically trained and educated working class, enormous possibilities exist for direct labor participation in production management and use of the proceeds. But its exact forms would have to be decided by the workers themselves, and nobody can say now what the decision might be.

We are told that under capitalism the consumer decides what shall be produced. Actually this consumer choice is very limited. Have certain brands of soft drinks come to the fore by the "free choice" of consumers, or by the power of monopoly capital to control distribution outlets and dominate advertising media? How much health information, necessary to make an intelligent choice, is kept from the consumer as a commercial secret? Nylon stockings can be made to last a year or a week. But the consumer has no choice at any price. DuPont and its associates have decided on short-term service, although the long-lasting quality is technically feasible and just as inexpensive.

Under socialism, the information needed for intelligent selection would be provided much more fully and easily than at present. And there would be no motive for high-pressure advertising misinformation, nor for suppression of more durable, high-quality goods. The techniques of public opinion surveys, so well developed in our country for private promotional purposes, would be utilized publicly, to enable national planning to establish a schedule of consumers goods production closely conforming to the wishes of the population.

Finally, each individual would have a high degree of freedom in choosing his own road in life, limited mainly by his personal capabilities. This would apply most pertinently to one's occupation. Today in an unplanned economy the individual has little choice. For the majority it is usually a matter of where a job can be obtained, rather than what kind of job. For those with a modicum of family property, it is the accident of what business or type of farm the family may own. Only for a comparatively few with inherited wealth is there complete choice of occupation—or of no occupation.

But suppose, under socialism, too many people want the same occupation? Of course not every aspiring youngster can become a Brooklyn Dodger, nor every would-be artist a concert performer. Such occupations would have to be filled by competition. Similarly, competitive examinations for various professional jobs would be necessary. However, the opportunities would be immeasurably improved over those now known. The demands for professional workers would multiply many times. With the rapid growth of atomic energy, and the massive introduction of automatic methods of production, the gap between manual labor and professional work would diminish greatly. Workers would have every opportunity to obtain the training necessary to operate the highest of new techniques—to become, as it were, engineers of automated equipment. And their children would meet with no economic handicaps on the road to whatever fields of education and training for a career they might wish to enter.

The role of planning would be to establish relative rewards and such other incentives as to influence the desires of individuals into approximate balance with the varied labor requirements of society.

People would also have a vastly increased freedom of choice in their place of residence, with government planners responsible for the smooth introduction of housing, schools, and all other amenities of life in growing communities—a notable lack in boom areas today.

In these and all the other ways in which man's freedom of choice should be multiplied, the various discriminations which exist under capitalism would be abolished. For example, no vestige of anti-Negro discrimination or of anti-Semitism, in any sphere of life, would be tolerated. Women would have genuine equality of opportunity.

To recapitulate: Under socialism in America a central body will carry out national economic planning. It will be democratically chosen, and will operate in closest conjunction with the population and their organizations. The aims of the plans will be to advance the welfare of the people. In this planned economy, individual initiative for the first time in our history will really flower. Human beings will be able to develop and express that vast potential which until now has only appeared in fragments, at times of great stress, and in unusual individuals.

Managerial Problems

By Carl Dreher

UNDER CONTEMPORARY CANONS of prestige and worth, almost everyone aspires to be an executive or manager. The universal and therefore unrealizable urge to be a chief, not merely an Indian, indicates an underlying social pathology, but it also points to the very real problem of coordinating billions of actions of millions of individuals towards the goals of production in the ever-growing complexity of modern industry. The high-level manager is, accordingly, a revealing figure; his characteristics tell us much of the society in which he bears the heat and burden of the day. It is especially revealing to examine the differences in managerial characteristics under different systems. These differences may easily be exaggerated by those who, like most Americans, know only the devil theory of communism, and equally by those who accept images of capitalism more consonant with the realities of the early nineteenth century than those visibly functioning twenty minutes' flight by *sputnik* from their own doorsteps.

CARL DREHER has had two careers. He was born in 1896, and twelve years later became a radio amateur. Following graduation from college he went to work for the Marconi Wireless Telegraph Company of America and subsequently was an engineer with the General Electric Company, Radio Corporation of America and National Broadcasting Company. He was Chief Engineer for RCA Photophone, 1928-1929, and Director of Recording for RKO Studios, 1929-1937. In 1937 Mr. Dreher began his second career—as a free lance writer. With time out for service in the army duing World War II, he has had several hundred stories and articles published. He is the author of "The Coming Show Down" (Little, Brown and Company, Boston, 1942) and "Automation: What It Is, How It Works, Who Can Use It" (W. W. Norton and Company, New York, 1957).

This essay also appears in *Virginia Quarterly Review*.

Yet differences there are, nor has social evolution come to an end either in the United States or in Soviet Russia. In the United States there would seem to be three possibilities.

The first is that the boom will be sustained indefinitely, with conditions of employment and division of the national product continuing substantially as in the postwar period. In that event socialism hasn't got a chance: the voters have been so thoroughly indoctrinated with the notion that it inevitably entails loss of freedom (which most of them haven't got anyway) that only very serious trouble could open their minds. Even so, capitalistic management may be expected to continue adapting appropriate socialistic techniques for anti-socialistic ends. Already large corporations are planning farther ahead than they used to; although theirs is a far cry from socialist planning, it tends to stabilize capital investment regardless of short-term changes in business outlook. At the same time management in government and in private industry are drawing closer together, through military procurement and interchange of personnel, in a fashion reminiscent of fascism rather than socialism.

The second possibility is nuclear war, followed by the socialism of ruination. The stresses and disabilities following such a catastrophe would be incalculably worse than those the Soviet Union and its allies have experienced in four decades of cold and hot war. There would be little point in speculating how these would be met, if, indeed, enough of industrial civilization remained to make rebuilding possible. Under such conditions socialism might scarcely be distinguishable from fascism.

The third possibility is that somehow, despite everything, peace will prevail and the United States will eventually be forced to cut back its military expenditures, with the Soviet Union following suit. Since an armaments race has diametrically opposite effects under socalism and capitalism, the communist countries could raise their living standards in proportion to the cutbacks, while the unbalanced American economy would be subject to large-scale unemployment, which might be aggravated by the trend toward automation. The welfare and salvage measures of the New Deal would shortly have to be reconstituted on a grander scale and despite the efforts of the mass media, which we may be sure would be valiant, the voters might begin to think along new lines. Socialism could in that case take over a modern industrial plant for the first time in history and be in a position to show what it can really do.

The order of improbability of some such sequence of events is no greater than that of a third world war; indeed, it may be less. The rest of this speculation, therefore, will be based on this perhaps wishful hypothesis of a peaceful and conservative transition to socialism and the role of the managerial profession under these conditions.

Not every business functionary who is called a manager falls within the true managerial group. Top executives who wield the real power and make far-reaching economic and political decisions, and those who are on the way to such status, are the ones we are mainly concerned with. Even among those of vice-presidential rank and higher in large corporations, the majority would not qualify under this definition. Many vice presidents exercising full operational authority in their own departments have no normal access to the chairman of the board and the president and no direct advisory power, much less a voice in policy decisions. These buck vice presidents usually report to executive vice presidents, who are beginning to proliferate as ordinary vice presidents did after the first world war.

There are, however, exceptions. The Radio Corporation of America, for instance, had no less than 31 active vice presidents at the beginning of 1957 and six executive vice presidents, one of whom had the especially honorific title of *senior executive vice president*. This man, together with the president, was also a member of the board of directors, under the redoubtable chairmanship of David Sarnoff. But one of the 31 vice presidents was likewise a member of the board. Obviously, despite his humble title, this was no common vice president and he would fall within the scope of our definition.

By all indications a similar managerial hierarchy would rule socialist industry, both in over-all planning and within individual producing, distribution and service units. The imperatives of powerized, mechanized, and automatized industry are much the same, regardless of the social system. Its operation calls for a certain amount of democracy but it appears utopian—at least within the calculable future—to expect really to democratize it. Prof. Arthur K. Davis brings out this point in his *Monthly Re-*

view article (September 1956) on "Juvenile Delinquency under Capitalism and Socialism". "An industrial society," Davis writes, "consists of a multitude of specialized, hence (in certain respects) unequal, roles . . . to unify this mass of immensely specialized roles, democracy based on a certain minimum of equal legal, political, economic, and social rights is indispensable. Among these rights is equality of opportunity for self-development and for attaining the more desirable jobs. Socialism is the extension and substantial raising of the minimum already achieved by capitalism . . . socialism will tend to equalize opportunities leading to, and the level of living derived from, various occupational roles, but it will not equalize the jobs themselves."

This is why soviets, factory councils and the like exercise power only during periods of revolutionary upheaval, and lose it when production once more becomes the main concern. Executive direction of industry, which nowadays is conducted as much by committees as by individuals, is necessary because mass meetings are too unwieldy and, even disregarding the complications introduced by the inevitable lunatic fringe, the difficulties of communication are so great that at best such gatherings cannot do much more than ratify or reject decisions reached by smaller bodies. But although the workers cannot run factories, even if they nominally own them, there must be not only machinery for the routine adjustment of grievances, but some sort of parliamentary representation in the operation of the plant. Otherwise we are back in the spirit of George F. Baer's famous dictum of 1902: "The rights and interests of the laboring man will be protected and cared for—not by the labor agitators, but by the Christian men to whom God in His infinite wisdom has given the control of the property interests of this country", with socialist administrators substituted for Christian men of property.

The reconciliation of these two necessities—the executive hierarchy and industrial democracy—is one of the tasks of democratic socialism. Under prosperous postwar capitalism, one would expect that, in lieu of a solution, the American managerial groups, with their corps of psychologists and public relations aides, would at least have succeeded in making themselves popular in their own organizations. But they haven't. In *Hu-*

man Relations for Management (Edward C. Bursk, editor) Elizabeth and Francis Jennings pose the question, "Why is it that every level of supervisors consider the next level above a bunch of s.o.b.'s?" And O. A. Ohmann bemoans the fact that "no people have ever had so much, and enjoyed so little real satisfaction".

Existing socialist systems have likewise made little progress toward the goal of happiness and dignity for human beings under industrialism, but with some excuse: poverty, technological backwardness, a cultural inheritance of repression and tyranny, the fascist onslaught followed by the cold war and the nuclear armaments race. A socialist America, free of all these handicaps, would have the opportunity to show its inventiveness in the field of industrial human relations, where innovation is at least as important as in automobile styling and guided missiles.

Although the managerial hierarchy will remain necessary under socialism, its numbers and functions will be considerably modified. Useless and parasitic managers will be transferred to other duties. For instance, there will be fewer advertising and publicity men, fewer lawyers and no patent attorneys, and fewer sales executives. In the United States about 25 per cent of executives now reach the top levels via sales and nearly half of the managerial staff is preoccupied with some aspect of selling. The symptoms point to the disease. But, although there will be drastic functional changes, it must not be expected that socialism will evolve, in the calculable future, a new, noble breed of managers. Many of the characteristics of successful managers under capitalism will be carried over, *mutatis mutandis,* into socialist administration. The primary executive characteristic is *sang-froid,* nerve, aplomb, ease under pressure, or, at a more, advanced stage, *kutzpa,* feebly translated from the Yiddish as gall, effrontery. An executive without *kutzpa* is like a bull without horns. An example of this invaluable trait is the remark of Gerard Swope when the government brought an anti-trust suit against the General Electric Company on the ground, among others, that it was selling 90 per cent, or some such figure, of the total of fractional horsepower motors produced in the United States. Swope was scheduled to address a mass meeting of GE sales executives a day or two after the indictment was handed down. "Gentlemen," he began, "I was shocked to learn that we are getting 90 per cent of this business. Go out and get the other ten per cent!" A watered-down version of Swope's crack, ascribed to Harlow Curtice, has circulated in the General Motors executive sodality in recent years, but this is not to say that Mr. Curtice has less *kutzpa* than Mr. Swope.

Ease under pressure is an indispensable factor in any command position. Business situations, for all the talk about "teamwork", "cooperation", "the family" (the Metropolitan Life Insurance Company bolsters the morale of its 80 officers and high executives, 19,000 agents, and 31,000 employees with "the family") partake of the nature of combat situations. The participants are not only trying to work together in a common front against outside opponents, but whether they like it or not they are also contestants in the intra-corporate struggle for personal advantage. These wars within wars are mostly carried on quietly in modern business, although some older executives still shout —Arthur Vining Davis, the eighty-nine-year-old board chairman of the Aluminum Company of America, is said to have been audible three stories below his office in the Pittsburgh headquarters in his younger days. But quiet or noisy, it is fatal to become confused or to show fear.

After *kutzpa* come, in the order named, "business judgment"; force and aggressiveness in relation to situations and people; and capacity for work. "Business judgment", a term worn thin in the vast current literature of management, is essentially a throwback to the faculty psychology of 50 years ago. It means simply a relatively high batting average in assessing situations for the profit of the corporation and the personal advantage of the decision-maker. Intelligence, experience, acute observation, intuition may be components of shrewd business strategy— luck certainly is. Managerially, the importance of specialized experience is diminishing, now that corporations are being agglomerated not on the basis of any common technological denominator, but for purely fiscal reasons.

Of the two remaining primary traits of the capitalist manager, aggressiveness, coupled with ambition, is correlated with nerve: since one can't stand still or retreat, one must attack. The editors of *Fortune* interpret aggressiveness as "desire to control one's environment rather than be controlled by it." The environment includes all the elements of production: materials, machinery, money, and people. To manipulate and coordinate these factors in their intricate and only partly predictable interactions means work. Typically, this is not merely an unusual endowment of horsepower, although that is generally a factor. The outstanding executive has acquired a liking for his work. He finds it exciting. He identifies himself with the job, often he *is* the job to such an extent that when he retires he doesn't know what to do with himself. While he is active, this absorption gives him an advantage over the man who has not acquired such an appetite and must drive himself, or who has reservations about the value of his work within a larger context than the corporation and the career. And of course, nothing succeeds like success: the ordinary man does ordinary, generally uninteresting, often poorly compensated work, perhaps under disagreeable or distracting conditions, while the manager, once he has arrived, is provided with a favorable and ego-enhancing environment—big desk, big office, big anterooms, decorative, high-powered secretaries, etc., He has something to fight for.

This summary of executive traits is not quite fair to the best managerial talent. Nobody who has worked for a first-rate administrator, after making all allowances for hero-worship and the tendency to be grateful if the big shot doesn't walk all over you, will deny that he may have an evocative quality over and above the items enumerated. Sarnoff's comparison of the head of a business with Toscanini is frequently quoted not only because it is apt but because Sarnoff is himself a prime example of the cult of personality in corporate business. The players made the music, Sarnoff pointed out, but Toscanini knew what he wanted, demanded higher performance than did most other conductors, and consistently got it. The hallmark of the top-notch executive is precisely that: he gets more out of people than they know they have in them. This quality of Sarnoff's has been a potent factor in the success of RCA.

With his stimulative power the typical capitalist executive usually combines traits which, from a socialist and humanist standpoint, can only be described as execrable. Many on the Left will resent the carry-over of such defects into socialized administration, but for a while compromises will be necessary on both sides. American socialism will necessarily evolve from American corporate organization and personnel. People are what prehistoric culture, slavery, exploitation, evolution, feudalism, capitalism, religion, fear, hope and all the circumstances of the past and the present have made them. They may be something else in the 21st century or the 22nd, but tomorrow socialism will have to deal with them substantially as they are today. American socialism in particular, stemming from the most successful variant of capitalism, must be expected to bear the marks of its origins for a long time to come.

The idea that industrial and business organizations can do without managerial compulsions is chimerical. Military organizations, with far harsher disciplinary controls at their disposal and the members united by a common peril and, in some cases, high *esprit de corps,* still find it difficult to control centrifugal forces. The best of them have to throw the book at an erring brother once in a while. Few rank-and-file people in capitalist industry have a strong sense of a mission, and among those who do, a large proportion must be fools. Many tasks in business are so trivial and meaningless, if not actually anti-social, that no self-respecting human being could apply himself to them without inner protest. Many such jobs would be eliminated under socialism; automation will take over others. But a certain amount of dull routine will remain. There will remain, also, a certain proportion of neurotics, child-minds, soreheads and troublemakers. Even these can make some contribution to society and to their own welfare. On the whole the advantages of industrialism outweigh the defects. Socialism will reduce economic disparities and eventually approach Veblen's ideal of a "republic of ungraded men", but today's children may not live to see that ideal achieved.

In some respects socialist managers will differ significantly from their capitalist counterparts. There differences should become more marked and eventually play a material part in demonstrating the superiority of the socialist order. Socialism will tend to unify the manager phychologically and make his job less nerve-wracking, thus improving not only his condition but, more important, that of the people under his direction and the larger population he serves. If the picture drawn by William H. Whyte, Jr. in *The Organization Man* is not a complete caricature, socialism should not find it difficult to produce managers with more individuality, intelligence, and originality than those now on the make. Some GE managerial trainees, asked what they would do if a brilliant engineer like Steinmetz were to apply to them for a job, were dubious. "I don't think we would put up with a fellow like that now," one said. Steinmetz was a socialist as well as an egghead. If this judgment is any criterion, socialism may be necessary to give the U.S. a chance to compete with the USSR, personnel-wise.

As events unfold, high-powered, rational managers may find that they actually prefer socialist to capitalist organization. Inherently socialism provides greater amplitude for the useful exercise of power than capitalism at its best. Even the most egotistical conventional manager, endowed with the strongest urge to control the environment rather than be controlled by it, seldom tries to dominate more than one trust or group of companies. But a basic principle of socialism is the control of the economic environment in toto, instead of leaving it to the mercy of competition shot through with price-fixing or monopoly masquerading as free enterprise. The socialist does not aspire to exercise such control individually. Nevertheless, as a member of a top management team, once he has reconciled himself to the primacy of the general welfare instead of the profitability of a particular enterprise, the reoriented entrepreneur can and does enjoy more power than he ever enjoyed under capitalism—and at times may have to take greater risks.

This socialized manager would be carrying on a process which is already in evidence in some sectors of the capitalist economy, but in a rather feeble way. Big businessmen and their publicists talk a great deal of the "fair", "suitable", or "managed" profit in place of the maximum profit, i.e., maximization of volume multiplied by unit price. As long as the titans of industry contended directly with one another, maximization was inevitable, since one titan could not see why he should get less than another, and none was inclined to take the long view. But with the transfer of ownership to scattered and largely impotent stockholders and the transfer of power to management, the managers now have to reckon with only a few large stockholders. Thus some management committees are in a position to set prices at a level which promises a stable income for man-

agement over a period of years, but which is short of the breakdown point where the consumers, even while heaping up debt,
still do not command enough purchasing power to keep the
economy going.

The theory is sensible enough. But this statesmanlike aim
looks to the future, while maximization remains a temptation
of the present—a temptation built into the system. Suitability,
therefore, is always open to attack, as all prudent policies are, by
the impetuous and passionate who, like dogs, want their satisfac-
tions here and now. Thus even enlightened managers are under pressure to maximize, not only from avid stockholders but
from their own unregenerate selves, which bid them rake it in
while the raking is good, get that promotion, earn that bonus,
or at least deflect the displeasure of the top dog who may be a
maximizationalist rather than a suitabilitist.

They are between Charybdis and Scylla. The more they
yield to the temptation to charge all the traffic will bear, the
more they feed inflation and the nearer they approach the
brink of the boom, with still higher levels of government spending as the only alternative to a bust. In the nature of the capitalist order, this normally means higher military spending. That
level is already too high, as intelligent conservatives like Charles
E. Wilson and George M. Humphrey were well aware. And
corporation executives know it too. In one case, sales of $1,125
billion resulted in profits before federal income taxes of $80
million (7.2 per cent) and net profit after taxes of about $40
million. A net of 3.5 per cent on sales is certainly nothing to
gladden the heart of a devout capitalist. Yet this tribute must
be paid to maintain earnings at their present level.

Only socialism can afford peace, and the socialist manager
will at any rate be rid of this incubus. The balance between
investment in new plant and meeting immediate consumer needs
will still remain a problem, and in the communist countries
today, aggravated by the armaments race, it is a sore problem
indeed. But it would be easily manageable under socialism in
an advanced economy like that of the United States. After the
needs of amortization and plant investment had been met, there
would be no one but the consumer to whom the savings of
advancing technology could be passed on.

Recently there has been added to the voluminous literature

on management in general a smaller but rapidly growing body of discussion on the miseries of managers. Actually, many seem quite happy, perhaps happier than they deserve to be. We have seen some of the conflicts which may account for their unhappiness, where it exists. There are others of a more personal nature, and even more readily remediable under socialism. Here again Whyte's citations are apposite, but, staying safely within the system itself, he can only exhort the burgeoning executive to *fight* The Organization (his italics and his capitals) while continuing to sleep with it.

A major count in any sophisticated indictment of capitalism is the unnecessary complexity it adds to the problems of production which, God knows, are complicated enough in a modern technological setup. It is pure slander to assume that managers don't have their share of Veblen's "instinct" of workmanship. It is likely that they have more of it, on the average, than mechanics. The only trouble is that by the basic requirements of the system they are debarred from freely exercising this "instinct", which is simply an impulsion based on reason and a preference for life over death. No wonder, then, that some of them are unhappy when they try simultaneously to produce, to cut their colleagues' throats and to be on terms of good fellowship with these same colleagues and on top of that to be part-time philanthropists, running fund drives, hospitals, symphony orchestras, universities and everything else, and in general behaving as if nobody else were competent to boss anything.

Another measure which would make the manager a healthier man under socialism would be to relieve him of the load of professional hypocrisy which he is now obliged to carry. He must pretend, or worse, actually try, to be a friend of the working man who, by some strange perversity, remains dissatisfied no matter what is done for him. But why? Almost all the books on management and human relations assume that the chief trouble is misunderstanding and other disorders of communication, and not a basic pathology in the relation of man to man under capitalism. They advocate some things which are good in themselves, such as attentive listening (in which socialists are just as deficient as capitalists) but they avert their eyes from the underlying morbidity which, however, does not disappear merely because it is unmentionable.

Mistakes can be made under socialism as under capitalism. Less often, we may reasonably expect, but there is no infallible barrier in socialist theory against every adverse visitation and error. Socialist and capitalist administrators are alike human and, though it may be straining a point, let us credit our adversaries with as good intentions as our own. But there remains a salient difference between the socialist administrator and his capitalist counterpart. The official stand of the socialist administrator is—and must be—that he is working for the worker. If he isn't, it will catch up with him in due time: one can say one thing and do another only so long. The capitalist administrator is not the worker's servant, officially, legally, or morally. He has only one fiduciary obligation—to the capitalist. Hence, when he pretends to be bleeding for the worker, he is putting on an act which will not convince the astute worker; if it does phychological damage to the administrator, he is only getting what is coming to him.

Under socialism, the capable and conscientious manager would be relieved, also, of the fear of finding himself out of a job merely because an essentially sound enterprise could not show a profit in the immediate future, or a profit not large enough, or because he happened to be in the way of some big-time operator muscling in on the company. Thus William White was booted out of New York Central after he had greatly improved the condition of the road during his presidency of 22 months. The Studebaker-Packard debacle is another example. The top man there got another job of lower rank but very likely, better than the one he lost, but his subordinates may not have fared as well. Yet a part of the merged company was in sound condition and the shotgun marriage of the two components proved to be the ruin of both. In 1956, also, the Crowell-Collier Publishing Company made some sort of record by throwing into the ashcan three magazines with an aggregate circulation of over 11.25 million, which, to make the situation more fantastic, was rising. Whatever the faults of these magazines, they did have a sizable readership, but others had drained away much of their advertising. If the Crowell-Collier magazines had been better, they would probably have got even less advertising.

The waste of such dissolutions, mergers, raids, and other financial legerdemain, and the only too well-founded anxieties generated in individuals, can occur only under a fundamentally maladjusted system. In an economy based on long-term centralized planning an executive's solicitude for his particular enterprise would be conducive to maintaining the most efficient balance between the extremes of over-centralization and parochialism. But under capitalism, the temporary health of one enterprise is often the mortal sickness of another—even during a boom.

The proportion of saints in the managerial class being no larger than in other classes, they must receive emoluments and perquisites which will induce them to apply their talents to the problems of production and distribution. But it does not follow that their compensation, under socialism, would have to follow the present American pattern, anymore than that their abilities would be employed in the same manner and toward the same ends. The master masons who supervised the construction of the great Gothic cathedrals were doing something quite as important as manufacturing automobiles or dishwashers, and they were paid only three or four times as much as the artisans who worked under their direction. The experience of semi-socialist enclaves like the Catholic clergy and the officers of the armed forces shows that able and dedicated men don't have to be paid six-figure salaries. Probably the maximum of $25,000 a year which was proposed during World War II but never adopted because "sacrifice" meant one thing for managers and profiteers and another for soldiers, would be ample under conditions where managerial prowess was not measured merely in terms of money, and where money income was not eaten away by inflation and taxation.

The salaries paid today are largely illusory. Even a top man like Harlow Curtice, although he is cushioned with about $4.5 million of General Motors stock, can keep only about $125,000 of his $750,000 in salary and bonuses. Today's more or less typical $60,000 man pays an income tax of $20,000 and the $40,-000 he has left will buy less than $20,000 bought two decades ago. He has less to live on and to sock away for his children than the $20,000 man of 1937, who paid an income tax of $1,000, bought a house baronial by today's standards for $12,000 (and paid cash), and lived well, if not lavishly, on half his income. As for today's $12,000-a-year "executives", half or more of them are deep in hock. And that's the way it's going to be as long as that $40 billion in annual corporate profit (before taxes) must be balanced by $40 billion in military expenditures.

One item in the cost of a violent revolution is that it alienates most of those who achieved success, or were born with status, under the old order, and so for a generation or more the economy suffers from a shortage of technological and industrial leadership. Under American conditions the transition to socialism could conceivably entail little of this waste and frustration. No group has less to worry about than the managers who actually play a creative role in the economy. Political executives will wither away when the state withers away (whenever that is) but industrial executives will remain, and so will their order, discipline, and force in a planned society.

The September 1956 *Monthly Review* said editorially: "Just imagine how much smaller the automobile industry would need to be if it were planned to turn out a relatively few models designed to last and to give the best and safest transportation service! How much less steel, nickel, chrome, and other scarce materials would be used up! And what a catastrophe it would precipitate if it were tried under capitalism! (Socialism *is* the only answer.)"

True—but there would still be managerial problems. The engineers would not always agree on the design of the relatively few models to be produced. The notion that engineers, or even scientists, left to their own devices, will swiftly come up with definitive answers is held mostly by those who have never had much contact with technological matters. There is a lot of trial and error in technology, a lot of opinion, hunch, and more or less educated guesswork, even a lot of prejudice, personal dislike, and childish pugnacity.

Scientists and engineers will reach agreement sooner than politicians, who thrive on disagreement, but: is the present rate of nuclear fallout dangerous or not? Not only are the scientists divided, but they are divided largely along political lines. Does ingestion of cholesterol predispose toward coronary thrombosis? The medical profession is split into three camps: yes, no, and maybe. And the same for the correlation between lung cancer and cigarette smoking. Should a particular Voice of America transmitter have been located where it was, or elsewhere? Senator McCarthy dived into that administrative cesspool and enjoyed himself hugely. Should the broadcasting system of the United States have been changed over from AM to FM in the late 1930's? The greatest of radio inventors staked and lost millions of dollars of his own money over that one, and finally committed suicide.

Such questions come up all the time. The areas of disagreement would be narrowed down by socialist technology, but disagreement would not disappear—nor should it. Decisions would still have to be made, and force applied when necessary. The decisions would be made by administrators who might oftener than now be engineers themselves (there has been a tendency in that direction even under capitalism), but who would be functioning as managers in the same predictive way as capitalistic managers risking other people's money.

Nor should it be forgotten that with the even greater importance of management under socialism, poor management can do proportionately greater damage, especially when an attempt is made to modernize a backward industrial country at top speed. What took place in Poland or Hungary, for example, prior to 1957, is scarcely conceivable in the United States, but the Poles and the Hungarians—and the Russians—are going to be paying for it for a long time. Central planning of that calibre is worse than no central planning at all. Another fact which it would be perilous to neglect is that neither capitalistic nor socialistic corporations are free from parasitic growths. The Polish Communist Party had 1.5 million members, many of whom got soft jobs at high salaries on the strength of party membership. There are times when managers have to be hatchetmen.

Since hierarchal managerial organization would not be radically modified by socialism, at least in its early stages, and since many of the ills of industrialism would remain for a generation or more, is it all one whether we continue under capitalism or risk the road to socialism? There could be no greater mistake than to let the similarities obscure the crucial differences between the two systems. Three counts alone in the indictment of the present order are decisive. Although it builds many technologically admirable plants and is manned by no small number of conscientious managers, technicians, and other workers, its over-all use of plant and personnel is grossly inefficient and wasteful. Although it has raised the general standard of living—or rather has been forced to raise it by labor organization and socialist competition—it can maintain these gains, such as they are, only by compensatory military spending of vast proportions and increasing hazard to the very existence of mankind. And although capitalist democracy is certainly to be preferred to the one-party state with no mechanism to make it responsive to popular pressures, only blind optimism could have much faith in the future of democracy under a two-party system which ducks the real issues and with the media of persuasion increasingly concentrated in the hands of vested interests. In a situation so precarious the problems of managerial reorganization are secondary. It is for the sake and in the name of political democracy that the way to socialism must be found.

Socialism Is Constitutional

By George Olshausen

IT IS SOMETIMES INSINUATED that the constitution requires "free enterprise". Nothing could be further from the truth. As Justice Holmes once said:

> A constitution is not intended to embody a particular economic theory, whether of paternalism and the organic relation of the citizen to the state or of *laissez faire*. (*Lochner v. New York* (1905) 198 U.S. 45, 75.)

The governments of the United States and of the individual states have operated countless businesses. *Business Week* for August 15, 1953, gives a list of 54 types of business, covering nine lines of print, from which the Eisenhower administration proposes to withdraw. It adds that the full list of enterprises now handled by the federal government alone (exclusive of the states) would cover several pages.

In many instances the constitutionality of governmentally owned enterprises has been tested before the United States Supreme Court. Constitutionality of government operation has uniformly been upheld. Moreover, the Supreme Court has repeatedly said that the government's power to operate industry

---

GEORGE OLSHAUSEN, a San Francisco lawyer, was born in Ithaca, New York in 1905. During his early years he was instructed by private tutors and in private schools, graduated from Northern High School, Detroit, Michigan in 1920. He received his A.B. degree in 1924, his J.D. in 1926 from the University of California. He was admitted to the California Bar in 1926, to the U.S. Supreme Court in 1935. A contributor of articles and book reviews to numerous periodicals, Mr. Olshausen is now engaged in writing a book—when not engaged in international law—on the legal and economic history of slavery in the United States.

Reprinted with permission of *Monthly Review*

varies with the needs of time and place. This bridges the gap between socialism and what has gone before. Until now, government ownership has been sporadic: socialism requires ownership of "the decisive sectors of the economy". When the country feels socialism is needed, socialism will also be held constitutional.

A brief survey of government ownership cases before the United States Supreme Court will show how far this is true.

Government ownership may be either by the federal government or by the states or municipalities. Decisions upholding the right of states to operate businesses are grounded on the states' reserved power to further the good and welfare of their inhabitants; decisions upholding the corresponding right of the federal government find it in one or more of the powers specifically delegated to the United States.

After World War I, North Dakota set up a State Bank and an Industrial Commission to conduct the business of manufacturing farm products, and to operate warehouses, flour mills, factories, and grain elevators. This program has sometimes been known as "the North Dakota experiment in state socialism". In 1920 the United States Supreme Court held the North Dakota plan constitutional. (*Green v. Frazier*, 253 U.S. 233.) The court was unanimous, the decision being written by Justice Day, an appointee of President Theodore Roosevelt. The opinion said in part:

> In the present instance, under the authority of the Constitution and laws prevailing in North Dakota, the people, the legislature and the highest court of the state have declared the purpose for which these several acts were passed, to be of a public nature, and within the taxing authority of the state. With this united action of people, legislature and court, we are not at liberty to interfere, unless it is clear beyond all reasonable controversy that rights secured by the Federal Constitution have been violated. (Pp. 239-240.)

The judges thought that it was not at all clear that the Constitution had been violated. They noted that, "In Many instances States and municipalities have in late years seen fit to enter upon projects to promote the public welfare which in the past have been considered entirely within the domain of private enterprise." (P. 242.)

The court also recalled its own decision of a few years before in which it sustained the right of the city of Portland, Maine, to operate a municpal coal and wood yard. (*Jones v. City of Portland,* (1917) 245 U.S. 217.)

So "North Dakota's experiment in state socialism" was held constitutional, with reference, it is true, to the particular conditions of North Dakota.

But the court had already upheld San Francisco's municipal railway. (*United R.R. v. San Francisco* (1919) 249 U.S. 517.) Since 1900 the San Francisco Charter contains a section declaring for municipal ownership of public utilities:

> It is the declared purpose and intention of the people of the city and county, when public interest and necessity demand, that public utilities shall be gradually acquired and ultimately owned by the city and county. (Sec. 119, as codified in 1935 Charter.)

The decision that the municipal railway was constitutional was written by Justice Holmes for a unanimous court.

Just as the Supreme Court had drawn an analogy with Portland, Maine, to uphold state operated business in North Dakota, it was soon to draw analogies with North Dakota to uphold similar enterprises in other parts of the country.

In 1922, *Boston v. Jackson,* 260 U.S. 309, unanimously approved Boston's right to own and operate the city's elevated lines.

Twelve years later, the Court once more gave the nod to municipal ownership of utilities—this time Seattle's electric electric light and power system. (*Puget Sound Co. v. Seattle* (1934) 291 U.S. 619.) Here the city of Seattle was competing with the Puget Sound Company in furnishing light and power to consumers. Such governmental competition with private industry was unanimously held constitutional. (Three Justices— Van Devanter, McReynolds, and Butler—also wrote a separate concurring opinion.)

Again in 1936, the Court considered California's State Belt Railroad, paralleling the San Francisco waterfront. A sentence was given to the problem of constitutionality:

That in operating its railroad it is acting within a power reserved to the States cannot be doubted. (*U.S. v. California*, 297 U.S. 175, 183.)

So much for the States. When the federal government enters business, the court has on occasion stretched a point to find the necessary constitutional authorization. Outstanding is the Boulder Canyon project, which with poetic justice may be called by its Republican name, Hoover Dam. It was set up "for the purpose of controlling the floods, improving navigation and regulating the flow of the Colorado River, providing for storage and for the delivery of the stored waters thereof, for reclamation of public lands and other beneficial uses exclusively within the United States, and *for generation of electric energy as a means of making the project herein authorized a self-supporting and financially solvent organization.*" (Emphasis added.)

This project was held constitutional as being an exercise of the federal government's power to improve navigation. (*Arizona v. California* (1931) 283 U.S. 423.) Justice Brandeis wrote the opinion; all Republican justices concurred. Justice McReynolds, appointed by President Wilson, wrote the lone dissent.

The Tennessee Valley Authority was likewise upheld under the power to improve navigation. (*Ashwander v. Tennessee Valley Authority* (1936) 297 U.S. 288.) Chief Justice Hughes wrote the opinion, which was supported exclusively by the old guard Republican judges. Justices Brandeis, Stone, and Cardozo thought that the Supreme Court should not consider the merits of the case but should summarily dismiss all objections to TVA; Justice McReynolds dissented.

The TVA controversy had a highly practical aspect: once the government entered the field, the private power company which had been there before, promptly sold out. (*Time*, August 28, 1939, p. 53.) There was no problem of taking private property for public use.

After three years, the Supreme Court said substantially the same thing again. (*Tennessee Power Co. v. TVA* (1939) 306 U.S. 118.)

Congressional debates as quoted in *U.S. v. San Francisco* (1940) 310 U.S. 16, show that the Hetch Hetchy water and power project was set up for the very purpose of having the

United States government compete with the Pacific Gas & Electric Company in furnishing hydro-electric power to San Francisco.

Almost simultaneously, the court summed up these decisions, saying, through Justice Frankfurter:

> In the light of all the exertions of state power, it does not seem possible to doubt that the state could, if it chose, go into the insurance business, just as it can operate warehouses, flour mills, and other business ventures, (*Green v. Frazier,* 253 U.S. 233; or might take "the whole business of banking under its control". *Noble State Bank v. Haskell,* 219 U.S. 104, 113. (*Osborn v. Ozlin* (1940) 310 U.S. 53, 66.)

The quoted definition[3] of socialism requires *first,* public ownership and *second,* comprehensive planning of production. Under existing law, ownership of property carries the right to plan its uses. If public ownership is found constitutional, the rest follows of itself. But the problem can also be approached from another standpoint: planning of production is one way of regulating property; if regulation of private property is constitutional, the same must all the more be true of public property.

Generally the issue of the government's power over property arises in three situations: (1) public ownership, already considered; (2) regulation of private property; (3) taking private property for public use (eminent domain). A single test is used throughout: the proposed action must benefit either all or part of the public. This rule has supplanted an earlier formula that, to be subject to government control, a business must be "affected with a public interest." For a time the Supreme Court seemed to hold that certain businesses inherently were not so affected; while also holding that the right of government to control business varied with the needs of the times. Most recently the court has expressly abandoned the "affected-with-a-public-interest" test, while retaining the principle that the power of regulation adjusts itself to economic conditions.

This idea stems from the first case on the subject, *Munn v. Illinois* (1877) 94 U.S. 113, 132. The state of Illinois passed a law classifying grain elevators as public utilities, though

grain elevators were not among the traditional public utilities
recognized by the English Common Law. The English law
as it existed in 1776 was retained at the time of the Declaration
of Independence, and where not changed by later legislation,
continued as the law of the United States. The Supreme Court
nevertheless held the regulation constitutional, saying that the
legislative right to declare businesses public utilities depended
upton circumstances of time and place. Lack of precedent was
of no importance.

> Neither is it a matter of any moment that no precedent
> can be found for a statute precisely like this. It is con-
> ceded that the business is one of recent origin, that its
> growth has been rapid, and that it is already of great im-
> portance. And it must also be conceded that it is a busi-
> ness in which the whole public has a direct and positive
> interest. It presents, therefore, a case for the application
> of a long known and well established principle of social
> science, and this statute simply extends the law so as to
> meet this new development of commercial progress. (P.
> 133.)

The same principle was followed in 1926 to uphold municipal zoning ordinances. The regulations imposed by such ordinances are comprehensive planning for real property. The court
did not treat them differently from any other type of regulation. In *Euclid v. Ambler Realty Co.*, 272 U.S. 365, it said,
speaking through Justice Sutherland (one of the Republican
old guard):

> Regulations, the wisdom, necessity and validity of
> which, as applied to existing conditons, are so apparent
> that they are now uniformly sustained, a century ago, or
> even half a century ago, probably would have been rejected
> as arbitrary and oppressive. . . . In a changing world it
> is impossible that it should be otherwise. (P. 387.)

Many other decisions have made the same point.[2] Among
the most interesting have been those concerning municipal
housing projects. Such projects involve a limited degree of comprehensive planning. They have been found constitutional on

the broad ground that the state's power varies with changing needs. (*Dornan v. Philadelphia Housing Authority* (1938) 331 Pa. 209; *Housing Authority v. Knoxville* (1938) 174 Tenn. 76.)

At various periods, to be sure, the Supreme Court has held social legislation unconstitutional. Examples are: *Lochner v. New York* (1905) 198 U.S. 45 (maximum hours for men bakers); *Adkins v. Children's Hospital* (1923) 261 U.S. 525 (minimum wages for women); *Chas. Wolff Packing Co. v. Kansas Court for Industrial Relations* (1923) 262 U.S. 522 (statute attempting to make meat-packing business a public utility); *Tyson Bros. v. Banton* (1927) 273 U.S. 418 (fixing prices of theatre tickets). All these were placed on the ground that the business involved "was not affected with a public interest," or that the contemplated regulation supposedly had no connection with the ends sought. But *Adkins v. Children's Hospital* was overruled in *West Coast Hotel Co. v. Parrish* (1937) 300 U.S. 379; *Nebbia v. N. Y.* restored the power to regulate prices; and in *Lincoln Union v. N. W. Iron & Metal Co.* (1949) 335 U.S. 525, 536, the court expressly discarded the "affected-with-a-public-interest" test.

The greatest resistance to government regulation has always been in the fields of price and wage-and-hour fixing. When it came to comprehensive planning otherwise, the opposition usually folded its tents without a whimper. As long ago as 1911, a compulsory statewide plan to insure the solvency of banks was instituted in Oklahoma. The Supreme Court unanimously found it constitutional. Justice Holmes said that the state could take "the whole business of banking under its control." (*Noble State Bank v. Haskell,* 219 U.S. 104, 113.)

There is another approach to the question whether socialism would be constitutional under the present United States Constitution. Setting up socialism means substituting a new economic system for the existing one. The reason for believing that this can be done within the present framework of government is that a previous economic change of comparable magnitude was accomplished with virtually no modification of the form of government.

The pre-Civil War system of chattel slavery differed from private wage capitalism at least as much as private wage capitalism differs from socialism. The labor of the slave was paid for in advance (upon purchase); thereafter the slave could not be "laid off"; the master could either work the slave and re-cover his capital investment plus profits from the products of the slave's labor, or he could sell the slave and recover his in-vestment in the manner of selling an installment note. After the slave became too old to work, the owner had to take care of him until death.

Slaves were held mostly by owners of plantations, and were for all practical purposes tied to the master's land.

According to Hinton R. Helper, the "slaveocracy" controlled the country almost up to the Civil War (Helper, *The Impend-ing Crisis of the South*, 1857, pp. 307-316.)

The Civil War marked the transiton from a slaveholding agricultural society to an industrial wage society. This transi-tion was accomplished with virtually no change in the structure of government. The framework of government set up in the Constitution could be used equally for a slave and for a capi-talist economy.

It is true, abolition of slavery was accomplished by the Thir-teenth, Fourteenth and Fifteenth Amendments. But while these altered the participation of persons in government, they did not alter the framework of government itself.

Not only could the existing structure be fitted to a slave and to a capitalist economy; it could likewise be fitted to one whose voters were exclusively whites or to one which en-franchised Negroes.

This fact is emphasized by the Confederate Constitution, specifically drawn for this slave system, but differing little from the Federal Constitution. It varies from the latter not so much in the structure which it sets up as in withdrawing certain addi-tional subjects from the scope of Congressional legislation.[4]

Thus the Constitution of the United States is a mechanical framework which fits different economic systems. In view of what the Supreme Court has already said on the subject of state regu-lation and ownership of business, there is little doubt that it will fit a socialist economy.

If not already constitutional, socialism may be set up by constitutional amendment.

The original constitution attempted to make three of its provisions unamendable. Before 1808, the slave trade could not be abolished; likewise, prior to 1808, there could be no change in the requirements that representatives and direct taxes must be apportioned among the states according to population; and no state might without its consent be deprived of its equal suffrage in the Senate. The first two are obsolete by their own terms. Apportionment of direct taxes was partly abolished by the Sixteenth Amendment. In the Constitution of today, only the equal suffrage of the states in the Senate is placed beyond the reach of amendment. It follows that Socialism, as already defined, is within the range of constitutional amendment.

Those who today suggest that constitutional amendment should extend only to matters which do not fundamentally change the existing system, forget that this issue was fought out in the Civil War. John C. Calhoun formulated precisely that theory in his "Discourse on the Constitution and Government of the United States," 1848-1849. He said:

> On the other hand should it [the federal government] succeed in obtaining the amendment, the act of the government of the separate state which caused the conflict, and operated as a negative on the act of the federal government would in all cases be overruled; and the latter become operative within its limits. . . . In this case, if the act of the latter [that is, of the federal government in securing a constitutional amendment] be predicated on a power consistent with the character of the constitution, the ends for which it was established, and the nature of our system of government;—or more briefly, if it came fairly within the scope of the amending power, the state is bound to acquiesce, by the solemn obligation which it contracted in ratifying the constitution. But if it transcends the limits of the amending power—be inconsistent with the character of the constitution and the ends for which it was established—or with the nature of the system—the result is different. In such case, the state is not bound to acquiesce. It may choose whether it will, or whether it will not secede from the Union. (Works of John C. Calhoun, 1854 ed., Vol. 1, p. 300.)

The Civil War denied the supposed right of a non-consenting state to secede where an amendment "transcends the limits of the amending power—be inconsistent with the character of the constitution and the ends for which it was established—or with the nature of the system". That is true even though the post-Civil War amendments touched lightly on the structure of government. In other words, no such limitations are recognized, and a constitutional amendment can set up any form of government or any economic system as long as it does not infringe the equal suffrage of the states in the Senate.

Under a constitutional amendment, moreover, private property may be taken without compensation, if desired. This was done for the first time by the Fourteenth Amendment. It is one of the ironies of American constitutional history that the Fourteenth Amendment, which provides in its *first* section that no person may be deprived of life, liberty, or property without due process of law, should provide in its *fourth* section that, "neither the United States nor any state shall assume or pay . . . any claim for the loss or emancipation of any slave; but all such debts, obligations and claims shall be held illegal and void". It all depends on whose ox is gored.[5]

The Eighteenth Amendment took private property without compensation for the second time in American history. It forbade "the manufacture, sale . . . transportation . . . or exportation" of intoxicating liquors for beverage purposes. This amounted to confiscation; but since the confiscation was expressly authorized by the Eighteenth Amendment, it was constitutional. (*Corneli v. Moore,* 267 Fed. 456, 457; affirmed by Supreme Court, 257 U.S. 491.)

Believing themselves threatened with a change to socialism, capitalists today echo the 100-year-old arguments of slaveholders who felt themselves threatened with a change to capitalism. In both cases, the Constitution is said to set up, or at least to entrench, a particular economic system. In both cases, it is urged not only that the Constitution as it stands prohibits abolition of the old system, but that the Constitution cannot be fundamentally amended.

So the anti-slavery fight assumes new relevance. On the one hand, decisions of the Supreme Court have traced a pattern, albeit piecemeal, indicating that socialism would be constitutional. But on the other, the slavery controversy established that, aside from equal representation of the states in the Senate, there are no limitations on the power to amend the Constitution. It follows that socialism may be established by constitutional means.

NOTES

1 As noted by the Supreme Court of Pennsylvania in *Dornan v. Phila-delphia Housing Authority* (1938) 331 Penn. 209, 233 n. 9.

2 *Rindge Land Co. v. Los Angeles* (1923) 262 U.S. 700 (what is public use for purposes of eminent domain) and *Nebbia v. New York*, 291 U.S. 502 (regulation of milk prices) are two typical examples.

3 As defined by the editors of *Monthly Review*, "By 'socialism' we mean a system of society with two fundamental characteristics: *first*, public own-ership of the decisive means of production and *second*, comprehensive planning of production for the benefit of the producers themselves."

4 In the Confederate Constitution, Art. I, Sec. 8 (1) prohibited the Con-federate Congress from imposing any tax or duty to foster any branch of industry; Art. I, Sec. 8 (3) forbade the appropriation of money for internal improvements (with certain exceptions). These two divergences were tailored to the agricultural interests of the time. There were also special guarantees for property in slaves. Otherwise the differences from the Federal Constitution were technical and not characteristic of the economic system.

5 Compensation for emancipated slaves was an open question until the adoption of the Fourteenth Amendment. Even the Thirteenth, while liberating the slaves, was silent on the question of compensation. Before that, opinion seems to have favored compensation, at least for those slaveholders who had remained loyal to the Union—principally in the non-seceded slave states of Maryland, Delaware, West Virginia, Missouri, Kentucky, and to some extent in Tennessee.

American Socialism, World Government and Peace

By Scott Nearing

FEW PEOPLE will question the desirability of world peace. Heavy
losses of life and property in recent wars and the increasing
efficacy of mass-destruction weapons and techniques have led
scientists, engineers and political leaders to join humanitarians
and ethical teachers in advocating the renunciation and abolition of war. In this stand they have had the support of multi-
tudes on every continent. World peace is desirable in theory.
The most important single obstacle to its realization is the per-
sistence of capitalism.

Wars have been a feature of capitalism from its early beginnings. Professor Quincy Wright and his associates in the University of Chicago produced an elaborate *Study of War* in which
they showed that from 1450 to 1940 nearly three hundred wars
had been fought—two-thirds of them entirely or partly in Europe. It was during these centuries that capitalism was developing in Europe and was extending its influence across the planet.

Professor Wright counted the number of wars in which the
principle countries of Europe had taken part during this period.

SCOTT NEARING, Ph.D., is a teacher, author, farmer, and world
traveller. Among his many published works are "Dollar Diplomacy", "The
Twilight of Empire" and "Economics for the Power Age". His most recent
book, written with Helen Nearing, is "Socialists Around the World", published by *Monthly Review Press*, 1958.

Britain headed the list with the greatest number of wars. France came second. The count reflected the duel waged between these two countries to determine which of them should hold trade routes, markets, raw materials, colonies. Britain came out ahead in this struggle, but France was a close second. Britain and France were the two chief war makers. Also they were the two leading colonial powers when war ended in 1945. The vast extent of their holdings, even as lately as 1956, appears in the United Nations *Demographic Year Books.*

Throughout their history, capitalist nations fought wars of conquest which brought weaker peoples under their control, and led to the establishment of the half-dozen great empires which dominated the life of the planet during the closing years of the 19th century. After 1870 the rival capitalist powers, face to face with rapidly rising productivity, seeking outlets in a limited world market, took part in an economic and diplomatic knock-down-and-drag-out struggle which led up to the Great War that began in 1914 and has continued, intermittently, since that time.

Throughout their history, the leading capitalist nations have used war as a means of adding to their wealth and increasing their power. Wars of conquest in the Americas, Asia and Africa have been accompanied by wars of rivalry fought to determine whether Spanish, Dutch, French, British, German or Russian ruling classes should get and hold land areas, natural resources, trade routes, markets and dependent peoples.

Unlike their feudal predecessors in Europe, capitalist nations did not look upon war as "the sport of kings and the king of sports." Since the capitalists were engaged in a competitive struggle for wealth and power, and since it was impossible to subjugate even the weaker peoples without the use of violence, they employed war as an instrument of policy in order to protect and advance their material interests. Repeatedly capitalist spokesmen have professed their desire for peace. At the same time they have insisted that their economies "must continue to expand." Peace and expansion stand opposed, one to the other. Where a choice has to be made, capitalist leaders have usually given priority to expansion, even though expansion meant war.

Until the opening of the present century, the United States participated only incidentally in the struggle to redivide the

planet. Its military expenditures and armed forces were less
than those of the leading European powers. Wars with Mexico
in 1846 and with Spain in 1898 were quite incidental to United
States capitalist expansion, which had been confined chiefly
to the North American continent. But the war of 1898 gave the
Washington government control of Cuba, Puerto Rico and the
Philippines. Twenty years later, in 1917, the United States
became an active participant in the war which was raging
in Europe.

Since then, and especially after 1945, the United States has
played a leading part in war preparations and in fighting. A
ring of more than 250 military bases girding the Northern
Hemisphere, a net work of military alliances in the Atlantic
and Pacific areas and the Western Hemisphere, the supplying
of arms to some sixty nations, and the stationing of more than
a million United States armed personnel abroad have put
the United States at the top of the list of world dominating
capitalist powers. With the rapid increase in military outlays which followed the outbreak of war in Korea (1950), United
States economy has become increasingly dependent on war-
spending as a means of maintaining full employment and high
productivity. These developments have committed the United
States to participation in almost any war almost anywhere.

Within the last forty years the area of world conflict has
been enlarged, and changed in character. Rapid transportation
and instantaneous communication have made different parts of
the planet increasingly interdependent. At the same time, war,
colonial revolt and social revolution have altered the world
power struggle. In the course of the Great War, nations and
empires have been destroyed, defeated and weakened economically. Colonial peoples, winning independence, have pulled
away from the great empires, weakening or shattering them.
Social revolution has threatened to undermine and perhaps to
destroy capitalist society. These forces have challenged the
United States as the richest and best-armed among the capitalist powers. They have also forced the capitalists of the West
to make common cause against the nations and peoples of East
Europe, Asia and Africa who are trying to build a form of society that can equal and excel capitalism.

This new rivalry between capitalism and socialism, known
since 1945 as "the cold war" has lined mankind up in three

camps: capitalism, socialism, and the very considerable group of nations and peoples committed to neither side and seeking to establish a middle way.

Intensified rivalry between capitalism and socialism has led to war on more than one occasion. Primarily the War of 1914-18 arose out of the transfer of the economic and diplomatic struggle between the big empires to the political field. Incidentally, however, the War of 1914 was welcomed by European conservatives as an opportunity to check internationalism, cripple organized labor and clip the wings of a rapidly growing socialist movement.

In 1919 the spokesmen for capitalism, assembled in peace delegations at Versailles, turned from treaty-making to stamp out the revolutions which were blazing across Europe and into Asia. To achieve this objective, armies from Europe, North America and Asia invaded the Soviet Union, and struck at the revolutionary movements in Central and Eastern Europe and the Far East. Japanese intervention in China had for its avowed purpose the destruction of the Chinese Soviets. German and Italian intervention in the Spanish Civil War (1936-39) was part of the Anti-Comintern drive launched in 1936. The declared purpose of the Anti-Comintern Pact was the overthrow of those powers which aimed to construct a socialist society. Hitler's massive drive into East Europe and the Soviet Union (1941) was aimed at "bolshevism," "socialism" and communism". Between 1919 and 1938 military preparations were being made and military expeditions were being readied and launched against the nations and peoples that were trying to build a socialist society.

General war from 1939 to 1945 aligned the chief capitalist powers against each other, and the 1941 invasion of the Soviet Union led to extensive collaboration between the Big Three capitalist nations and the Union of Socialist Soviet Republics.

War's end in 1945 brought a realignment of anti-socialist forces. Britain, Germany and France and Italy—the backbone of European capitalism, had been crippled and bankrupted by war losses and by revolts among the colonials. Only one of the big capitalist powers, the United States, was solvent and strong enough to face the tide of socialism sweeping over Europe and Asia.

Once the "capitalist" enemy (Germany, Italy and Japan) was

defeated, the remnants of capitalist imperialism rallied their scattered resources and lined up their armed forces for the cold war.   Backed by United States subsidies and equipped, in part, with United States military supplies, the Western nations organized alliances, mobilized weapons, recruited personnel and prepared to meet the Soviet invasion of the West, which, according to Western propaganda sources, was planned for 1951, or, at the latest, 1952. From 1927 to 1948 Chiang Kai-shek, with some Japanese and much Western support, fought a series of wars aimed to crush the Chinese Soviets. French armies in Indo-China and British forces in Malaya battled for years to destroy native "socialist" or "communist" regimes.

The local wars of 1945-55 were fought chiefly between Asian and African peoples seeking independence and the right to establish some form of economic collectivism, and the scattered fragments of Western imperialism, which, with United States subsidies and supplies were striving by force of arms to contain, turn back and defeat erstwhile colonial peoples demanding self-determination.

Until 1900 the United States had been a lightly-armed, isolationist, minor power. In 1945 the U.S.A. emerged, armed to the teeth, with productive capacity multiplied, and a volume of national income exceeding that of all other capitalist nations combined, to assume the responsibility of defending and promoting the interests of world capitalism and undermining and eventually destroying not only the outcroppings of collectivism in Viet Minh, Indonesia, Korea, British Guiana, Mexico and Guatemala, but also the centers of socialist construction—the Soviet Union and the Chinese People's Republic.

Speedy shifts on the stage of history, during the four decades following 1914 shattered the capitalist empires, destroyed or seriously crippled all but one of the big capitalist powers, loosed a tidal wave of colonial unrest and revolt, turned two-fifths of the human race to the task of building socialism and tossed upon United States shoulders the chore of restoring, holding and strengthening the capitalist world in its struggle to check and throw back the advancing tide of socialism.

United States policy-makers were convinced that this program could be carried out only through the build-up of positions of military strength, expressed in the land, sea and air forces of NATO, plus the armed forces of individual nations,

backed by the latest developments in guided missiles and nuclear weapons. Capitalism had reached a level of deterioration
at which its chief defense was armed violence and its champion
was a United States equipped with designs, production lines
and destructive power "second to none".

Whether a super-armed United States, supported by its allies
and dependencies, can preserve capitalism is a question that need
not detain us here. History will answer that one. What does
concern us is that these stockpiles of death-dealing destructives,
and the long assembly lines from which they come, are numerous enough and lethal enough to atomize the human species.

How can this menace best be met, and the ominous threat
of war transformed into the promise of a stable peace? The answer is simple: By making the United States socialist. When
the United States takes up the task of building socialism,
Japan, Canada and the NATO countries and the members of
the Bandung Bloc will easily fall into line, if they have not
previously joined the peoples dedicated to the building of a
socialist world.

Once the balance has been tipped toward collectivism, the
large segment of the world engaged in building socialism, plus its
new recruits and allies, could ignore or laugh off scattered
vestiges of capitalism in Switzerland, Spain, Australia, New
Zealand, South Africa and parts of Latin America.

Social engineers, humanitarians, idealists and utopists are
face to face with this task: Make the United States socialist.
Having tipped the world balance decisively away from capitalism toward socialism, the builders of a new social order will
face the next problem: making sure that a socialist world can
coexist without resorting periodically to armed violence.

Collectivists never tire of asserting that a collective world
will suffer from war and benefit from peace. Of course this is
true. But in the long run the same truth applied to the capitalist world. While capitalists who won wars made short-term
gains, their economy as well as their political and social structure were undermined, upset and finally wrecked by war. The
mere fact that a practice like war wrecks a society does not prevent human beings from following practices that end in destruction.

Collectivists insist that since a collective community is organized around the principle of cooperation instead of around

the competitive principle and practice of capitalism, collectivism
will lead to peace rather than war. Certainly an argument
can be made in support of such a contention, but several decades of experience with socialist construction bring this argument into serious question.

Whether under capitalism or under collectivism, the modern
world is closely knit by interdependence, trade, transport and
communication. Each center of industry requires certain resources and raw materials. Petroleum and cotton are indispensable in modern industry, whether it be capitalist or collectivist. Petroleum is scattered irregularly across the earth.
Cotton production requires peculiar soil and climatic conditions. Since all industrial areas are dependent on natural resources and materials which are unequally distributed, geo-
graphically, it follows that the need for 'have-not" areas to secure such commodities and the tendency of "have" areas to
keep them will result in pressures, tensions and perhaps conflicts.

Similarly, easy and quick transportation and communication pose questions of migration and exchange which may result
in misunderstandings and difficulties. Equally fraught with
possibilities of irritation and conflict are problems arising out of
trade, pricing, lending and borrowing. Interdependence will
increase with the growth of production and its corresponding
demands for raw materials, food supplies and markets.

Economic sources of tension and possible conflict, arising
out of conditions prevailing in modern industrial communities, are directly related to the unequal levels of cultural development which confronts us on all hands—sometimes within
small nations and invariably in large areas like the diverse
territories embraced in the United States, the Soviet Union,
China and India. So far as we can judge, cultural inequalities
will persist for an indefinite period, with corresponding possibilities for misunderstanding and friction.

Again, there is nationalism—one of the most widely prevalent
manifestations of the present era. Nationalism was one of the
outstanding features of capitalist society. It reached notable
intensity among the colonial peoples who have won their independence during the period of the Great War. It has been
prominent in the socialist areas of the world. "Socialism in one
country", translated into current experience, would read "so-

cialism in each country". Nationalism of a very intense order has persisted throughout the collectivist areas.

There is no use in arguing that nationalism is a hang-over from capitalism. Whatever its origin, nationalism is a factor of major present-day importance. Among the survivals of capitalism, among the self-determining colonials and among the peoples building socialism, nationalism persists. There are many reports of its growth. There is no present sign of its abatement. Closely tied in with cultural inequalities, nationalism is a local unifying force and an international cause of isolationist loyalty, friction and conflict.

Varied interests, unequal cultural levels, and sharply accentuated national loyalties are features which may be met in every corner of present-day society. They are not limited to capitalist countries but are products of the times. All are divisive. All point toward tension and conflict. To these forces, inherent in the structure and function of present-day society must be added the generously subsidized and elaborately developed projects to subvert and overthrow those areas engaged in socialist construction. Emigres and paid agents of the old order join hands in these organized efforts to offset and upset the attempts to build socialism.

During the first decade when socialist construction was being carried on in a number of countries (the decade 1946-56), unequal cultural development, nationalism, subversion and sabotage threatened peace and pointed toward conflict—cold and hot. There is no need to go into detail. Ten years after fighting stopped in 1945, each of the nations building socialism was a sovereign state, enjoying the full rights and privileges of sovereignty, including the right to wage peace and make war. Moreover, each state building socialism was armed and equipped for defense and was jealously guarding ts frontiers and its "national honor".

Before world peace can be maintained, even under socialism, a firmly knit international government must be established. Presumably, such an international structure will consist of agencies which bind nations and peoples into flexible but workable whole.

At the base of the structure will be national or regional units. Unitary, closely knit structures like France and Italy are such national units. Federations such as the United States of Mexico and the United States of America are such regional units. Four-score of these political units would make up a workable United Nations Authority or United States of the World.

Such an organization, to be effective, must be flexible, because of the wide range of cultural institutions to be found even among the socialist nations which are in existence at the time of this writing. Attempts to reduce these nations and peoples to a uniform pattern would produce hostility, resistance and finally rebellion against the world authority. An effective world authority would undertake to ensure the widest possible range of choice, decision and action in the areas composing the world organization. The component elements of the world body would enjoy home rule in the same sense that the cities of Illinois enjoy the right to handle their own city problems or the provinces composing Canada determine their own provincial affairs.

Theoretically, at least, the more local autonomy or home rule exercised by the nations and regions composing the world authority, the more vital and dynamic would be the entire organization of world life.

Side by side with local home rule, the United World Authority must have the means to deal effectively with matters which concern two or more of the nations or regions which make up the world organization. Home rule in local affairs must be paralleled by a central organization with delegated powers sufficient to deal with problems concerning the welfare of several nations and areas. This federal principle of home rule in local affairs and central administration of matters of general or common concern has worked with varying degrees of effectiveness in S.   land, the United States and the British Commonwealth.   the federal principle lies the key to effective world organizati

Under ex   ng world conditions, the extreme emphasis placed on "independence", "self-determination" and "national sovereignty" tips the ba nce against the workableness of a world authority. The prov   in the United Nations Charter limiting the function of the   al Assembly, and giving five nations permanent seats in t   rity Council and therefore permanent veto power, preserv   sovereignty of the Big Five by providing each of them with the possibility of obstructing or crippling United Nations action and thus outlawing measures which are distasteful to one among the fourscore members of the United Nations organization. A socialist world federation, which aimed to preserve peace and order and to provide for the general welfare, must limit national sovereignty sufficiently to enable the world organization to make and implement decisions in matters concerning the general world welfare.

Events of the past decade make it increasingly evident that the world economy, as at present constituted, will grow more collective rather than less as the years pass. A collective world economy will necessitate a collective political and social superstructure. The collectivist trend, progressive for this historical period, is blocked at the moment by capitalist survivals, chiefly those in the United States and the British Commonwealth. Making the United States socialist would open the way to world progress at the same time that it increased the probability of world peace.

PART III. WANTED: AN AMERICAN PEOPLE'S PARTY

"Socialism is a growing idea, an expanding philosophy. It is spreading over the face of the earth. It is as useless to resist it as it would be to try to arrest the sunrise on the morrow. It is coming, coming, coming, all along the line. . . . The greatest movement in history.

"It bears the scars of a thousand defeats but it grows stronger and braver and more invincible through them all, and it will never lay down the weapon of its peace-loving crusade, never cease its holy war until its triumph is complete and sets the whole world free.

"What a privilege to serve it. It is your duty to help build. . . . Need I say, comrades, that the crying need of the day is organization?"

From the speech of Eugene V. Debs, *delivered at Dayton, Ohio, on June* 16, 1918.

"Isn't it about time that the working people of our country took a good look at a rigged political setup which still has all of us in a straight-jacket?

"It's a sad state of affairs when a country like ours has to go through a national election in which the millions in labor unions, the Negro people, the small farmers and the many decent, honest liberals have no real candidate of their own and no party which truly speaks for them.

"In no other major capitalist country—England, France, Italy, Australia, New Zealand—could such an election be held today without a labor or socialist party of sorts campaigning from labor's point of view and with labor candidates from the unions bidding for the people's vote.

"Labor needs its own fighting program and its own party to carry this program forward".

From a statement by Harry Bridges, *President, International Longshoremen's and Warehousemen's Union, in* The Dispatcher, *Nov.* 9, 1956.

"TIME AND AGAIN I HAVE SAID that organized labor should not be the captive of any political party. We belong in nobody's pocket. The labor movement is staggering under the blows of the Taft-Hartley law, the Right-to-Work laws and the shadow of future restrictive and destructive legislation.

"Under these circumstances, it is of the greatest urgency that the organized working people of this country begin to think about building their own political party. . . . More than ever, I believe there should be a political party which represents 95 per cent of the American people—the workers and farmers of America, without regard for color or religious affiliations. The slogan of such a party might well be, WHAT IS GOOD FOR 95 PER CENT OF THE PEOPLE IS GOOD FOR AMERICA!"

From the report of MICHAEL J. QUILL, *as President of the Transport Workers Union of America, AFL-CIO, delivered at the 10th Biennial Convention of the Union, October 21, 1957, in New York City.*

"THEREFORE, BE IT RESOLVED: That this 16th convention of the UAW, AFL-CIO, call upon the AFL-CIO to convene in the near future a Congress to which shall be invited delegates of all interested union bodies and representative farm groups and liberal elements, including those from the Republican and Democratic Parties, and which shall have the function of determining a program and setting in action the mechanics for the establishment of a Farmer-Labor Party in the United States."

Resolution almost unanimously adopted by the General Council, Ford Local 600, United Automobile Workers, CARL STELLATO, *President, February 16, 1957.*

Public Power Speeds the Pace to Social Planning and Ownership

By Reuben W. Borough

FEW AMERICANS ARE AWARE of the importance of the struggle around public power or of its vast potential in relation to the future economic and social transformation of the nation.

And yet this power issue blazed across the horizons of the closing nineteenth and opening twentieth centuries, is firmly enmeshed in the current economy, and looms in the minds of our business monopolists as tomorrow's major menace.

Public power is closely allied ideologically with the earlier Greenback and Populist demands for a government-issued and a government-controlled currency ("fiat money") and government-owned and government-operated railroad systems. It appeared as a campaign issue in the Socialist Party's forthright platform of the twentieth century's first decade and among the planks of the more conservative progressive ("Bull Moose") Party platform of 1912.

From 1882, when there were only four municipally owned

REUBEN W. BOROUGH was born in 1883, in Sylvania (a suburb of Toledo), Ohio. His background of intellectual independence was in part provided my his father, a carriage manufacturer and ardent Populist, his paternal grandfather, a circuit-riding German Evangelical Lutheran preacher in Southern Michigan, and his maternal grandfather, a devout follower of the agnostic, Robert G. Ingersoll. Successively a University of Michigan student, country school teacher, newspaper reporter (Fort Wayne and Chicago), and a travelling salesman for his father's business (toward the end of the horse and buggy days), Mr. Borough migrated to California in 1912. He edited *Epic News*, Upton Sinclair's gubernatorial campaign organ, 1934, helped unseat a corrupt Los Angeles mayor, 1948, served as a member of the Los Angeles Board of Public Works under Mayor Bowran, 1939-45. Running for the United States Senate as candidate of the Independent Progressive Party of California in 1952—the sole opponent of Senator William F. Knowland—Reuben Borough polled more than 542,000 votes.

electric utilities in the United States, municipal ownership
spread persistently for half a century, particularly in the West
and Mid-West. By 1923 municipally owned plants had reached
a total of 3,801, a figure reduced to 2,300 today, due to the integration of the smaller public plants in the larger inter-lacing
private systems: a process resulting, in part, from the greater
assurance of unbroken service to consumers from the inter-
meshed distribution of the private companies and, in part, from
"power trust" propaganda against the slothful management of
some of the smaller public plants.

In the hundreds of political campaigns that marked this over-
all progress the grass-roots leadership of the Socialist Party and
the advanced elements of the labor movement gave effective,
though some times none too welcome, support to the real estate,
commercial and professional groups clamoring for cheap power.

In the 1930's came the public power achievements of the
Roosevelt New Deal. Greatest among these was the Tennessee
Valley Authority, whose multiple-purpose dams formed the base
for power-generating, power-distributing, flood-control, irrigation, navigation, conservation and recreational projects—a veritable new American frontier. The pattern of TVA was followed in whole or in part in the maze of works which the Interior Department's Reclamation Bureau and the U.S. Army's
Corps of Engineers laid down in 21 states, outstanding among
them Grand Coulee and Bonneville of the Columbia River
Basin in the Northwest and, in the Southwest, Boulder Dam
of the Colorado River Basin and Shasta of California's Central
Valley Project.

All this is public record which cannot be expunged by the
zealots of "private enterprise". It stands as proof that the people
of the United States do not reject but, on the contrary, willingly
accept non-profit, production-for-use instrumentalities and techniques to meet their pressing needs and that they do this, not
under compulsion of imported manifestos, but easily, naturally,
in line with their established traditions. The home-grown social revolution is already under way and, in its New Deal
phase, it has turned out its own native mechanism for the
penetration and transformation of the areas of capitalist monopoly: the authority, a public corporation specifically empowered by government to engage in business for the general
welfare.

The case for public power and the authortiy which is its distinguishing instrumentality rests, it must be remembered, not upon theory but upon proven performance in an extensive field.

The physical properties of the public power domain, alone, are awe-inspiring. Topping the 2,300 municipal plants and the other federal power structures are 80 federal dams, all more than 200 feet in height. These dams, fixed in rivers draining more than 30 states, are mountains of poured cement, a total of a half billion cubic yards, and behind them can be stored enough water to flood to a depth of one foot the states of Massachusetts, Connecticut, Rhode Island, Delaware, Pennsylvania, Maryland, North Carolina, South Carolina, and Florida. The Tennessee Valley Authority's integrated dams constitute an unparalleled production equipment. Its output is large enough to serve, through the distributing systems of 98 municipalities and 51 rural co-operatives, more than 1,200,000 electrified homes and farms in a territory of 80,000 square miles—nearly twice the size of Tennessee.

In 1953, according to the Federal Power Commission, the installed generating capacity of the federal plants (the thousands of smaller municipal, state and public utility district plants *not* included) was 38.6 per cent of the combined installed capacity of all public and private plants in the nation—8,293,520 kilowatts as against 21,463,872. By 1955 the installed capacity of the federal plants had grown to 10,266,120 kilowatts—a figure that will soon be increased, by plants under construction or authorized, to 17,000,000 kilowatts; and this, in turn, under reasonable expectations will be raised to a total of 47,000,000 kilowatts by 1960.

Moreover the federal plants, per kilowatt of capacity, turn out more product in kilowatt *hours* than the privately owned plants. For 1953 the ratio of federal plant output to total output of all plants, publicly and privately owned, was 42 per cent— 47 billion kilowatt hours against 112.5 billion—and the federal plants did this (as noted above) with only 38.6 per cent of the total installed kilowatt capacity.

In addition to the monumental stature of the physical plant and its impressive performance (and, of course, explanatory of these) is the superiority of public power as a competitive economic unit. The public power plant is lean and strong.

The annual reports and the book records of hundreds of municipal, public utility district, rural co-operative and federal properties underscore these impressive facts:

1. Public power is free from the perpetual drain of dividends to non-producing stockholders.

2. Public power capitalization (the sum of government loans and/or the proceeds from bond sales for the basic investment) includes only the original cost of producing the physical plant.

3. This honest capital obligation is liquidated from public power's earnings in annual installments running through periods varying from 25 to 50 years. TVA, as one example, is paying off on a total investment of $968,365,000 (net after depreciation, 1954 fiscal year) at the rate of 4 per cent a year although its commitment is for only 2½ per cent.

4. The debt eliminated, the only factor determining rates, aside from taxes, depreciation and upkeep, is the operating cost (salaries, wages, materials and supplies).

5. Generally public power pays taxes or sums in lieu of taxes to local government (municipal, county, state). It does *not* pay federal income taxes. But the amount it turns back annually to the federal government to pay off obligations on original capital investment equals—or more than equals—the amount which the private company would have paid in federal income taxes if it had owned the property. (Failure of performance along this line, if any occurred, could be obviated by foregoing a rate reduction or two!) TVA's comment in its 1956 report on the fact that it does not pay federal income taxes is that "all of TVA's income belongs to the government; and, if a share of TVA's power earnings were earmarked for income taxes in the same proportion as for utility companies, there would still be enough left over to cover the government's cost of providing the money invested in the power system".

In marked contrast to the above-outlined capital structure and mode of operation of public power under the authority is that of the private companies, as disclosed in the records of the great controversies before various state public utility commissions. Private power conventionally carries, in additon to the parasitic dividend requirements, a heavy burden of over-capitalization—an unjustified expansion of the "rate base" upon which the company is allowed by the regulatory state commission to collect a return, or profit, for its "investment". The result is an indefensible drain upon the rate payers, or consumers. This over-capitalization includes the following extraneous "values", some of which are obviously fictional but all of which have been established as property rights in the courts of many states: good will, going concern, franchise value, promotion stock, issues of stock dividends, padded construction costs (pay-offs to subsidiaries or financial allies). The capital structure is further unduly extended by the perpetual refunding of the bonded debt. (It is pertinent here to observe that the capitalization of the other great monopolies, both inside and outside the public utility category, are weighted with similar, or even worse, extortions.)

6. Public power charges to consumers over the nation are from 25 to 50 per cent lower than private company charges—the logical consequence, in part, of the variations noted above in the structure and functioning of the two systems. There is another important factor—the contrast in operating costs. In the TVA area, for instance, the average charge per kilowatt hour to consumers for the 1955 fiscal year was 1.21 cents as against 2.67 cents throughout the nation. This difference in retail price represents substantially the difference in the total cost in these specific fields: producing, transmitting, distributing, and selling electricity. According to Federal Power Commission reports, this total operating expense for public power is about half the average for the private utility industry.

It should be apparent to all that the organism under examination here is a vigorous and earthy embodiment of secular socialism operating aloof from the saints in a contaminating capitalist society but nevertheless successfully. The jittery power trust's characterization, to change the metaphor, is correct—public power, with its catalytic agent, the authority, is "creeping socialism". And tomorrow it may walk, then run!

It is one of the paradoxes of our time that the defense of the public power domain should fall, in the main, not upon the social ideologists of the Left, but upon conservative groups whose vested interests and community loyalties impel them to protect it. Most directly involved of these are the keepers of the plant, the management and operating personnel. Thus, for instance, TVA in its 1955 annual report notes that those responsible for guiding the operations of its municipal and rural co-operative distributors (some 900 directors and trustees) come from more than 90 businesses and professions and constitute a cross section of the business and social life of the region.

These keepers of the plant run the business well. Acting out of pride in their function and a desire to entrench and strengthen it, they maintain a logical alertness against the evils of bureaucracy, which are apt to invade large-scale business, both public and private. They critically discard routine patterns of work which have become outmoded. Their publications and the omnipresent specialists addressing their public gatherings relentlessly drive for improvement of techniques in accounting, financial, public-relations, and physical plant operations. Right now they are much concerned with the pending problems of automation, which are of arresting proportions in electrical energy.

Moreover, these keepers of the plant possess a sensitivity and retaliatory strength which, in the past decade of political retreat, have been the chief obstacle against the raids of the power monopolists. When public properties and public projects have been attacked these responsible functionaries have struck back promptly. Their official organization, the American Public Power Association, representing more than 700 publicly-owned electric utilities in 39 states, keeps an eye on Washington, D. C., reporting on the latest strategies of the enemy there and elsewhere. In its annual convention in Los Angeles in August, 1956, the association frankly met the public power crises of the hour. In harmony with its opposition to the ill-fated power trust conspiracy to inject—through the notorious Dixon-Yates contract—high-cost private monopoly power into the TVA system, it condemned the Idaho Power Company's maneuvers, later successful, to prevent Congressional appropriation for the building of a high multiple-purpose federal dam in Hells Canyon on the Snake River. It supported Congressional action for public development of power at Niagara Falls, resisting—unfortunately, without success—the move to turn the remaining power potential of the Falls over to five interlaced private power companies. In a score of unanimously adopted resolutions the association urged Congressional action to rescue beleaguered public properties, large and small, across the nation.

Next to the keepers of the plant in its direct interest in public power development and operation is the electrical industry (as distinguished from the private power corporations which are the chief support of the power lobby): the manufacturers of the costly power plant equipment and the plethora of appliances for homes, factories, commercial establishments. For such capital goods and consumer commodities the public power domain is a major market in which sales range from generators of the 1,500-ton magnitude of the Northwest's Grand Coulee plant down to toasters and light globes. The electrical industry is now engaged in the production of turbine generators and the auxiliary installations for 37 new public dams under construction—almost a doubling of the present federal plant capacity of 8,293,520 kilowatts. Neither General Electric nor Westinghouse is on public record as objecting. Because of low electric rates and the skillful exploitation of the advantages of domestic appliance use 62 per cent of TVA area's electrified homes have electric ranges as compared to 27 per cent for the nation and 42 per cent have electric water heaters as against a national average of 15 per cent. During the decade following World War II appliance purchases in the TVA area totaled $1.5 billion.

The major benefits from public power, however, are not to those who sell capital goods to the public power authority— the electrical, cement, steel, aluminum, or copper industry— nor to those who sell commodities to its customers. The major benefits are to the purchasers of the authority's product, electric energy, and to the economy which indirectly gains thereby. Residential consumers in the TVA area paid $40,000,000 less for their electricty during the fiscal year ended June 30, 1955, than they would have paid if average rates prevailing over the nation had been charged. This release of purchasing power in itself would have proved a welcome stimulus to business activity but, when joined to the attraction of new industry which TVA's low power rates have demonstrably brought, it becomes the basis for an almost unbelievable economic and social expansion and change.

Net increases in manufacturing in the TVA area since 1929 are reported by Alex Radin, APPA general manager, to number 1,600 plants. Employment opportunities in manufacturing establishments increased 72 per cent between 1929 and 1950 as against a nationwide increase of 41 per cent. The purchasing power of the area for consumer goods increased for the year,

1952, to $5,900,000,000—about $1,650,000,000 more than it would have been if the per capita income of the area had moved upward no faster than in the nation as a whole. This meant an increase in the purchase of food produced in the Middle West, Far West, Florida and elsewhere by $440,000,000. It meant the spending of $110,000,0000 more for the purchase and operation of automobiles than would have been spent if only the national rate of income increase had been maintained. It can be seriously argued that if TVA's power rate base and low domestic rates were to be suddenly wiped out tomorrow by surrender to the private power monopoly the economy of the area would be wrecked, with disruptive repercussions throughout the nation.

Unquestionably the power authority's wide penetration of the capitalist order and its easy acceptance by surrounding private enterprise has done much to strengthen the case for public ownership. It has banished the bogey man—it is a proven source of benefit next door. Nevertheless public power today is in the greatest peril of its existence. It is under assault not only from private power company bludgeoning and propaganda flooding press, radio, and television at an annual cost of more than a million dollars. It is, in addition, the target of the entire sector of monopoly capital, now politically organized against "Big Government" in any financial or industrial realm. Oil, coal, steel, transport, insurance, the banks—a complex of the profiteering trusts—are all in the fray, concentrating first against public power. Their proud standard bearer is the Eisenhower Administration, supported by a bi-partisan Congressional majority in an obvious determination to destroy the most vital legacy of the Roosevelt New Deal: the Interior Department's resource-conservation and resource-expansion policies. Here are the enemy objectives:

1. No more publicly owned and publicly operated power dams, whether single or multiple purpose.

2. This failing, isolated Congressional appropriations for water development projects into which private power is tied in either of two ways: (a) the power plant to be built into the dam structure by private capital and owned by private capital with rights of lasting ownership by private capital or (b) the power plant to be built by the government and turned over to the private company on a long-term basis. This "appropria-

tion approach", it is to be noted, by passes the Interior Department's troublesome Reclamation Bureau, which has not only protected the public distribution systems (cities, public utility districts, rural co-operatives) in their right to purchase publicly generated power ahead of the profiteering private companies but has doggedly enforced the 160-acre limitation on water rights in defense of the family size farm and its citizen operators. Thus the "appropriations approach" opens the way for outrageous land speculation on the one hand and, on the other, for the creation of semi-feudal agricultural holdings worked by impoverished tenants and stoop-labor hirelings.

3. In lieu of the above two objectives, the hypocritical partnership. The government will build and operate the multiple-purpose dam, generating and delivering the efficiently produced low-cost power exclusively to the private company, which will then distribute it to the ultimate consumer at the old-time exorbitant private monopoly profit.

The only force that can avert the threatened economic and social catastrophe is the power of an aroused people, a political movement that will embrace the working populations of cities and towns and their logical allies, the farmers and business and professional folk of "the free enterprise" world. For the leadership of such a coalition the keepers of the plant (management and operating personnel) are—despite their privately stated virtues—distinctly inadequate. They are a-political and a-social. They decline to relate their key economic role to historic transitions. They fight their battles as holding actions only. They will not go on the offensive—they will not declare war.

Their eminent spokesmen are on record as being opposed to "nationalization of the power industry" (or, for that matter, any other industry) and as declaring that "the electric industry is big enough for private and public power". They would maintain public power with all its economic and social stimuli in the Tennessee Valley but would leave New England floundering without hope in the stagnation of private monopoly exploitation.

If the potential of public power and its chief instrumentality, the authority, is to be realized, the leadership of the new political movement must project public ownership as the means of economic penetration and transformation—a daring and comprehensive program around the public authority that will fire the imagination of the entire nation.

Its demands should stress revision and broadening of the authority concept to cover not only power—hydro-electric, steam-generated (whether derived from coal, oil or atom) and combustion-produced—but the whole range of captive monopoly industries in the United States, each under an authority of its own. This governing body, a public corporation, set up by constitutional legislative action, either of nation or state, should be given *carte blanche* to engage in any business necessary to fulfill its general welfare scope. Such authorization is by no means without precedent—the California-granted charter of the City of Los Angeles, as one instance, confers such power.

In harmony with the American scene the particular authority covering power, it would seem, should be of two types: national, governed by a commission appointed by the president of the United States and officially represented in the president's cabinet; and state, operated by a commission whose members preferably (as in the case of Nebraska's state-wide Consumers' Public Power District) are elected by constituent districts on a non-partisan basis and for fixed terms.

The responsibility of the national power authority would be the maximum public development of hydro-electric energy, together with flood control, irrigation, navigation, etc., in every river system of the United States. Complementary development of steam-generated electricity (coal- and oil-derived) is, of course, implied. Steam-generated electricity, *atom-derived,* since it is still in the realm of experimentation, might well remain the business of another governmental agency.

The obligation of maximum public development necessarily involves a repudiation of the Eisenhower Administration's plan for "partnership" with the power trust. Maximum development cannot be achieved without invasion of the inefficient and under-developed power trust empires and the purchase of their utility properties through condemnation proceedings or negotiation and on the basis of physical value only; and, if this proves impossible, the duplication of their power plants and the paralleling of their distribution lines for an all-out and final competitive struggle.

As for the state power authority, its function (also aimed at exclusive control in its field) would be the supplementation and coordination of the activities of the municipalities, public utility districts and rural co-operatives.

In any advocacy of these militant objectives the fact must be emphasized that hydro is still the cheapest power available, with only 20 per cent of its potential developed in the nation. Moreover, with its multiple-purpose dams, it is the conservationist's well deserved darling. It implements the drifting ocean mists, rains and snows upon mountain and plain. It does not waste our natural resources but helps to build them. In this connection, it is well to note that the Soviet Union, aware of the importance of cheap hydro at the base of its economy, is literally making over its European and Asian maps by damming rivers, large and small, and transforming them into inland seas.

One of the major purposes of the expanded power authority would be to develop and test out a rounded, integrated, socially planned and socially operated regional economy. Thus, under the revised concept, the authority in charge in the Tennessee Valley would not be limited to the fields of hydro generation and distribution, flood control, irrigation, forestation, recreation. It would, of course, continue to manage its socially created water ways (a function which enabled TVA in 1954 to save shippers using the Tennessee River instead of rails $14,-000,000 in transportation charges). But it would go beyond that—in the interest of further savings, it would own and operate the harbors and the transport systems upon those water ways.

Such an expanded authority would grow forests, not only for conservation ends, but for timber to be converted into lumber in its own mills for the building of the people's homes and for sale on the market. It would own and operate the region's mass transportation system, including a set-up for collecting and delivering the raw and the co-operatively processed products from the region's family-size farms for sale in the municipal markets. It would provide regional banks for the easy extension of credit to rural co-operatives, consumer co-operatives, and individual farmers and business men.

The scientific methods of the authority would transform community wastes into community wealth, possibly at an over-all profit, and would forever end the current defilement of earth, streams, lakes, sea and air by private greed and political incompetence. An ample community health service would be open to all at cost. Old-age security benefits would be generous and compulsory. Of course, the authority would own and operate the regional communications systems, telegraph, telephone, radio and television, with full freedom of public discussion guaranteed over the latter two media. The conscious purpose would be to shape the region into a convenient, safe and attractive community that would stand out with withering effect against that monstrous excrescence, the smog-ridden, filth-exuding, congestion-cursed megalopolis. Thus the authority would play an important part in the badly needed redistribution of the population, as well as the income, of the United States.

Since the authority liquidates its investment debt as it goes, from operating revenues, it is an absurdity that an extraneous political body such as the United States Congress should dictate the rate of its expansion by requiring—as at present in the case of TVA—legislative appropriations for such purpose. The revised authority would have independent power to issue its own revenue bonds in amounts adequate to meet the needs of growth.

There are at least two convincing reasons why the development and use of nuclear power for peaceful purposes should be the exclusive responsibility of public agencies, either national or state.

The first is that such development and use—divorced, though they be, from the ends of destruction—are loaded with danger to the human race. No irresponsible private interest with an eye single to profits should locate, operate and control any of its plants, whether experimental "pilot" or nuclear reactor in going industrial production. The risk of accidental leakages of radio-activity is still here to menace both plant workers and surrounding populations. Furthermore, from the view-point of love and care of this earth home of ours, both its land and its water, and of future generations that are entitled to it unpolluted by greed (not to mention freedom from dread of gene mutations), there is as yet no satisfactory long-range answer to the problem of the disposal of the ultimate wastes: the contaminated plant equipment and the radio-active materials that have passed the limit of effective use and must be discarded.

The second reason for government "monopoly" is that, while atomic power, because of greater cost, is not immediately feasible in countries with ample hydro-electric resources, its use will nevertheless be mandatory within several decades unless science and engineering open up fresh sources of non-depletable cheap energy such as the sun, tides, ocean currents. According to a January 1, 1953, report of the federal power commission, if the hydro-electric resources of the country were at present totally (instead of 20 per cent) developed, they would yield an annual generation of 491 billion kilowatt hours. But this amount, according to an October, 1955, report of the commission, would only scantily exceed the total load demand of 447.9 billion kilowatt hours for the year 1954. The commission estimates that by 1975 the total annual power requirements of the country will mount to 1,419.5 billion kilowatt hours. Imperative as is the need for immediate development of hydro and inexcusable as is the present delay, it is obvious that this source of power cannot contribute importantly to a final solution of the shortage problem.

It is a certainty that basic power, upon which the operation of the entire economy rests, is due for disruptive shifts, if not painful constriction, during the remainder of the twentieth century. There is eminent backing for the prediction that oil and pressurized gas will be off the scene in the '70's; that coal will have disappeared as a fundamental fuel, supplanted temporarily by coal-derived fluids; that uranium and the split atom will thereafter rapidly take over a field in which hydro will play a shrinking role.

Theoretically the shift to uranium and nuclear fission should bring increased security. As a world resource the nuclear fuels boast twenty times the magnitude of the doomed conventional fossil fuels. Actually, however, there is no ground for social optimism. For atomic power is seemingly on the way to complete private monopoly and its extortionate toll upon the industrial order with the inevitable result of curtailed use.

What are the pertinent developments as to peaceful use of atomic energy under present national policy? Despite the flurry of rebellion in the first session of the 85th Congress against the "sell-out" program of the Atomic Energy Commission, the national government is still effectively prevented from extending its "know how" through wide-scale experimentation in this new field (nuclear reactor "pilots") and it has no program for the launching of government-owned and government-operated commercial plants based on such acquired information. President Eisenhower, with his specious "partnership" pronouncements, dominates the field of battle.

It is true that the 1957 Congress passed legislation emanating from its Joint Atomic Energy Committee which authorized the construction of two experimental reactor plants (one at Hanford, Washington, and the other at Arco, Idaho) and appropriated the necessary funds—but Senator Gore's "crash program" of six nuclear reactors of varying types and in widely separated locations went to the dump heap. The important consideration is that the licensing system, riveted on the nation by the Atomic Energy Act of 1954, still controls. The business of developing atomic energy for peaceful purposes will be farmed out systematically to private corporations. This is straight betrayal of the public interest.

The inevitable effect of this fundamental policy of the Eisenhower Administration is hailed with enthusiasm by the private power interests. The *Los Angeles Times,* voluble spokesman for this group, foresees with ill-concealed delight the day, perhaps not fifty years away, when the hydro-electric plants of TVA and the network of similar governmental agencies "will produce only an insignificant part of the power the country will need" and the atom (property of the power trust) will "turn most of the wheels in America".

Against such crippling private exploitation of the whole American economy the nation's public ownership forces must be set to work. The situation calls for a bolder program than Senator Gore's isolated six nuclear reactor plants. The first demand of this program must be the prompt abolition of the system of licenses and the second the promulgation of a new national policy whose objective will be the feeding of ample atomic power into the steadily expanding network of public power systems as rapidly as such power justifies itself economically. To accomplish this, nuclear reactors in adequate number and size should be built and operated by the envisioned national atomic energy authority. There is no moral or economic ground for special interest monopoly in any part of this field. The economic order in which all of us must live is entitled to— and, in self-defense, must have—power at cost of production, shorn of profit to any limited class.

But the national atomic energy authority should be charged with wider responsibility than the development of atomic energy solely for power purposes, basic though that be. The authority should at once embrace the plan of Nebraska's Consumers' Public Power District for the realization of the indirect as well as the direct benefits of atomic fission. These indirect benefits include the by-products of the nuclear reactor plant: the "spent fuel elements" (rods of uranium) which, during the cooling off process ("decay of radio-activity") can be used to sterilize and preserve food products such as pre-packaged meats, fresh vegetables, flour, milk, eggs, cheese. Additional by-products not to be overlooked are the radioisotopes, which open up to medical science a new wonder world for human service.

The above are only a few of the more pressing fields in which "socialist solutions"—action by public ownership—are plainly indicated. A cursory glance at today's financial and industrial set-ups will suggest many others.

Rail transportation, anarchistic and obsolescent, is in need of re-organziation and revitalization. A nation-wide transport authority should take over this job, beginning with the weakest links, and weld a system that will open up, on a logical cost basis, the markets of the land to the producers of both capital goods and consumer commodities. The same re-organization and revitalization should be undertaken for the heavily subsidized ocean transport and the airlines and, by the local authorities, for the mass transport systems of the nation's great cities, practically all of which are disintegrating under the greed and stupidity of the system's owners. There are other crippled enterprises and services—notably among them, coal—which for the general welfare should come under authority rule.

But the need is perhaps greatest in the areas of highest profits pre-empted by the big monopolists of oil, steel, insurance, finance, the war enterprises—important among the last-named, aircraft manufacture.

In all the comprehensive studies of our economy's weaknesses from Henry Demarest Lloyd to Harvey O'Connor oil stands out as outrageously wasteful, inefficient and conscienceless. The November, 1956, campaign in California around a so-called oil "conservation" measure (Propositon No. 4 on the ballot) disclosed both sides to the controversy (the "independents" and the "monopoly") to be concerned solely with profits, short- or long-range, and incompetent to conceive any over-all program for the cautious and orderly development and use of this fast-dwindling natural resource. The national authority here advocated would take over this jungle of private enterprise, pool by pool, for the production of oil and its finished products and ration out these commodities at cost for the general welfare. Such a nationalization program, it is important to note, would prove a powerful factor in removing the threat of war continuously arising from oil imperialism's attempted dictation of politics in the Middle East and elsewhere.

Steel, too, lies at the base of industry. Its nationalization would have a stimulating effect upon the entire business world. The steel authority's lowered costs of non-profit production would beneficially affect not only the varied categories of capital goods (heavy and light machines) but the multiplicity of articles fabricated by private enterprise for sale in the consumer markets. Lowered prices—as in the case of TVA and public power generally—would release purchasing power in every direction.

Particularly is it important that the war economy be invaded by the appropriate public authority. Unless the peoples of the earth fail in their demands for a peaceful world—unless final tragedy encompasses us all—the manufacturing, testing and stock-piling of atomic weapons must be stopped. This is the authority's first job. Its next is the taking over of this sector's subsidized "free enterprise" corporations and their operation, if they are usefully creative, not for national pillage, but for public benefit. This means, among other things, the nationalization of airplane research and production.

It is a fact to be welcomed and not deplored, as must be emphasized again and again, that every penetration by public ownership of a new monopoly capital field will result in the birth of additional private enterprises, mostly of small dimensions. These, when and if the need arises, can be socially absorbed through voluntary co-operation or action by the authority.

The anti-monopoly social programs urged above can be achieved, as stated, only through a militant movement of the people embracing the workers of cities and towns and their logical allies, the farmers and business and professional folk of the "free enterprise" world. In its beginnings this movement functions through propaganda accompanied by direct presssures upon the existing political organizations and the state. But such activity is inadequate for major accomplishment. It would soon become apparent that the commitments to the *status quo* of the "old parties", and of the state which they dominate, rule them out as agents of a changing order.

Specifically as to the Democratic Party, the fallacy of any strategy of invasion and capture must never be obscured. Adventures of this sort by American radicals have uniformly failed —the "capturers" wind up the "captured". A notable example is Upton Sinclair's EPIC campaign (1913-14), which took over the Democratic Party in California and was dissipated in factional struggle. Another was the attempt of the Middle-of-the-Road Populists in 1896 to appropriate William Jennings Bryan and indoctrinate his Democratic following through "fusion", the result of which was the annihilation of the "fusionists".

In its preliminary phase the rising socialist party is necessarily engaged in doctrinal inquiry, discussion and debate: in self-education. But, unless it moves out of this involvement into the living world, eager for impact upon the society around it, it will shrivel and die without fruit. Through democratic techniques and democratic political victory it must try, with all its might, to assume direction of the existing state and the going economy.

In the parliamentary democracies, in which a large measure of civil liberties is either already realized or within the grasp of a determined people, the major function of a successful socialist party is clearly indicated. It must strive for genuine statesmanship. Its representatives in office—largely legislators, at first—must be persistent planners of the coming commonwealth, tireless advocates of social exploration. They must be ready with practical blue prints and road maps for setting governmental agencies at work in strange fields.

Facing the national threat of mass unemployment and conscious of the devastating role of private profit in a monopoly-capitalist society, the socialist leadership must strike at soundly chosen points for the elimination of profiteering and the expansion of the workers' share of the national income. Among other things it might, for example, seriously propose two five-billion-dollar projects for the development of water and power with the attendant flood-control, irrigation, navigation, and conservation benefits: one for the Missouri River Valley and the other for the Columbia. And these proposals could be genuine lessons in economics. They could spell out for the people the meaning in dollars: first, of the huge capital-goods and construction-labor investment in the proposed plants, and second, of the savings, and therefore of the increased purchasing power, of the people from reduced charges for water, power, and transportation. Not, of course, overlooking the highly significant fact that these socialist projects, while vitalizing the economy, would at the same time be retiring their investment debt.

In a realistic move for world peace the socialist leadership could well isue a spectacular factual report exposing the fallacy of the "permanent war economy" as an asurance of full employment. Such a report might establish, through a study of the war economy's outrageous profits, its tax burdens upon the masses, and the resulting contraction of purchasing power; that the over-all effect of war-economy operations is not the multiplication of jobs, but their destruction; not to mention the highly inflammatory concentration of wealth and political mastery around the Pentagon. On such a basis the new popular advocates would be able successully to propose the scrapping of the war plants or their transformation into government-operated enterprises of social value.

Fortunately, there is no end to this sort of specific approach.

Are we, then, still out to "abolish capitalism"? Certainly, but not through a single flaming proclamation or push-button decree; rather through ceaseless exploration, strategic penetration and transformation. What are the most likely points of entry? And how can entry best be effected? These are the questions that must command and absorb the attention of the emerging peoples party.

The under-lying strategy of this program of public ownership is that of an economy functioning in unbroken line through social change in which the citizen—and not the dictator—makes the great decisions. This strategy rejects the dogma of abject misery as the necessary forerunner and precipitant of social advance. It accepts the world-shaking premise that the path of revolution, if wisely chosen and courgaeously pursued, leads not through catastrophe, violence and bloodshed but through ever increasing prosperity and security for the common man.

The Negro and Socialism

By W. E. B. Du Bois

THE UNITED STATES, which would like to be regarded as a democracy devoted to peace, finds itself today making the greatest preparations for war of any nation on earth and holding elections where citizens have no opportunity to vote for the policies which they prefer.

What are the causes of this contradictory situation? First, we know that our main reason in preparing for war is the fact that slowly but surely socialism has spread over the world and become a workable form of government. Today for the first time in history the majority of mankind live under socialist regimes, either complete socialism as in the Soviet Union and China, or partial socialism as in India and Scandinavia. Most Ameri cans profess to believe that this spread of socialism is mainly the result of a conspiracy led by the Soviet Union and abetted by a section of American citizens. For fear of this group, we have curtailed democratic government, limited civil liberties, and planned war on a gigantic scale.

The spread of socialism in the last one hundred years is unquestionably a fact. It stemmed from growing protest against

---

WILLIAM EDWARD BURGHARDT DU BOIS was born in 1868, reared in New England and educated at Fisk, Harvard, and the University of Berlin. He was one of the incorporators of the National Association for Advancement of the Colored People; has been an aggressive proponent of peace among all the nations; a progressive political leader—active in support or the national Progressive Party in 1948, and American Labor Party candidate for the U. S. Senate from New York, in 1950. Dr. Du Bois has published fifteen volumes, including "The Suppression of the African Slave Trade to the United States of America", "The Souls of Black Folk", "Black Reconstruction", "The World and Africa", "In Battle for Peace", and "The Ordeal of Mansart".

that tremendous expansion of business enterprise which followed the French revolution. This private initiative and economic anarchy resulted in the factory system, which stemmed
from the American slave trade, the sugar empire and the cotton
kingdom. All this was concurrent with such suffering and degradation among the laboring masses that by the end of the nine-
tenth century there was harldy a man of thought and feeling,
scarcely a scientist nor an artist, who did not believe that socialism must eventually supplant unbridled private capitalism, or
civilization would die.

All over the earth since the Civil War in America, socialism
has grown and spread and become more and more definite. It
has emerged from dream and doctrinaire fantasy such as charac-
terized Fourier and St. Simon into the rounded doctrine of Karl
Marx and finally into the socialist states of Lenin and Mao Tse-
tung. In all this struggling advance lay the central idea that
men must work for a living, but that the results of their work
must not mainly be to support privileged persons and concen-
trate power in the hands of the owners of wealth; that the welfare of the mass of people should be the main object of government.

To ensure this end the conviction grew that government
must increasingly be controlled by the governed; that the mass
of people, increasing in intelligence, with incomes sufficient to
live a good and healthy life, should control all government,
and that they would be able to do this by the spread of science
and scientific technique, acess to truth, the use of reason, and
freedom of thought and of creative impulse in art and literature.

The difficulty of accomplishing this lay in the current culture
patterns—in repressive religious dogmas, and in the long inculcated belief that nothing better than private ownership and
control of capital could be planned, with human nature as it is.

Democratic control, therefore, while it increased, tended to
be narrowly political rather than economic. It had to do with
the selection of officials rather than with work and income.
Discovery of new natural forces and of increased use of machines
with intricate industrial techniques tended to put land, labor,
and the ownership of capital and wealth into control of the few
who were fortunate or aggressive or unscrupulous and to emphasize a belief that, while the mass of citizens might share in
government by electing officials to administer law, and legisla-

tors might make laws in certain areas of government, the people could not control industry or limit income.

As science increased its mastery of nature and as industry began to use world trade to expand markets, an entirely new problem of government arose. Industry realized that, unless industrial organization largely controlled government, it could not control land and labor, monopolize materials, set prices in the world market, and regulate credit and currency. For this purpose new and integrated world industry arose called "Big Business"—a misleading misnomer. Its significance lay not simply in its size. It was not just little shops grown larger. It was an organized super-government of mankind in matters of work and wages, directed with science and skill for the private profit of individuals. It could not be controlled by popular vote unless that vote was intelligent, experienced, and cast by persons essentially equal in income and power. The overwhelming majority of mankind was still ignorant, sick and poverty stricken.

Repeated and varying devices for keeping and increasing democratic control over industry and wealth were regularly rendered useless by the superior training and moral unscrupulousness of the owners of wealth, as against the ignorance and inexperience of the voters. Bribery of the poorer voters; threats and even violence; fear of the future and organized conspiracy of the interested few against the unorganized many; lying and deftly spread propaganda used race hate, religious dogma and differing family and class interests to ruin democracy. In our own day we have seen that the income tax, designed to place the burden of government expense on property owners in ratio to income, actually lays the heaviest weight of taxation on the low income classes, while the rich individuals and corporations escape with the least proportion of taxes.

When the American farmers and workers revolted against the beginnings of the British colonial system and set out to establish a republic of free and equal citizens, it seemed to most thinking people that a new era in the development of western civilization had begun. Here, beyond the privilege of titled Europe, beyond the deep-seated conditioning of the masses to hereditary inequality and subservience to luxury and display, was to arise a nation of equal men. That equality was to be based on economic opportunity which, as Karl Marx later preached, was the only real equality.

But unfortunately while the United States proclaimed, it never adopted complete equality. First, it prolonged the European recognition of property as more significant than manhood. Then it discovered that theft of land from the Indians was not murder but a method of progress. Next, America reduced the African labor, which rising British commerce had forced on her, to slave status and gained thereby such fabulous income from tobacco, sugar and cotton that Europe became the center of triumphant private capitalism, and the United States its handmaid to furnish free land and cheap labor.

This nation had to fight a Civil War to prevent all American labor from becoming half enslaved. Thus, from 1620 when the Puritans landed until 1865 when slavery was abolished, there was no complete democracy in the United States. This was not only because a large part of the laboring class was enslaved, but also because white labor was in competition with slaves and thus itself not really free.

In the late nineteenth and twentieth centuries, while socialism advanced in the leading European nations and in North America, in most of the world European monopoly of wealth and technique—strengthened by theories of the natural inferiority of most human beings—led to the assumed right of western Europe to rule the world for the benefit and amusement of white people. This theory of world domination was hidden behind the rise of the western working classes, and helped keep democracy and social progress from eastern Europe, Asia, and Africa; from Central and South America, and the islands of the seven seas.

In western Europe a labor movement, and popular education kept forcing increasing numbers of the workers and of the middle classes into a larger share of economic power. But on the other hand, the mass of colored labor, and white labor in backward Latin and Slavic lands, were reduced to subordinate social status so that increased profit from their land and labor helped to maintain the high profits and high wages of industry in Western Europe and North America. Also it was easy there to hire white soldiers to keep "niggers", "chinks", "dagoes", and "hunkies" in their places. This was the essence of colonial imperialism. It was industry organized on a world scale, and holding most of mankind in such economic subjection as would return the largest profit to the owners of wealth.

Meantime, the new effort to achieve socialism, fathered by Karl Marx and his successors, increased. It declared that even before the mass of workers were intelligent and experienced enough themselves to conduct modern industry, industrial guidance might be furnished them by a dictatorship of their own intelligent and devoted leaders. As knowledge and efficiency increased, democracy would spread among the masses and they would become capable of conducting a modern welfare state. This social program the world governed by owners of capital regarded as impossible without the dictatorship falling out of their well-meaning hands and into the hands of demagogues. Every sort of force was employed to stop even the attempt to set up such states. Yet the first World War, caused by rivalry over the ownership of colonies, resulted in the effort to start a complete socialist state in Russia; and after the second World War, arising from the same causes as the first, a similar attempt was made in China.

Despite wide and repeated opposition, which used every despicable and criminal method possible, both of these states have become so successful and strong that their overthrow by outside force or inner revolt does not today seem at all likely. Also and meantime, in all leading countries, socialistic legislation steadily increased. It did not creep. It advanced with powerful strides.

This development has emphasized the fight between beleaguered private capitalism and advancing socialism, the Communists pointing out the unnecessary lag of socialization in western lands and the capitalists accusing communism of undemocratic dictatorship.

In order to fight socialism super Big Business, as contrasted with ordinary small business enterprise, had to become itself socialism in reverse. If public welfare instead of private profit became its object, if public officials supplanted private owners, socialistic government would be in control of industry. However, those Americans who hope that the welfare state will thus be realized under a system of private capital are today having the carpet pulled from beneath their feet by the recession of democracy in the United States. This has come about by the repudiation of socialism by organized labor and the consequent refusal of the labor vote to follow even the goals of the New Deal. This surrender of labor has been led by the new industrial South, with favorable climate, cheap labor, and half that labor disfranchised and most of it unorganized. The mass of Southerners do not vote. In the Congressional District where the black boy Till was murdered, there live 400,000 Negroes and 300,000 whites. Yet only 7,000 voters went to the polls to elect the present Congressman. The disfranchisement of the black half of the labor vote in the South keeps Negroes poor, sick, and ignorant. But it also hurts white labor by making democratic government unworkable so long as the South has from three to ten times the voting power of the North and West.

Because of this systematic and illegal disfranchisement, a majority of American voters can often be outvoted by a minority. Laws like the McCarran and Smith Acts can become illegal statutes, because a minority of voters can prevail over a majority. Figures to prove this are easy to adduce, but I only mention now the fact that former Senator Lehman of New York represented the vote of 5 million citizens who went to the polls, while Senator Eastland of Mississippi represented less than 150 thousand voters. Yet Eastland was far more powerful than Lehman.

This loss of democratic control of the government of our nation can be even more clearly demonstrated. There was no effective candidate for the Presidency in the last national election who stood pledged for peace, disarmament, abolition of the draft, lower taxes, recognition of the right of the Soviet Union and China to have the government which they choose and for stopping our effort to force other nations to do as we want them to do. Not only did we have no chance to decide our foreign policy, but we were equally helpless in deciding our course in domestic affairs. Our system of education is falling to pieces. We need teachers and school houses by the millions, but we cannot have them if we continue making weapons at the present rate and setting our youth to learning death and destruction instead of building, healing, and teaching.

Is this curtailment of democracy the result of knowledge and discussion? On the contrary, knowledge and discussion are today so far curtailed that most men do not even attempt to express their opinions, lest they be accused of treason or conspiracy.

Why is this?

At the very time when the colonial peoples were trying desperately to have food and freedom, powerful Americans became obsessed by the ambition to have North America replace Britain as the empire upon which the sun never dared to set. They demanded high profits and high wages even if the rest of the world starved. In order to restore world rule of organized industry, shaken by war and depression, the United States prefers preparation for universal and continuous world war, until a colonial imperialism in some form is restored under our leadership.

To this program most people of the United States have submitted. How was such submission brought about? Such a national policy found unexpected support in our long encouraged prejudice against people with black or colored skins and against all groups of foreign-born who were not of Anglo-Saxon descent. This provincial point of view, repudiated by science and religion, still remains in America a living and powerful motive guiding our lives and likes. This support of the colonial system by American race prejudice has resulted in our present program of war. How was this accomplished? How have the majority of American people been convinced that preparation for war, suspension of civil liberties and curtailment of democracy are our best paths to progress?

America is an intelligent nation, despite large illiterate groups and the lack of an integrated background of culture. We still have large numbers of the poor and sick, but our average income is far higher than that of most nations. This nation wants to do right, as evidenced by a plethora of churches and a wide and loud profession of religion. If any country is ready for increase of democracy, it is the United States. Yet we are preparing our sons for war, because we actually have been induced to believe that the Soviet Union is behind a world-wide criminal conspiracy to destroy the United States and that socialism is the result. The statement is so fantastic that most foreign peoples cannot conceive how it can be true that we really accept this fairy tale.

To restore our lost opportunity to make huge profit on private investment in Russia, the Balkans, and particularly in China, Big Business has restricted and guided public access to truth. It has dominated news gathering, monopolized the press and limited publishing. By fear of losing employment, by secret police and high pay to informers, often confessed liars; by control of education and limitation of radio and television and censorship of the drama—by all these methods and others, the public opinion of the nation has been forced into one iron channel of disaster.

In order to let the nation return to normal sanity we must realize that socialism is not a crime nor a conspiracy, but the path of progress toward which the feet of all mankind are set. Some of the greatest intellectual leaders of our era have been advocates of socialism: Charles Kingsley, Leo Tolstoi, Edward Bellamy, William Morris, Henry George, Robert Owen, Bernard Shaw, Sidney and Beatrice Webb, Kier Hardie, H. G. Wells, Harold Laski. The footsteps of the long oppressed and staggering masses are not always straight and sure, but their mistakes can never cause the misery and distress which the factory system caused in Europe, colonial imperialism caused in Asia and Africa, and which slavery, lynching, disfranchisement, and Jim-Crow legislation have caused in the United States.

Our way out of this impasse is straight and clear and as old as the struggle of freedom for the mind of man: Americans must face the facts at all costs. Walking with determination through a morass of deliberate distortion, we must insist on the right to know the truth, to discuss it and to listen to its interpretation by men of intelligence and honesty; we must restore to all citizens their civil rights and the right to vote, no matter whether they are Negroes, Communists, or naturalized foreign-born. We must insist that our foreign policy as well as our domestic problems and especially our problem of industry, be subjects on which we shall have the right to vote.

Meantime, we are prisoners of propaganda. The people of the United States have become completely sold to that method of conducting industry which has been so powerful and triumphant in the world for two centuries that Americans regard it as the only normal way of life. We regard the making of things and their purchase and sale for private profit as the chief end of living. We look on painting and poetry as harmless play. We regard literature as valuable only as handmaiden to industry. We teach Business as a science when it is only an art of legal theft. We regard advertising as a profession even when it teaches the best way to lie. We consider the unselfish sacrifice of one to the progress of all as wasted effort. Wealth is the height of human ambition even when we have no idea of how to spend it, except to make more wealth or to waste it in harmful or useless ostentation. We want high profits and high wages even if most of the world starves.

Putting aside questions of right, and suspecting all our neighbors of being as selfish as we ourselves are, we have adopted a creed of wholesale selfishness. We believe that, if all people work for their own selfish advantage, the whole world will be the best of possible worlds. This is the rat race upon which we are set, and we are suspicious and afraid of folk who oppose this program and plead for the old kindliness, the new use of power and machine for the good of the unfortunate and the welfare of all the world of every race and color. We can and do give charity abundantly, particularly when we are giving away money or things which we cannot ourselves use. We give to beggars but we hate the beggars who recoil from begging. This is what stands back of our murderous war preparation as well as back of our endless itch to be rich. At any cost, or in any way, this is our reason for living, gambling on radio, on stock exchange or on race track is our way of life.

The power of wealth and private industry extends itself over education, literature and art and we live in fear, with a deliberately low standard of culture, lest democracy displace monopoly of wealth in the control of the state.

One of the devastating effects of our current education on our youth is the training of them by military officials. They are indoctrinated by propaganda against socialism, by ridicule for their attachment to their mothers, and with disrespect for all women. They learn to kill and destroy, and force as a social method of progress is extolled. Small wonder that what we call "juvenile delinquency" increases among us.

One of the contradictions of our day is our argument about the distribution of property and the relative size of incomes, at a time when secrecy as to the truth about these matters is a matter of official compulsion, and most carefully guarded on the ground that a man's income is his private business and the ownership of property concerns the owner primarily. These propositions are false and ridiculous. The distribution of income is a public affair since it is increasingly the result of public function. Property is a matter of state control, permitted to rest in private hands only so long as it is of public benefit that it should so rest. For any reasonable thought or action concerning property, there should come first open information as to its ownership. Without that, no science or ethic of wealth is possible. We can only guess madly and conclude erroneously. Taking the meager guesswork of the United States census, as some approximation of the truth: it is clear that the poor are still with us in this rich land.

There are nearly 40 per cent of our families who receive less than $2,000 a year and over six million of our 46-½ million families receive less than $500. In addition to this there is a psychological poverty, in some ways more frightening than actual lack of income: there is the great number of artisans, white collar workers and professional men who could live plainly on their incomes but who skimp and borrow and gamble, and sometimes steal to "keep up with the Joneses"; who drive a car and spend too little on food and medicine; who buy fur coats and crowd into one room. American culture is made uneasy and insane by the millions among us who expect in some way to get flamboyantly rich and cannot be satisfied with that simple life which all experience teaches is the finest and best.

Especially must American Negroes, awaking from their present fear and lethargy, reassert that leadership in the American world of culture which Phillis Wheatly began in the eighteenth century, Frederick Douglass led in the nineteenth, and James Weldon Johnson and Carter Woodson advanced in the twentieth. American Negroes must study socialism, its rise in Europe and Asia, and its peculiar suitability for the emancipation of Africa. They must realize that no system of reform offers the American Negro such real emancipation as socialism. The capitalism which so long ruled Europe and North America was founded on Negro slavery in America, and that slavery will never completely disappear so long as private capitalism continues to survive.

The fight to preserve racial segregation along the color line in the United States only helps to drive the American Negro that much faster into the arms of socialism. The movement of the whole nation toward the welfare state, and away from the concept of private profit as the only object of industry, is bound to show itself sooner or later in the whole nation. But if the Negro tenth of the nation is forced ahead by color discrimination, the socialization of the nation will come that much sooner. Consider the situation: there are today about 16 million Americans of admitted Negro descent. They are by reason of this descent subjected to public insult, loss of opportunity to work according to ability or to receive wages level with white work-

ers; most of these people are disfranchised and segregated in
education, travel, civil rights and public recreation. Ten million of these Negroes are poor, receiving less than $50 a week
per family. Half of them cannot read or write. They live mostly
in the rural districts and small towns of the former slave states,
whence their efforts to escape are hindered by law, mob violence,
and scarcity of places of refuge which welcome or give them
work or places to live.

Above this depressed 10 million are 4 million Negroes who
are economically insecure and on the edge of poverty. They work
as laborers and servants in the towns and cities. They can read
and write, but among them are a class of criminals. Next come
1½ million middle class Negroes living in cities. They have education and property and are engaged in semi-skilled work and
white collar jobs. Many are trained in the better paid work of
personal service, some are teachers and ministers of religion. Out
of this group have come the leading intelligentsia. At the economic apex of this middle economic group are a half million
Negroes who are well-to-do, receiving at least $10,000 a year.
They are professional and business men, civil servants and public entertainers. They have good, sometimes elaborate homes,
motor cars and servants. They live mostly in the larger cities.

When discussing American Negroes, one must distinguish
among these classes. Southerners raving about the degradation
of Negroes are usually talking about their disfranchised and exploited serfs. Negroes talking of their progress are usually
referring to their bourgeoisie. But the Negro intelligentsia must
ask how it happens that in free, rich America so many Negroes
must be poor, sick and ignorant while in Communist Russia,
peasants who were emancipated at nearly the same time as
Negroes, live without poverty, with universal education and with
national attack on disease? Why is it that the Chinese coolie,
who recently was as low as the Negro slave, is today a man in his
own country, with the blood-sucking whites driven out? Every
effort is made in America to suppress this line of thought among
Negroes; but as thought in America regains its lost freedom,
as democracy begins to replace plutocracy, the social thought
of the nation will find increasing support from Negroes.

Even before such freedom comes, the segregated Negro
group will increasingly be forced toward socialistic methods to
solve their inner problems. They will unite in boycotts as in
Montgomery, Alabama; they will turn to consumers' coopera-

tion; a new Negro literature must soon burst out of prison bonds and it will find in socialism practically its only voice. Negro schools and colleges, so long as students are excluded from public education, will become centers of thought where the Soviet Union and China cannot escape intelligent discussion.

The modern rise of Africans in the twentieth century to self-expression and organized demand for autonomy and freedom was due in large part to the Pan-African movement started by American Negroes. Today every part of Africa has a national congress fighting for the ends which the Pan-American movement started in 1919. Further leadership of Africa by black America has been stopped—but too late. Already the Africans have their own leaders, and these leaders like Nkrumah and Aziwiki are quite aware of the Soviet Union and China and are building their new nations on socialist lines.

Moreover as the mass of the colored peoples of the world move toward socialism in Asia and Africa, it is inevitable that they influence American Negroes. I had long hoped that American Negroes would lead this procession because of their chances for education. But "philanthropy", disguised in bribes, and "religion" cloaked in hypocrisy, strangled Negro education and stilled the voices of prophets. The yellow, brown and black thinkers of Asia have forged ahead. But nevretheless the black folk of America will hear their voices and, what is more compelling, will see their outstanding success. On March 6, 1957, when ancient Ghana was reborn in West Africa, American Negroes realized how far toward socialism this group of black folk had gone. Soon, too, socialism in the black Sudan, in East Africa, the Belgian Congo and South Africa will place the Black world in the train of Soviet Russia, China, and India and tear loose from the allegiance, which American Negroes try now to profess, to the dictatorship of wealth in the United States.

One thing and one alone keeps socialism from growing even more rapidly than it is—that is fear of war and especially of attack by the Soviet Union and China. Most of our vast national income is being spent for preparation for such war and we have but small funds left for education, health and water development and control which we so sorely need. The frantic and continual cultivation of the national fear goes on just as the danger of war decreases. The class structure of our nation grows tremendously at the very time that our prapagandists are fiercely denying it. We have a privileged class of men with more income than

they can possibly spend and more power than they can hire
brains to use. In the guise of idle rich, with trained executives
and with a vast and useless military organization throwing away
the taxes piled on the workers, this ruling clique outrivals the
aristocracy of George III or Louis XIV. We have a middle class
of white collar workers, technicians, artisans, artists, professional
men and teachers able to live in comfort so long as they restrict
their thought and planning, and deceive themselves in thinking they will sometime join the "independently" rich.

Our last presidential election was a farce. We had no chance
to vote for the questions in which we were really interested:
Peace, Disarmament, the Draft, unfair taxation, race bias, education, social medicine, and flood control. On the contrary we had
before us one ticket under two names and the nominees shadow-
boxed with false fanfare and advertisement for the same policies,
with infinitesimal shades of difference and with spurious earnest-
ness. Small wonder that half of the American voters stayed
home.

Thus it is clear today that the salvation of American Negroes
lies in socialism. They should support all measures and men
who favor the welfare state; they should vote for government
ownership of capital in industry; they should favor strict regulation of corporations or their public ownership; they should vote
to prevent monopoly from controlling the press and the publishing of opinions. They should favor public ownership and control of water, electric, and atomic power; they should stand for
a clean ballot, the encouragement of third parties, independent
candidates, and the elimination of graft and gambling on television and even in churches.

The question of the method by which the socialist state can
be achieved must be worked out by experiment and reason and
not by dogma. Whether or not methods which were right and
clear in Russia and China fit our circumstances is for our intelligence to decide. The atom bomb has revolutionized our
thought. Peace is not only preferable today, it is increasingly
inevitable. Passive resistance is not the end of action, but the
beginning. After refusing to fight, there is the question how to
live. The Negro church which stops discrimination against bus
riders must next see how those riders can earn a decent living
and not remain helplessly exploited by those who own busses
and make jim-crow laws. This may well be a difficult program,
but it is the only one.

The Farmers and Independent Political Action

By Homer Ayers

THE POPULATION LIVING on farms has dwindled to less than 14 percent of the total, but their political direction is of tremendous importance to workers, middle class groups and all those who would like to help bring about a socialist America. In addition to the actual farmers, there are perhaps 15 percent of our population in small towns or in cities working at jobs directly dependent on servicing a mechanized agriculture. Tied economically to farmers, these town and city folk may well identify politically with the outlook of the farmers themselves.

It is important for progressives today to understand the background and tradition that made for rural radicalism, and for its perversion at times, if they hope to organize a pro-socialist movement with a tune people will recognize. For this reason I will dwell on background more than on programmatic schemes for a future which might be at quite a distance.

The United States actually has several agricultural regions, each with different backgrounds and problems. The South with its background of slavery and its special problems is highly important, as the issue of civil rights and integration is tied to the whole plantation system of exploitation. The Far West, where truck and garden farming has been established on a

HOMER AYERS is a South Dakota sheep rancher and cattleman. His grandfather was a Greenbacker, his father a Populist and Non-Partisan Leaguer. He has long been a member of the Farmer's Union; was formerly editor of the *Iowa Union Farmer;* a columnist of the *Federated Press,* and is the author of numerous pamphlets. In addition to his activities among the farmers of the Middle West, Mr. Ayers was for some years the director of farmer-labor relations for the Farm Equipment Workers of America.

"factory on the farm" scale, is another problem. The New England pattern based on dairy and poultry farming, and gardening, is another. The great Middle West, the bread basket of the nation, is a key region that bears special attention.

Living as I do in the Middle West I propose to base most of my observations on the problems and background of this region, with cursory references to other regions from time to time. It was in the Middle West that farmers developed a radical tradition. It was here that the Free Soil Movement flourished before the Civil War; and it was the Free Soilers who sparked the newly formed Republican Party to oppose slavery and plantation farming and to secure passage of the Homestead Act.

In the relatively short span of 30 years, after the passage of the Homestead Act in 1862, the territory west of the Mississippi was settled, mainly by poor immigrants who were forced to go into debt to the "money lenders" to get a small start as independent farmers. It was a period when the young trusts were beginning to feel their oats—as they fleeced the nation of its lumber, coal and mineral resources. Encouraged by great land give-aways, the railroads were extending their lines across the country.

Wheat began flowing from the rich farm land to the ports of the world. There was plenty of hustle and bustle on the surface But farmers were plagued by hard winters, bad roads, grasshoppers, high freight rates and exorbitant interest. The landless masses from Europe who came looking for the "promised land" soon learned that there was also the "promissory note." So the bust end of capitalism's boom-bust cycle found farmers going under the auctioneer's hammer even when crops were bountiful, because the crops wouldn't fetch enough to meet notes signed when prices were higher and money cheaper. All this kept the kettle of farm politics boiling.

While the farmers were well aware of the collusion between the stud ducks in the economic puddle—the railroads, machinery companies, elevators, processors, middlemen and bankers—for the most part they felt that most of their misfortunes came either directly or indirectly from a "plot" involving eastern capitalists and "International Bankers". The "Money Power," farmers told one another, "had its headquarters in Wall Street—and its hindquarters in Washington, D. C.".

Then, as now, the question of "fair prices" was uppermost.

It is quite understandable that the farm leaders hung to the simple means of boosting prices—money inflation. Then the debts could be paid with the same number of bushels the loans equalled when contracted. But voices were raised, too, to nationalize the railroads—the main villains—and the telegraph and telephone lines, for government loans on produce stored in government warehouses, for cooperatives, as well as scrapping the "whole damnable system of exploitation".

The very nature of the frontier economy, however, was fertile soil for an ideology which held that no fundamental change in the social system was necessary, although the influence of Marx was already beginning to be felt. Production might be held to a small size—on a par with the 160 acre farms—most farm leaders reasoned, although the laws of capitalist development lead to greater and greater accumulation, and the ruination of the small producers—including the self-reliant family farmer, long exalted as the "foundation of civilized society". By the same laws, the loss of the fertility of the land itself occurs.

The farm discontent took the form, eventually, of the Populist Party and from 1890 to 1896 the farmers took seriously the admonition of their leaders to "raise less corn and more Hell". The political pot boiled furiously, not only in the Middle West but also in the South as well. Much of the legislation to prevent Negroes and poor whites from voting in southern states was passed in the 1890's to stop the growth of Populism.

Judged by New Deal standards neither the reforms demanded by the farmers nor the money inflation schemes were radical enough to sow terror among the capitalists. It was the fear deep in their guts that the zeal and enthusiasm generated by the mass movement, already anti-capitalist and anti-imperialist, would lead to a separate class party of farmers and labor, and upset the two-party system they had always owned and controlled.

The Populist movement might push to higher levels and include government ownership of the whole economy, along with the railroads and communication lines. *The New York Tribune* warned of a "modern tendency toward socialism everywhere".

Capitalism's political bosses were able to canalize the great rumbling anti-monopoly discontent up the currency blind alley, after it had already been compromised on the issue of white supremacy, by maneuvering a fusion of the Populists and the Democrats. The radical Henry Demarest Lloyd said that they lacked all grasp of fundamental principles which might hold a genuine party together. "Free Silver is the cow-bird of the Reform movement," he said. "It waited until the nest had been built by sacrifices of others, and then it laid its eggs in it. . . . The people's party has been betrayed."

The Populist Party was all but dead by 1900 but the ideas of Populism lived on, changing the whole political pattern. Even in relatively good times the old battlers kept hammering against their enemy—Wall Street. They formed cooperatives, and they organized the Farmers Union which had its birth in 1902. The Utopian clubs formed already before the Populist movement collapsed spread the gospel of Bellamy's *Looking Backward.*

After 1900 farmers turned increasingly to Eugene V. Debs for intellectual leadership. An aged former Farmers Union organizer in Iowa related how he left his bride the very day after he was married, for an extended trip with a team and buggy south through the state and into Missouri, holding socialist meetings as he went. Those were the days of great zeal.

Then, there is a story oldsters in South Dakota tell—how the Debs "Red Special" pulled onto a siding for a meeting on the sparsely settled prairies between the Black Hills and Pierre. Ranchers and sod busters drove in from miles around. The state's U.S. Senator Pettigrew, the arch-foe of Mark Hanna and the trusts, accepted socialism. His books, *The Course of Empire* and *Imperial Washington,* had a profound influence on the farm movement in the Dakotas and elsewhere during the farm crisis in the 1920's.

Socialists won political offices in many small towns in the countryside and even such a position as Mayor of Minneapolis. Caught in the cost-price squeeze during and after World War I farmers again showed signs of revolt. Socialists sparked the Non-Partisan League "political prairie fire" which got started in North Dakota in 1915 and spread rapidly to six or seven other states. Socialists and Leaguers wrote into farmers' programs of immediate demands against the predators of agriculture planks for state-owned enterprises. North Dakota still has a state bank and flour mill while South Dakota has a cement plant, set up by the GOP when it got panicky and stole the League's thunder.

Until conditions were ripe for a mass people's movement on

a national scale the Non-Partisans and the Farmer-Laborites who followed were willing to try it on a state scale. Their theory was that the common people had to gain control of the government and use governmental power to protect the people from the trusts.

Many immigrants had come from Europe to escape military conscription so the farm movement had little enthusiasm for America's entry into World War I. This sentiment was combatted by the "home guards" with tar and feathers, beatings and prison terms. Socialists and League leaders were branded "pro-German". Later, after the Russian revolution, the term "Bolshevik", a more sinister sounding name, was hung on them.

Capitalism thwarted the first real threat to its existence—Populism. To forestall further Populist or League movements a next move was to split off a section of the farmers and enlist them on the side of capitalism. Agricultural education was a politically safe and sane program, and its leaders believed farmers should be neutral in the struggle between capitalists and workers. Infecting certain farmers with bigshotitis was made easier by the disparity within agriculture itself, a change already perceptible by the turn of the century. The way to solve the farm problem was to "produce more efficiently", to beat the cost-price squeeze. Farm organizations should "keep out of politics". Big Business fostered and financed new farm organization (such as the Farm Bureau) which would "keep down unrest", and "stop Bolshevism".

"Efficiency" made little difference, however, when the "diligent, intelligent, and above all frugal elite", were wiped out along with the "lazy rascal", and the smiles left their bankers' faces, when 2.5 million farms went through forced sales during the deflation of the 1920's in the attempt of the big banks to "get back to normalcy" after World War I.

Agriculture hadn't recovered from the crisis of the 1920's when the crash came in 1929. The 1920's found the whole countryside in a desperate situation. In 1931 the parity index figure, indicating the ratio of farm prices to costs, slid to the all-time low of 58 percent of parity. (The period between 1909-1914 equals 100.) The number of farms producing an annual income of less than -600, one-fourth in 1920, rose to nearly one-half of the total. Few could meet their obligation and hundreds of thousands lived in dire poverty—poverty amidst plenty. "The new

4-H Club", farmers moaned, "Hoover, Hyde, Hell and Hard Times". (Hyde was Hoover's Secretary of Agriculture.)

Farmers raised plenty of Hell, this time leaving their farms to picket the highways when they went on strike or to stop foreclosure sales or evictions when their neighbors were threatened with being forced into the lanes. Many farmers were heard to predict: "There will be a revolution if things keep on the way they are going." They didn't want a revolution, they simply wanted "something done in Washington" so they could continue to stay on their farms and begin to retire their debts. "Just give us cost of production," they said. Farmers, of course, formed part of the great landslide that covered Hoover and brought in the New Deal. Their militant mass action had much to do with waking up Washington to their plight.

Hitler was on the march and some of his ideas found their way to the corn fields in the Middle West. Always more or less infected with racism and anti-Semitism, it was not neglected when the Nazi fifth-column launched its hate-the-Jew propaganda campaign in the U.S. Thousands of copies of the *Protocols of the Elders of Zion* were distributed to farmers. The "International Bankers", berated by the Populist leaders and radicals as the source of the farmers' woes in the 1890's, quickly became the "International Jewish Bankers". The International situation confused thousands of farmers and made some of them anti-Roosevelt because they thought him a "war monger". It was doubly difficult to secure legislation in Washington which the farmers greatly needed, especially the family farmers, at a time when excitement and spending for armaments took priority over domestic issues.

The New Deal's Agricultural Adjustment Act, passed in May, 1933, declared that its purpose was to bring about and maintain such a balance between the production and consumption of agricultural commodities as would give farm commodities parity, or a purchasing power with respect to articles farmers buy, equivalent to the purchasing power of the farm commodity in the base period of August 1909-July 1914. It was based, however, on the theory that agriculture was over expanded and a great reduction campaign was in order—the scarcity theory.

Its three main principles were: (1) to increase farm buying power by paying farmers to reduce production (2) to cut interest rates on many farm mortgages and scale down the principal on

many more, and (3) inflation. It gave little comfort to those on
the lower rungs of the economic ladder, who needed direct
federal cash for food, clothing and medical aid, a permanent
moratorium on foreclosures and evictions, low-interest rehabili-
tation loans on a long-time basis, and feed and seed loans.

It was proposed by some "planners", out with a "solution"
for poor farmers, that they be declared "surplus". From one-
fourth to one-third of the farm population—on the poorer land
—could pack up their kids and belongings in the Model T and
rattle away. Whole areas were called submarginal and mapped
for government purchase, to be turned into great pastures for
the stock on the stronger units.

It wasn't conducive to happiness for a busted farmer to start
off into the great unknown looking for work, with several million unemployed ahead of him—the goat for a broken-down
economic system.

Then, in those days, there were the humiliating "bean checks",
not good for tobacco, gasoline or even pepper, in some places,
handed out for relief work—the relief work along the highways
on cold days, or hot; the "grant" checks, not enough to keep a
family of birds. The New Deal politicians in Washington
wondered why so many farmers were deserting them.

A sort of left-wing grew up among the farmers, bombarding
Washington for help for the small farms and for more democracy in the program. In the eastern part of the country milk
producers got into the struggle, and in the South the tenants
and sharecroppers, most of them Negro farmers, began to push
against the plantation owners and landlords for a bigger share
of the New Deal benefits.

There is no doubt that the Nazi grand strategy called for
making capital of the New Deal's failure to actually grapple
with many of the farmers' most pressing problems, so they could
build a mass base in the heart of the country, turning the old
anti-imperialist sentiment into "isolationist" sentiment.

It can't be considered accidental that the radio priest and
silver speculator, Charles E. Coughlin, started a third political
party with the "funny-money" Congressman Lemke as its candidate, to take away from Roosevelt the votes of farmers who
wouldn't go back to Hooverism. Nor was it an accident that
Col. Lindberg, decorated by the Nazis, came to Des Moines, in
the heart of farm politics, to test his anti-Semitism.

Dozens of fascist hate-groups and newspapers, financed by Big Business, made a bid for the farmer's ear. Not a few ardent New Dealers among the farm leaders bought in on Huey Long's Every-Man-A-King demogoguery, and promoted Lemke's ridiculous money speeches at farm conventions before they awoke to the fact that the Coughlin-Lemke crowd were out gunning, not only for Roosevelt's farm program, but for Roosevelt—and for them too.

To the everlasting credit of the left-wing, a coalition of radicals, socialists and Communists, hundreds of thousands of farmers were rallied in support of the positive features of the New Deal program, while pressing Washington for greater concessions (such as the Farm Security Administration) for the small and middle-sized farmers. Much of the pressure was exerted through the awakening Farmers Union movement. The left-wing exposed the fascist demagogues and their foreign policy helpful to the Rome-Tokyo-Berlin Axis. Pearl Harbor sent the Lemkes, Coughlins, Nyes, Wheelers, and others of the same ilk scurrying for cover, while the farmers united in a great productive effort behind the war. This brought better prices and farm prosperity—and neglect on the part of farm leaders to speak of a "cooperative commonwealth" as the way out of capitalism's nose-on-the-grindstone way of life for farmers.

Mechanization and electrification, especially after the war, increased the man-hour output so that today each full-time productive worker turns out enough farm products to support himself and 20 others. In 1945 one farm worker produced enough for himself and 13 others, in 1920 himself and 9 others, in 1820 himself and little more than 3 other persons. Henry Wallace claims that now it requires only six minutes to produce a bushel of corn, and that an efficient Iowa farmer, with the help of one man, can grow corn enough to produce meat and livestock products to feed 300 to 400 people in town.

Farm machinery and motor vehicles on farms have more than doubled in the past ten years, but production expenses, as a percent of gross farm income, have risen from 50 percent to 65 percent.

As farmers are at the mercy of the big monopolies now more than ever before, having no say as to prices they have to pay for power fuel, machinery and supplies, or prices they receive for their products, the battle lines are quite sharply drawn. The cost-price squeeze is the crux of the farm fight today, as in 1890.

With this great disadvantage the average farmer can no longer make a go of it, and is forced to go deeper and deeper into debt to buy more and more machinery to stay in the game. He is compelled to pay continually higher rents and land taxes, as the stronger units reach out for more land on which to use their great outlays of equipment. Therefore the farmer requires federal help in the form of price supports, or payments.

The farm fight against monopoly is now more simple, as larger numbers must unite on the issue of price support floors. The "funny-money" cure-alls and panaceas so common in past decades seem to have been shelved along with the horse liniment —at least for the present.

Congress now holds the fate of practically all farmers in its hand. A workable program was proposed several years ago by a group of farm leaders and presented to Congress by Agriculture Secretary Charles Brannan, which provided that farmers would receive payments direct from the government to make up the difference between what they got at the market place and the "fair price" decided by Congress. The products would move into the market, as now, at supply and demand prices, with no artificial restrictions. Consumers could take advantage of lower market prices when an abundance pushed them down. Abundance would be a blessing to both farmers and consumers, not a curse. The Brannan plan was linked to soil conservation practices, and a limitation placed on its benefits to family type farms —those grossing less than $26 thousand a year (about 98 percent of all farms).

The Brannan plan was howled down by the mouthpieces of capitalism as "socialism", then deserted by its sponsors in the Truman administration when Korea opened up possibilities for a solution by war spending—and more inflation.

Capitalism hsa always wanted "cheap food", but now, more than that, it wants agriculture operated as "agribusiness" or "vertical integration",—from top to bottom, production of farm products, processing and merchandizing by corporations. It wants a continuing stream of farmers moving from the land to the city streets as a reservoir of labor willing to work for low wages rather than starve. It doesn't want the countryside populated with small owners, who use the power of government to help preserve the family farm communities—which could be strongholds of democracy, where the atmosphere might be unhealthful for corporate agriculture.

Thus, junking any federal farm programs which would help keep family farmers solvent is the chief objective of capitalism. They do not favor kicking them out of the plane without parachutes, however. They debate among themselves the question of the exact size of the chutes with which the farmers will drift to the desert sands below.

Suggesting that as many as 3,800,000 should go, as *Life* did in 1947, business groups have dozens of interlocking farm committees, councils, forums, institutes, foundations and what-not to influence and pressure Congress, farm and labor leaders in a great Madison Avenue style to destroy the farm program left from New Deal days. The Eisenhower-Benson farm advisory commission has several members direct from the U.S. Chamber of Commerce agriculture committee, not to mention the connections of the others.

The U.S. Department of Agriculture has, in reality, become a department of packers, processors and big agriculture. The rate of growth of capitalist concentration in agriculture is increasing. Big outfits eat up small farms as the smaller ones go busted, with low prices and inadequate capital for mechanized operations, and consolidate with still larger ones.

Some socialists say the process of centralization has gone so far it can't be halted, and take a dim view of the family farmers' fight for survival, seeming to join the spokesmen for capitalism. Such an attitude, instead of winning friends, makes farmers who are in the fight with their backs to the wall hopping sore at socialists.

What all socialists and labor should realize is that it is not inevitable that family farming be wiped out and that America break with the Jeffersonian philosophy and its allegiance to small ownership and the family farm.

The fight for family farming is tied up with the fight for maintaining labor's organizations, for civil rights, for democracy and for world peace. Ships can be made to sail against the wind, but it takes an experienced and determined crew. The principal role which farmers will play from now on will be as allies of labor on the political field. Or, if labor turns a deaf ear, the farmers can play a role on the side of reaction. Farmers are no longer the numerical force as in the days of Populism, or even in the 1920's. The outcome of their struggle to survive will depend on the size and strength, the understanding and steadfastness of a labor-farmer coalition into which can be drawn certain sections of small business.

The experience farmers gain in this long struggle will determine how many of them go to the left, remain neutral, or follow a racist, anti-labor, McCarthy-type program. A deepening of the crisis will bring thousands of farmers into the fight actively who today are suffering from cold war paralysis—wondering if "they" won't finally "do something", so everything will come out in the wash. Likewise, a deepening of the crisis will draw in thousands of small business and service men in the countryside who would be pushed out along with the farmers.

Socialists have always maintained that the majority will be happier, and economically better off, under socialism. This also applies to farmers. Even under the best conditions farming is no picnic. Today, for most farmers, it is a rat race. Such tremendous problems as long hours of work, drought, floods, erosion (the world loses two inches of top soil annually, and it takes 1,000 years to build an inch) and the loss of fertility generally, can only be solved under a system of socialism. As population gains are made, experts tell us that a food problem will have to be faced. In time this problem will have to be solved with socialist planning. Simply telling farmers, however—even those living under the most miserable conditions of exploitation and poverty—of socialism's great advantages to them and to all humanity will bring only a few to its support. The great majority must be won through struggle, where farmers learn at first hand that socialists and the working class are on their side.

A farm program for a labor-farmer coalition should be based on the proposition of maintaining family farming as a pattern for agriculture, as against factory-type farming. Federal price supports, long-term credit and a brake on big agriculture, along with soil conservation, should be its guiding principles.

A farm program might well begin with a Brannan-plan-type arrangement of production payments and support floors at parity (or more) for all farm commodities. Wool already has such a program with supports during the 1954-56 marketing at 106 percent of parity.

To discourage big agriculture and suitcase farming the

amount of production on which each farm family could claim full support should be limited to, say, $10,000 or $15,000. Supports should be scaled down on production over that amount, with all over $25,000 annually with no supports at all.

Of course, all government programs should be tied to a soil conservation program, and soil conservation should be enlarged and extended, as it is vitally important from a health and nutritional standpoint as well as for prevention of wind and water erosion.

Low interest, long-time loans should be provided by the government so that farmers could settle their pressing obligations and repay the government gradually; also, so that poor farmers with insufficient equipment, buildings, livestock, or land could become more efficient and productive.

The government should launch a sort of new homestead act. When large holdings come up for sale the government would have priority, and could resell to young family farmers, splitting up the tracts into economic units; or sell the larger tracts to groups who wished to organize and farm cooperatively.

The time is already here, perhaps, when socialists should be reviving the ideal of a cooperative commonwealth, and thinking about practical applications of this ideal for modern agriculture. The cooperative movement has gained a solid foothold in rural America, both in selling supplies to farmers and in marketing farmers' products. Why not stimulate farmers to think about the challenge of big-scale agriculture? Perhaps we should advocate federal loans up to $100,000 to help a group of farmers pool their resources and buy new and modern machinery for a large-scale cooperatively-owned operation. The group of farmers involved could elect officers and weekly meetings could be held to plan for the coming weeks or months. A method could be evolved so that new members could be invited to join the co-op to replace retiring members. For many farmers the prospect of this kind of farming, with a division of labor, shorter hours, except in the very busy season, and annual vacations, might prove particularly attractive in comparison with the nightmares and tortured days under the present system.

Farmers have always helped one another, and working together on a cooperative farm for a common objective would be one way of building for a future society. I do not, however, offer cooperative farms or ranches as a solution for the farm problem under capitalism. But with the price and credit problem solved, cooperative farms, for many, might lead to a much better cultural and intellectual life and prove to people everywhere that "dog-eat-dog" can go the way of the hand corn planter.

There should be a federal old age retirement plan so the tillers of the soil, regardless of their past incomes, could live out the balance of their lives in peace, comfort and decency after the age of 55 or 60.

The above farm program can be begun under capitalism, and much more, when labor and the farmers show political teamwork and get down to the business of repudiating Cadillac and mink coat government. Actually what both farmers and labor need is a new New Deal, much broader, much deeper and much more liberal. The anti-imperialist sentiment among farmers must be revived and the government spending that capitalism requires, to keep it from falling apart at the seams, can take the form of spending for domestic purposes rather than for military hardware.

In building a farmer-labor coalition labor will need to take the initiative, and the left will need to give guidance and aid to both farmers and labor. In the course of this long and difficult struggle the farmers will plow out new leadership, and plow under some of the old. Those farmers, who have become so preoccupied with the profits of oil stations, farm-hardware stores, insurance companies or other enterprises that they have forforgotten their members, will begin to find rural leaders, tried and true, in their own ranks. Socialists will come down out of their ivory towers and walk in the fields to learn for themselves what farms are like and where milk comes from. The people can win, but it will not be easy. As the late Marcantonio once told us, "There is no substitute for hard work." Let us get going with it.

The Trend of American Labor Toward Socialism

By Philip S. Foner

THE SEPTEMBER 1, 1957 ISSUED OF *The Record,* official magazine of the Retail, Wholesale and Department Store Union (AFL-CIO), featured a Labor Day editorial which raised timely questions for the American labor movement. Conceding that American labor had much to boast of, especially the growth of trade union membership from 3,500,000 to over 16,000,000 within two decades, the editorial went on to state frankly that despite this unprecedented growth and the increasing strength and influence of labor that accompanied it, the labor movement was on the defensive. Organization was down "to a mere trickle"; anti-union laws were being adopted in many states; in the political arena, "labor's recent accomplishments" could scarcely "be called spectacular" and, as a result of the exposures of the McClellan Committee, the American people were becoming

PHILIP S. FONER graduated from the College of the City of New York, where he was a member of Phi Beta Kappa. He received his Ph.D. degree from Columbia University, taught history at the College of the City of New York and has taught Labor History for many trade unions. Dr. Foner is the author of "History of the Labor Movement in the United States". Volumes I and II, covering the period from colonial times to the beginning of the 20th century, and is at work on Volume III. He is also the author of "Business and Slavery;" "The Fur Workers Union;" "Jack London: American Rebel;" "Jews in American History", and the four-volume definitive "Life and Writings of Frederick Douglass", Dr. Foner is editor of the two-volume "Complete Writings of Thomas Paine", "The Basic Writings of Thomas Jefferson," and of "The Selected Writings of George Washington, Abraham Lincoln and Franklin D. Roosevelt". He has completed a new book, "Mark Twain: Social Critic", to be published early this year.

convinced that the labor movement was a cesspool of corruption. "What can labor do about it?" the editorial asked. And it answered:

> "It seems to us that what's needed right now is a revival—a revival of idealism, of the crusading spirit that built the labor movement against all the odds, of the social outlook that goes beyond the bread-and-butter issues to grapple with the larger problems facing all mankind. . . . What is needed is the dedication, the sense of mission, that once animated the labor movement."

If one glances back over the course of American labor history, he will see that again and again "the crusading spirit" that played such a large part in building the labor movement was supplied primarily by the socialist-minded workers and their leaders. They were not alone in making this contribution, but it was they who supplied the dynamic impetus and the program that "animated the labor movement".

Socialist influences in the American labor movement were evident as early as 1853 when Joseph Weydemeyer, an associate of Karl Marx, helped organize the American Workers' League which called for building of trade unions and for independent political action by a united labor movement cutting across lines of craft and national origin. Over a century ago, this movement raised a slogan which was to reverberate again and again through labor's ranks: "Forward to a great association of workers, not only to fight for higher wages and for political reforms, but for the creation of a platform which can unite all workers for the welfare of the working class."

It was not, however, until the 1880's, with the spread of the modern factory system and large-scale, mass production and the emergence of monopoly capitalism, that Socialist influences in the labor movement began to be felt in a real way. The Marxists organized in the Socialist Labor Party, having defeated the Lassallean Socialists with their indifference to trade unionism, and the need to organize workers along trade union lines began to play an important role in the building of national and local unions and state and city central labor bodies all over the country. Influential in the Knights of Labor, the Socialists were also an active force in the formation of the American Federation of Labor. Indeed their influence is clearly reflected in the preamble to the Federation's constitution which emphasized: "A struggle is going on in all the nations of the civilized world, a struggle between the capitalist and laborer, which grows in intensity from year to year, and will work disastrous results to the toiling millions if they are not combined for mutual protection." By 1894, socialist influences in the union affiliated with the American Federation of Labor were so strong that a majority of these organizations went on record in favor of a political and legislative program which included such features as government ownership and operation of the national telegraph and telephone and railroad systems, endorsed collective ownership by the people of all means of production, and supported the formation of an independent labor party to achieve the program. While Gompers and his associates on the A. F. of L. Executive Council were able by parliamentary tactics to prevent adoption of the program by the Federation's convention, they could not hide the fact that a majority of the affiliated unions had endorsed the demands set forth by the Socialists.

Socialist activity for the formation of an independent labor party was reflected in the independent political movement of labor in the municipal elections of 1886. These labor parties laid the foundation for a farmer-labor coalition against the forces of monopoly capitalism. In the election of 1888 a National Union Labor Party was formed with backing from the Farmers' Alliance and from groups both within the Knights of Labor and the American Federation of Labor among whom the Socialists were an active force. This party failed to make much impression either in the Federal or State elections, but the very existence of such an organization showed that the time was ripe for the building of a farmer-labor alliance against the common enemy of both classes.

These ideas saw effective realization in the next decade through the Populist Party. By the end of 1892 Populism had attracted so much enthusiasm and interest among the organized worker that many A. F. of L. unions, particularly those in which the Socialists were influential, openly endorsed the Populist program as one of the effective answers for the problems which American labor faced. By 1894 the labor groups became so active in Populism that, in the industrial areas, they represented the driving and dominant force in the movement. Labor-Populist alliances were achieved in key industrial states such as Illinois, New York, Ohio, Indiana, Massachusetts, Minnesota, and California. The platform of these alliances went far beyond the demands advanced by Populism in the rural areas, calling for nationalization of the mines; municipal ownership of street railways, gas and electric plants; abolition of the sweating system; sanitary inspection of mines, factories, and homes; compulsory education, a legal eight-hour day and, in several states, even advocated "collective ownership of the means of production and distribution".

The achievement of unity between urban labor and the agrarian forces, symbolized in the rise of labor-Populism, resulted at first in sweeping victories for the new political movement. The Populist vote in the congressional and state elections of 1894 was over forty-two per cent more than that of 1892. Unfortunately, by this time forces were at work to shelve the advanced program of the labor-Populist alliance for a narrow program of currency reform, embodied in the demand for free silver and, within the next two years, these groups became dominant. In 1896, the Democratic Party framed its program in such a way as to steal as much of the Populist fire as possible. In addition to coming out for the free coinage of silver, it stressed such measures as governmental regulation of railroad rates and a federal income tax, and attacked government by injunction.

The result was easily foreseen. The Populist leaders who favored diverting the movement from one with a broad program such as advanced by the labor-Populist alliance into one based essentially on free silver, went over into the Democratic camp, and in the course of William Jennings Bryan's whirlwind campaign in the West, the great bulk of the Populists followed their leaders into the Democratic ranks. The Populist movement faded away.

After the defeat of Bryan in 1896, a general rise in farm prices and the spread of prosperity put an end to independent political action for the time being, but the ideas embodied in the program of the labor-Populist alliance were to have a rebirth in an even more intensified form in the first decade of the twentieth century with the growth of the American Socialist Party.

The propagation and spread of Socialist ideas in the American labor movement was unfortunately impeded by the weaknesses of the Socialist Labor Party. Dominated on the one hand by the German-Americans who did little to learn the language of the country of their adoption and confined their propaganda primarily to their own national groups and, on the other, by the followers of Daniel De Leon who regarded any labor organization which was not fully committed to Socialism as reactionary and worthy only of being destroyed, the Socialist Labor Party was sinking into an insignificant, sectarian movement.

In 1900 many persons in the Socialist movement, who were thoroughly disgusted with the doctrinal nature of De Leon's leadership, joined together to form the American Socialist Party. The new party was actually an amalgamation of various groupings of Socialist-minded Americans: the Socialist Democratic Federation, led by Eugene V. Debs, the Milwaukee Socialists, led by Victor Berger, and the New York sections of the S.L.P., led by Morris Hilquit. In addition, the new party drew many recruits from among the ranks of the former supporters of Populism in the West.

Because of the force of Debs' own personality and the tremendous respect for him in labor's ranks—he had himself been a leading railroad union official and founder of the American Railway Union, the great industrial union among the railroad workers—and the general interests in progressive reforms at the time, the Socialist Party grew in influence. This influence, so far as the labor movement was concerned, was reflected in the considerable following the Socialists gained among such unions as the Brewery and Bakery workers, the Clothing, Cap and Millinery Workers, the Ladies Garment Workers, the United Mine Workers, and the Western Federation of Miners. In addition it was reflected in the annual conventions of the A. F. of L. The Socialist Party, while aiming primarily at the setting up of a collective system of production and distribution in the United States, with government ownership of industry, did not make the mistake of ignoring immediate issues facing the workers. Convention after convention of the A. F. of L. resolved itself into clear-cut battles between the A. F. of L. leadership and the Socialist delegates over these issues. Four Socialist proposals in particular were the cause of constant dispute between the Socialists and the A. F. of L. administration. These were the establishment of an independent political party, the adoption of the industrial union form of organization, the approval of social legislation, and the cessation of affiliation of the A. F. of L. officers with the National Civic Federation.

While Socialists inside the A. F. of L. were battling for a progressive labor program others, convinced that the Federation was too completely dominated by conservative forces to achieve such a program and who found the Socialist Party tactics too mild for their liking, joined forces to form the Industrial Workers of the World. In the eyes of its founders the untimate goal of the I.W.W. was the creation of a socialist commonwealth in the United States, in which economic exploitation and unequal distribution of wealth would be ended. But the partisans of the movement were a very mixed lot; they ranged from moderate socialists to extreme anarchists and they had much disagreement about the methods by which this goal was to be reached.

Although its successes were always transitory, the I.W.W. did conduct tremendous organization campaigns among the unskilled workers in the great lumber mills, the dockyards, the copper and silver mines, the wheat, fruit and vebetable ranches, the textile mills, the fish canneries, whom the A. F. of L. had largely overlooked in the past. During the period after 1907, the I.W.W. conducted a series of spectacular strikes and free speech fights among the lumber workers of Washington and Oregon, among the Copper miners of Idaho and Montana, and among the textile workers in Massachusetts and New Jersey, which succeeded in attracting nation-wide attention to the movement.

The widespread agitation of the I.W.W. had an immensely vitalizing effect on the American labor movement as a whole. The A. F. of L. National Executive Council realized that they would have to wage a more vigorous fight on the industrial and political front if thousands of members of its affiliated unions were not to drift over en masse to the ranks of the I.W.W.

Meanwhile the Socialist Party was making slow but steady progress in the industrial cities of the North and Middle West. Debs ran as presidential candiate in every election, and each time his support climbed, until in 1920 he was able to pile up almost a million popular votes. More and more unions in the Federation were becoming permeated with socialist ideas.

At the 1911 annual convention, the Socialist candidate for
president of the A. F. of L., Max Hayes of the Typographical
Union, received 5073 votes as against 11,974 for Gompers.

Many different factors—the organizational drives of the
I.W.W., the pressure of the Socialist groups within the Federation, the open shop drive of the employers, particularly as reflected in court decisions outlawing boycotts, picketing, etc.—
impelled the A. F. of L. leaders to adopt a more progressive
labor program. By 1914 the program of the A. F. of L. had come
to embrace a large part of the program for social legislation
advocated by the Socialists. Whereas the resolutions adopted at
the annual convention of the Federation around the turn of
the century were limited almost entirely to subjects that dealt
with wages, hours and working conditions, the 1914 convention
extended felicitations to the New Carranza government in
Mexico, requested a bill from Congress for the unemployed,
asked for citizenship for Puerto Ricans, recommended a presidential primary law, favored an easier method of amending the
United States Constitution, demanded of the states free and
uniform text books in the public schools, went on record for
the abolition of child labor, a general campaign of education,
an old age pension law and government loans of money for
municipal sanitary housing, and declared that it should support any plan which would bring disarmament. While it is
true that it was not too difficult for the A. F. of L. leaders to
ignore these resolutions once the convention adjourned, the
very fact that they were adopted was a tribute to the pressure
of socialist-minded workers and their allies.

The A. F. of L. leadership remained a constant foe of the
Socialist clamor for an independent labor party, but was compelled to abandon its attitude that the trade unions would
be ruined if they entered politics. By 1906 it had become clear
that political action was no longer an issue to be fought over
between the Socialist trade unionists and the "pure and sim-
plers", but was a vital, practical, requisite necessitated by the
elementary principles of self-defense and self-preservation. To
be sure, the A. F. of L. leadership adopted the political method
of "reward your friend and punish your enemy," and refused
to support any plan for an independent labor party, but even
this was a step in advance of its previous attitude of "No Politics in the Unions".

Moreover, the demand for independent political action continued very much alive, and it increased in intensity during and after World War I. The workers had become more and more restless and dissatisfied as a consistently larger slice of their pay envelope kept going for food and other necessities, while their wages remained almost stationary. This mood of dissatisfaction became intensified when the war plants began to shut down and the transition was made from wartime to peacetime production. The end of the world conflict saw a great upsurge of radical political activity in all regions of the country. The Socialist Party suffered a decline as a result of persecution of many of its leaders for their continuing opposition to the war, but the general atmosphere was full of unrest. Labor felt that the victory of the Allies should be followed by a genuine attempt to create a new social order in the United States, in which inequalities of income should be abolished and the society recast along more democratic lines. The soul-stirring and momentous events of 1917 and 1918—the collapse of the Romanoff despotism in Russia and the establishment of the Soviet Union, the downfall of the Hapsburg and Hohenzollern regimes in Central Europe and their replacement by democratic and socialist regimes, the establishment of Communist regimes in Hungary and Bavaria—created new hope and optimism in labor and progressive circles in all parts of the United States.

The year 1919 was one of social disturbance in the United States as in Europe. As the cost of living climbed to record peaks a strike wave, climaxed by the great steel strike, developed and threatened to engulf the whole industrial structure of the country. The radicalization in the thinking of the workers was also reflected in the 1919 A. F. of L. convention. Criticism of Gompers' policies had already become open and widespread among the affiliated unions and, at the convention, it was reflected in the proposals advanced by the Socialist delegates. These included the endorsement of a labor party, approval of the recognition by the United States of the new Bolshevik regime in Russia, backing the Plumb Plan which had been sponsored by the four railroad brotherhoods for the government operation of the national railroad network, and election of the officers of the Federation by referendum. The Socialists were defeated at the convention on the issue of the

American recognition of Russia and on the labor party question, but they succeeded in getting the approval of a majority of the delegates on the Plumb Plan. The provisions of this plan called for continuation of government ownership and operation of all the railroads, a process which had begun during the War, with full support of the American Federation of Labor and the Railroad Brotherhoods. The railroads were returned to private enterprise but the socialist trend in the labor movement continued.

Although the Federation refused to endorse a labor party, the forces favoring independent political action took steps to realize their goal. In the summer of 1919, they formed the National Labor Party, whose program emphasized plans for the democratic control of American industry by the workers and for the government ownership and operation of public utilities. Led by Max Hayes and John Fitzpatrick, an influential Socialist trade unionist and the President of the Chicago Federation of Labor, the party soon became the rallying point of socialist-minded A. F. of L. members in New York, Pennsylvania, and some of the Middle Western states.

The new party failed to win the endorsement of the A. F. of L. at the Federation's 1920 convention, but its influence was felt in the adoption by the delegates of resolutions approving the Plumb Plan and the nationalization of mines and public utilities. In the 1920 presidential campaign, the National Labor Party allied itself with Midwestern farm organizations and nominated Perley Christiansen, a Utah lawyer who had been prominent in labor affairs, as presidential candidate. The results were disappointing. Far more impressive was the vote polled by the veteran Eugene V. Debs as the Socialist Party candidate—running for the presidency from behind the walls of Atlanta Penitentiary, where he had been imprisoned for his anti-war stand in 1918.

After 1920, the impetus for independent political action came from the Northwest where hatred of Eastern capitalism, which had been so widespread in the days of the Populists, now formed expression through the Non-Partisan League. The early success of the League was very rapid, and it gained control of the state legislature of North Dakota, Minnesota and Wisconsin and elected several representatives to Congress. The Farmer Labor Party in Minnesota built up a considerable following among the workers and farmers of that state, which was more industrialized than North Dakota. In the years after the Armistice the collapse of farm prices, and the loss of rich overseas markets in Europe for agricultural products kept this agitation alive all over the Northwest.

Gradually, as this new agrarian reform movement began to build up its strength in the West, it obtained increased representation in Congress. By 1922 the progressive farm bloc was strong enough in Congress to merit the attention of the national labor movement, and several members of the A. F. of L. Executive Committee advocated a policy of cooperation with the farm bloc in Congress on the ground that both labor and the farmer had the same foes. In 1922 the Federation's Executive Council made a public declaration that "all legislation in favour of the farmer or of labor benefits both"; in a letter published in the same year calling for a joint conference of labor and farm organizations, it declared that "Whatever injures labor injures the farmer. Whatever is for the interests of labor or of the farmer is for the best interests of all people except the privileged few".

Cooperation between the farm groups and the progressive elements in the trade union movement became close. In 1922 members of these two groups came together to form a new political pressure movement under the name of the Congress For Progressive Political Action, which was designed to be the possible nucleus of a new national party. Its first conference was held in Chicago in 1922 and was widely attended; some of the larger unions in the A. F. of L., such as the United Mine Workers and the Garment Workers, sent delegates and, all told, twenty-eight international unions, eight state labor federations, the Chicago Federation of Labor, and a number of Farm Leagues took part in the proceedings. The conference decided upon a policy of working on an independent and non-partisan basis for the election to Congress and to the state legislatures of candidates with progressive records and platforms.

During the next two years, the C.L.P.E. attracted the allegiance of a considerable number of officials in the A. F. of L. unions who were impatient with the static and unprogressive nature of the Gompers' leadership. In July, 1924 it assembled again at Chicago with about 600 delegates from the international unions, the Socialists, the progressive parties and various reform groups. The Conference decided to nominate as its presidential candidate Senator Robert La Follette who was the undisputed leader of the progressive forecs in Congress.

Having failed to convince the Republican and Democratic conventions of the need to adopt a labor program the A. F. of L., in disgust, decided to abandon the policy which the Federation had followed continuously since the beginning of its national political activities, and came out publicly in support of the La Follette ticket. They did so on the grounds that this "proferred a program within which the economic interests of the day are met in a manner much more nearly conforming to labor's proposals than any other program". The A. F. of L. leaders made it clear, however, that they were backing La Follette as an independent candidate and not as the leader of a third party movement.

In the election La Follette succeeded in poling up about 4,800,000 popular votes, although he carried the electoral college only in his native state of Wisconsin. This was by far the largest popular vote picked up by a third party or independent presidential candidate since the end of the Civil War. But the failure of the third party campaign was used by the A. F. of L. leaders as a further and even more convincing proof of the complete futility of any departure from the traditional non-partisan policy by the Federation. At the next annual convention, the Federation endorsed the continuation of traditional political policies, with only one dissenting vote.

After the failure of the La Follette movement, whatever radical agitation in labor's ranks existed was that conducted by the Communist Party and the Trade Union Educational League. The League kept alive the issues of industrial unionism: the mass organization of the unskilled workers who were outside of the ranks of A. F. of L. unions, and the formation of a national American farmer-labor party. The League began a policy of penetrating unions in the A. F. of L. with its progressive ideas and doctrines. In spite of bittered opposition by the Federation's leadership, the League managed to carry on a ceaseless agitation against the conservative policy of the A. F. of L. Executive Council, and worked for amalgamation of the existing craft unions into larger unions, carrying whole industries and for independent political action.

The League, its work becoming impossible within the Federation as a result of wholesale expulsions of progressive A. F. of L. members, advanced its program outside the Federation through the Trade Union Unity League, organized in 1928. That there was a burning need for the program it advanced is indicated by the fact that these years represented an era of retreat on all fronts for the Federation. Few advances were made into new fields and there were serious losses in industries which had been strongholds of unionism ever since the early days of the Federation. Between 1925 and 1929 nearly sixty per cent of all unions in the Federation either remained stationary or lost members. Although Gompers finally passed from the scene in 1924 his ideas and conception, based on conditions which had existed in the United States nearly half a century before, still governed the minds and actions of the members of the National Executive Council.

It is easily understandable that, after so many years of stagnation, the Federation was placed in a parictularly vulnerable and weak position when the first blasts of economic depression swept across the United States in 1930. The Federation's leadership refused to take a definite stand on the pressing question of providing relief for the million of jobless workers, confining themselves to issuing futile appeals to employers to avoid lay-offs and wage cuts—to which the latter paid absolutely no heed. But as the general industrial situation rapidly grew worse in 1930 and 1931, the influence of the left-wingers, many of them Communists, began to be felt inside the Federation. One after another, the A. F. of L. unions were won around to the idea of compulsory Federal unemployment insurance as a means of combatting the depression. By 1932 this pressure had become so strong that the Executive Council announced publicly that it had instructed President William Green to draw up plans for a Federal unemployment insurance bill which was to be presented to Congress. Although the Federation did not take this very important legislative step until two and a half years after the start of the depression, and at a time when hundreds of thousands of jobless workers were prowling the streets of the great industrial towns and cities, the very fact that it was compelled to do so, gave proof of the widespread dissatisfaction with the A. F. of L.'s political methods of action, both inside and outside of the ranks of the Federation.

With the coming of the New Deal, this feeling of dissatisfaction reached new heights. The National Recovery Act's labor provisions not only gave a mighty impetus to union organization but also helped to intensify the keen interest in political and legislative questions among trade unionists all over the country. The painful experience of the depression years, between 1930 and 1933, made the average worker much more keenly aware than ever before of the extent to which his own personal well being and that of his union were dependent on the nature of the policies which were pursued by the Federal Government in Washington. A great new labor federation sprang into existence—the Congress of Industrial Organizations. Its policies and program were based upon a basically different conception of the functions of government, in the labor and industrial sphere, from those held by the disciples of Gompers. Ever since Gompers' time, the A. F. of L. leaders had tended to adopt an exceedingly suspicious and mistrustful attitude towards all forms of legislation and of state action and regulation. This outlook had resulted in such a remarkable phenomenon as the Federation's refusal to approve the setting up of a national system of unemployment insurance and relief until the depths of the most severe economic crisis the nation had ever suffered had been reached—at a period when the jobless in the Uinted States numbered in the millions. The leaders of the C.I.O. did not fight the intervention of the Federal Government in the relations between capital and labor. Instead they welcomed this new trend in American politics because of their belief in the vast potentiality of the powers of the State to give the workers a life which would be relatively free of fear and insecurity. Like the leaders of the A. F. of L., they favored retention of the free enterprise system, but experience of the depression had shown that this system had created very serious abuses—grave inequalities of income and economic opportunity. It was the duty of the Federal Government to correct these abuses and to use its great legislative power to give the underprivileged third of the nation decent houses, adequate educational facilities, proper low-cost medical care and, in general, the full benefit of the great advances which had been made in social and technical fields during the past several decades.

The adoption of this new approach towards the functions of the government, on the part of the C.I.O., brought the new

organization quite close to the policies advocated by the Socialists and other progressive forces in the American labor movement, who had fought for such a policy for many decades. This
is to be seen in the first legislative program of the C.I.O. which
was drawn up in 1936. It included a publicly administered
and financed federal housing program; new federal legislation
to raise general wage scales and to improve working conditions
in exploited and sweated industries, and the nationalization
of coal mines, railroads, marine transportation and telephone
systems, as well as banking. This involved a degree of government intervention in social planning which would have in-
furiated most of the A. F. of L. leaders of an earlier day, but
every one of these demands had already been raised by the
Socialists within the Federation before World War I, and were
raised again by the Communists after the war. What had then
been the position of the minority forces in the American labor
movement had become the program of the majority.

The great strides in organization and membership strength
which the American labor movement made after 1935, with
the adoption of industrial unionism, organization of the unskilled and semi-skilled, especially Negroes, women and the foreign-born—again a program advanced by the socialist-minded
workers over the previous decades—brought with it a corresponding increase in labor's general political power. It was no longer
an insignificant minority group whose demands and wishes
could be ignored by the politicians and party leaders with im-
punity. After 1935 the labor vote began to exercise a very important influence in the outcome of presidential and congressional contests. Indeed, without this mass backing on the part
of organized labor, it is doubtful if the Roosevelt administration
could have remained in office for so many years.

In the main the New Deal discouraged any further third
party activity, since its broad program included so many reforms
for which progressive groups in the labor movement had been
fighting for several decades. Nevertheless, many socialist-minded
workers, while prepared to support the New Deal under Roosevelt against the opposition of Big Business, were not willing
to do so under the Democratic emblem. These workers were
mainly members of the clothing workers' and ladies garment
workers' unions. The two leaders of these unions—Sidney Hill-
man and David Dubinsky—with other union leaders, including

those even further to the left, organized a special labor party whose immediate goal was to gather the vote for the New Deal under the banner of the American Labor Party. In November, 1936 its work certainly helped in the victory of Franklin D. Roosevelt in New York State and the re-election of Governor Herbert H. Lehman. The following year it aided in the re-election of Fiorello H. La Guardia as mayor of New York.

The sentiment for independent political action increased after 1940, as the trend away from the New Deal policies and in the direction of conservatism became pronounced. With the reactionary groups in the two national parties forming an alliance for the purpose of undoing many of the social reforms of the New Deal, the forces favoring a labor party on a national scale raised their voices increasingly at conventions of the C.I.O. The C.I.O. leaders, however, insisted that a third party movement would split the progressive vote to the benefit of the Republicans, and favored instead the creation of a new high-power political pressure organization which would be allied with the C.I.O. and which would work for the election of pro-labor candidates. This organization was given the name of the Political Action Committee. In the contests of 1944, the P.A.C. worked actively to ensure the re-election of Roosevelt and the pro-labor and progressives forces.

Four years later, a new third party movement appeared on the national political scene. Henry A. Wallace, seeking to rally the New Deal forces throughout the nation, announced his intention of heading a new national progressive movement which would continue and expand the work of reform begun by the Roosevelt regime. Knowing well that the only real hope for such a movement lay in his support by the two national federations of labor, Wallace made very definite overtures to the A. F. of L. and the C.I.O. He was rebuffed by both organizations, although a number of progressive unions in the C.I.O. and not a small percentage of the rank and file of both labor federations did swing in behind Wallace's Progressive Party.

The lack of support by the labor movement doomed the Progressive Party almost from the outset. Still the movement was significant as yet another manifestation of the desire of American progressives of all shades of opinion for independent political action and for social goals that could not be attained under the old parties. Moreover, although it was only for a brief period, the Progressive Party did show that Communists, Socialists, rank and file trade unionists and other progressive forces could work together for a common goal.

By the middle of the twentieth century, the American labor movement had reached the conclusion that it must build up a tremendous unified political force which would give labor a far more decisive vote in the determination of national politics of all types than it had ever possessed in the past. There were, however, two main currents in the labor movement regarding the way in which this unified political force was to exercise its influence. One opposed creation of an independent labor party, insisting that conditions had not matured for it and that, for the foreseeable future, labor could best achieve its aims by working for a coalition of progressive forces within the old parties, particularly the Democratic Party. The other contended that both old parties were dominated by big business, that it was dangerous for the labor movement to become a tail to the kite of the Democratic Party, and that the times required that labor organize a third party in order to achieve its legitimate goals.

Even though there may not be enough support at this moment for the immediate launching of a labor party, work and education should be carried on towards a labor party, and labor parties should actually be formed in certain states. "I believe," declared Michael Quill, President of the Transport Workers Union, in advocating this position at the 1954 C.I.O. Convention, "that a national party of labor could be formed that would bring our people by the hundreds of thousands to our banners."

This outlook is still a minority current in the labor movement, but even the most irreconcilable foes of the formation of an independent party of labor have had to concede that conditions may arise that would make a labor party an absolute necessity. Even George Meany, President of the AFL-CIO, has declared publicly: "If we can't act as unions to defend our rights, then there is no answer but to start a labor party."

Everything, then, points to the continued growth of political consciousness in the labor movement. Accompanying this will be an ever-increasing broadening of the aims of the labor movement. In October, 1956, the AFL-CIO distributed millions of pieces of literature to voters from coast to coast in which the newly-formed united labor movement outlined an eight-point program to end a condition in which "more than 31 millions of Americans" were in want. The AFL-CIO "Program to End Family Want" called for: (1) a "minimum standard of schooling" for all Americans in "all parts of the nation"; (2) elimination of discriminatory employment practices based on race, color, creed, or sex; (3) extension of minimum wage coverage to millions now unprotected by federal or state laws and establishment of rates "which reflect rising minimum needs"; (4) extension and enforcement of the right to organize and bargain collectively; (5) aid to the chronically distressed areas "which exist in half the states" to restore employment opportunities; (6) restoration of farm families to "full participation in our rising national income"; (7) improvement of our system of social security by legislative action to enable the aged, the widows, and dependent children to "live in dignity and decency", unemployed families to maintain an "adequate" living standard, permanently disabled and dependents of the fatally injured to "receive "just compensation" and so all American families can obtain "prepaid medical care and insure income support during illness and disability"; (8) alleviation of the "unjust tax burden" now borne by the lower-income families, and substitution of tax levies based on "ability to pay".

"Is it not high time," the AFL-CIO Program asked, "for this rich and humanitarian nation to end the impoverishment of its lowest fifth? Surely, in a great country that produces goods and services in excess of $400 billion yearly, want in the midst of such plenty is neither morally nor economically justifiable."

Although the AFL-CIO does not favor socialism, its "Program to End Family Want" clearly raises the question of socialism. Capitalism does not have the answer.

In sipte of the discouraging picture of the status of the labor movement drawn by *The Record* of September 1, 1957, and quoted at the very beginning of our discussion, it is not an exaggeration to say that the opportunity of bringing the message of socialism to the American workers has rarely been as great as it is today. Here are some of the reasons for this conclusion:

1. Whereas a little more than two decades ago, the labor movement was small, split and with a limited program for a progressive America, today there is a large trade union move-

ment with a program, such as is exemplified by the AFL-CIO program to end want, the programs of the UAW, Amalgamated, Packinghouse and other unions. These raise demands which open the opportunity to discuss the possibility of achieving the goals raised in these programs under capitalism and the need to achieve socialism to realize them fully.

2. Labor is moving inexorably toward political independence, and is doing so at a time when it embraces more than 15 million members. This is a far cry from the situation which existed in the last century or even the first three decades of the present century when the trade union movement represented a very small minority of the total working class. The labor movement is in the position to exert decisive influence in an independent political party.

3. The Negro people are a powerful and compact, increasingly organized political force, particularly in the North, but now also in the South. There are 1,500,000 or more Negro trade unionists. The base for progressive political activity has thus been considerably broadened.

4. The farmers are becoming increasingly aroused over the current farm crisis, and a new opportunity exists to revive the alliance of the past between the labor movement and the poor and middle-income farmers.

5. The prestige and influence of the conservative and reactionary bureaucrats in the labor movement has received a damaging blow as a result of exposures of corruption in trade union ranks. While it is true that these exposures have weakened labor's public influence and have split the labor movement as a result of impending expulsion of graft-ridden unions from the AFL-CIO, the workers are no longer as intimidated by the entrenched bureaucracy, and they are beginning to speak out vigorously for a progressve labor program.

6. The atmosphere in the country, and in the unions, has improved considerably since the heyday of McCarthyism. It is no longer easy to dismiss a progressive labor program with the ancient cry of "red".

7. A major battle is shaping up over issues which affect millions of workers intimately. Such issues as the fight against unemployment, for job security, especially arising out of problems of automation, and for the guaranteed annual wage open up new opportunities to point out the fact that there is no

basic solution to these problems under capitalism.

8. The achievements of socialism in other countries has been brought home sharply to American workers with the launching of the earth satellites by the Soviet Union. Consequently, many workers are becoming more receptive to evidence that, on the basis of our industries, farms, natural resources, and democratic forms and traditons, socialism would make giant strides towards full realization of the American heritage of "Life, Liberty and the Pursuit of Happiness".

The socialist-minded workers have a clear duty to perform —that is to participate actively in the everyday struggles of the working class, introducing a greater degree of class consciousness in the course of these struggles, and constantly popularizing the advantages that socialism would bring in America. We have seen that the socialist-minded forces in the labor movement before and after World War I performed a function that all progressives in American history have traditionally performed, even when they did not carry through their program in their own day—namely, to bring new issues before the people and to force new policies upon the majority. Today it is the duty of socialist-minded forces to carry on this tradition, raising in the course of the day to day struggles the issue of independent political action, with the ultimate goal of socialism.